Celluloid Mushrooms

Critical Studies in Communication
and in the Cultural Industries
Herbert I. Schiller, Series Editor

CELLULOID MUSHROOM CLOUDS

Hollywood and the Atomic Bomb

JOYCE A. EVANS

Westview
PRESS
A Member of the Perseus Books Group

Critical Studies in Communication and in the Cultural Industries

Copyright © 1998 by Westview Press, A Member of the Perseus Books Group

Published in 1998 in the United States of America by Westview Press, 5500 Central Avenue, Boulder, Colorado 80301-2877, and in the United Kingdom by Westview Press, 12 Hid's Copse Road, Cumnor Hill, Oxford OX2 9JJ

Library of Congress Cataloging-in-Publication Data
Evans, Joyce A.
   Celluloid mushroom clouds : Hollywood and the atomic bomb / Joyce
A. Evans.
      p.   cm. — (Critical studies in communication and in the cultural
industries)
   Includes bibliographical references and index.
   ISBN 0-8133-2613-3 (hardcover) — ISBN 0-8133-9141-5
   1. Nuclear warfare in motion pictures.   I. Title.   II. Series.
PN1995.9.W3E82   1998
791.43'658—dc21   98-2752
                                                                                   CIP

The paper used in this publication meets the requirements of the American National Standard for Permanence of Paper for Printed Library Materials Z39.48-1984.

10   9   8   7   6   5   4   3   2

for Costi

Contents

Acknowledgments

I am grateful to the many individuals who have contributed to the final completion of this project, at long last! I thank Dan Hallin and Robert Horwitz for their invaluable critical judgment and guidance in the early stages of this manuscript. DeeDee Halleck provided much needed insight into nuclear culture and popular media, and was a great influence upon the development of this work. A special thanks to Gene Chavira, who was always there when I needed him.

Thanks are also due to John Elmore, Kathryn Evans, and Christos Karastamatis for technical assistance with this project. At Westview Press, I thank Cathy Pusateri, Melanie Stafford, and Norman Ware, who handled and edited the manuscript with patience and care.

Domestically, I have endless appreciation for my parents, for their moral support, general stamina, and eternal hours of baby-sitting. I thank both of them. My mother, Marian Evans, also provided editorial advice on multiple versions of the manuscript. I am eternally grateful to my son Costi for teaching me the meaning of patience, and to my daughter Marina for expanding its boundaries to unimaginable limits.

In the final instance, however, this book could never have been completed without the tireless support of my friend and mentor Herbert Schiller, who continues as always to be a constant source of inspiration.

Joyce A. Evans

Introduction

Hollywood and the Atomic Bomb

WITH THE BLINDING BURST OF AN ATOMIC MUSHROOM CLOUD, the action begins! The audience is transported to a desert wasteland, or plunged to the ocean depths in a nuclear submarine. All is not well. Strange gigantic insects and monstrous crustaceans, the horrible consequence of American scientists' unnatural tampering with the atom, terrorize the unfortunate public. Extraterrestrial aliens, fleeing from the results of their own misuse of nuclear technology, seek to invade the Earth and rob it of its scientific knowledge and resources. Even more pernicious communist agents subversively attempt to destroy American society after stealing its atomic defense secrets. Or perhaps the willing audience in the theater is offered a glimpse into its own future, as post–nuclear holocaust survivors battle subhuman mutants while beginning life anew in the confines of a fallout shelter. Sometimes the military and the scientific community intervene as saviors in these movie scenarios, taking control of the ensuing mayhem; at other times the Earth's population succumbs to toxic global fallout, which transforms the planet into a lifeless orb.

These all-too-familiar themes form the range of film narratives that were created by the Hollywood studios and presented to the American moviegoing audience between 1946 and 1964. From Hollywood's first experiments with the new and potentially controversial topic of atomic development to the evolution of a science fiction genre exploiting the fear of radiation and its transmutational effects, a set of representations associated with all that atomic energy entailed gradually developed.[1] Such representations addressed and exploited popular concerns and anxieties over the role of the new atomic scientists, the possible consequences of an atomic war, and the imagined, unforeseen effects of the atomic bomb testing program with its accompanying radiation.

In the popular culture of today, depictions of the mad nuclear scientist attempting to destroy the world, secret experiments with exotic substances that transform flesh-and-blood humans into horrible apparitions, and heroic military geniuses saving Earth's civilization from malevolent nuclear terrorists are all so familiar, such an integral and accepted part of American culture that the origins of these representations are seldom investigated and the motivations of their creators never questioned. What is surprising is that the same restricted set of representations that evolved during this fifteen-year period still cling tenaciously to nuclear discourse today and can be found throughout American popular culture as well as in contemporary public debate.

The examples are endless: The supermarket boycott of irradiated food, the debate over how the use of the atomic bomb over Hiroshima would be presented in the Smithsonian's fiftieth-anniversary display, the television commercial depicting the shrinking of a confectioner's truck and its contents into "mini cinnamon buns" after it passes through a mysterious cloud in the desert, and the transmutation of common turtles into child-captivating "mutant ninjas" after their exposure to toxic waste all in part represent the continued reliance upon a set of definitions developed at the dawn of the atomic age. It seems as if texts of popular culture have stubbornly remained lodged within the confines of the established repertoire developed in the aftermath of the creation of the atomic bomb. Why have these narrow representations, concocted in part by the Hollywood movie industry and perpetuated through its offshoots, come to represent all that nuclear development embodies?

The answer lies in the understanding of Hollywood as an extremely influential producer of industrialized, commercialized popular culture. As a technologically dependent industry regulated by government and financially reliant upon mass audiences, Hollywood studios must function in a constantly changing network of relationships with other institutions that operate both within and without the film industry, and that ultimately shape the thematics and stylistics found in Hollywood film. And, as in all cultural industries, Hollywood also functions in a "selective tradition" in which choices of topic, discourse, and image are constantly being made, selected from a realm of possible representations. Hence, the composition of a film, the selection of certain specific images and themes over others, is always overdetermined by an array of influences such as technology, economics, competing commercial forms, individual producers and filmmakers, other media from which film texts may be adopted, prevailing ideologies, political influence, historical events, and audience preference.[2]

Direct and indirect political pressure, the interests of studio ownership, and audience expectations, combined with the standard operating procedures of film production, ensure that Hollywood, for the most part, produces film content that supports, or at least does not contradict, the dominant ideological assumptions of American society. This dominant ideology consists of a specific set of rhetorical and representational techniques that can give rise to particular ways of constructing, perceiving, and acting in the social world, ultimately reinforcing the prevailing institutional setup. As a system of representations (images, myths, ideas, or concepts), ideology provides a way of conceptualizing the world and sets the boundaries of reality.[3] Film works to create, reflect, and reinforce the central system of practices, meanings, and values operating within a society during a particular period, which helps to form this dominant ideology. Some meanings are reinterpreted whereas others are excluded, diluted, or reconstructed into forms that support or at least do not contradict other elements within the dominant culture. Perhaps the most pernicious aspect of Hollywood's perpetuation of the dominant ideology is its ability to appropriate potentially oppositional views and incorporate them into the dominant ideological position, thus delegitimating genuine opposition.[4]

However, despite its unintended ideological function, Hollywood's overreaching motivation is purely economic. Hollywood film has always been tailored to appeal to the largest potential audience and is constructed to embody values meaningful and appealing to current audiences. To accomplish this, most movies have steered clear of controversial issues, using stories based on the lowest common cultural denominators. But the public's taste is to some extent unpredictable; it cannot always be gauged.

In order to remain competitive, Hollywood producers must continuously appropriate the changing cultural attitudes and values of their audience, attempt to satisfy the needs of diverse interests, and thus meet the wishes of the public and of competing political, social, and cultural interests. Hence, although dominant ideological views are prevalent in film texts and reveal important information about the society in which they are produced and viewed, other potentially challenging and contradictory views are to some extent incorporated as well into the ever changing entertainment fare in the constant search for box-office appeal. This process by which Hollywood perpetuates the dominant ideological stance while meeting the diverse needs of its audience in its production of popular culture is exemplified by the industry's negotiations in presenting the potentially controversial atomic issue.

Hollywood Meets the A-Bomb

Hollywood's exploitation of the atomic bomb took place during a period characterized by many convergent elements. Changing political pressure on the Hollywood studios was accompanied by drastic economic structural transformations within the industry. This period coincided with broader social and technological changes. The years between 1948 and 1960 marked a time when the American population became highly dependent upon the mass media for entertainment and information and when changing economic priorities largely brought on by the widespread adoption of television gradually forced Hollywood to cater to a shifting and shrinking film audience.

Also during this period, the military rose to a peak of influence within the American power structure and the Cold War brought on an era of general political, social, and military fearfulness. The Cold War ideology constituted a set of values, judgments, and ideas that became deeply embedded in American culture and that resulted in direct political influence over the context of studio production and the content of Hollywood film as its products and personnel were subjected to the intense scrutiny of the House Un-American Activities Committee (HUAC).

But perhaps the most important social and political factor of this era was the development of the "atomic age," during which American society enlarged its perception and knowledge of atomic weaponry and the potential ramifications of its development and use. The seminal point of the widespread public discussion and uneasy acceptance of this technology began with its use in ending a military conflict at great human cost. The historical fact of the American use of the atomic bomb not only became the most pervasive sociopolitical problem of this time but also can be regarded as the defining symbol of the era.

What the American public knew and comprehended about atomic energy and the bomb evolved from information disseminated by government information releases, by the newly formed Federation of Atomic Scientists, and by the discourse and assumptions presented in all forms of the mass media.[5] This wide range of information was fleshed out with ideas and images, some based on a level interpretation of facts and the appropriation of factual circumstances, others developed from residual themes already present within the culture that were appropriated by participants in this public discussion in order to make sense of and give meaning to the new issues surrounding atomic technology. The majority of the mass media appeared intent upon convincing the public that employing the bomb had been the only rational course of action and was necessary to achieve a final settlement in the war with Japan. The policy of a continued atomic weapon buildup was also presented as crucial for the survival of the American system, as a developed Cold War ideology worked to frame the sentiments concerning the new and evolving technology of nuclear weaponry.[6]

Atomic technology had been forever linked to military interests due to the circumstances of its development during World War II, while the escalating Cold War between the United States and the Soviet Union destroyed all attempts at some sort of international control over weaponry development. For the sake of national security and the need to build up the country's defense arsenal, the atomic tests at the Bikini atoll demonstrated to the American public and to the world the destructive power the U.S. military harbored. Soon, the Atomic Energy Commission (AEC) was occupied with discovering and eliminating alleged spies seeking to steal atomic secrets as well as overseeing new weapons development.

The Soviet Union shocked the nation as it detonated its own atomic bomb in 1949, and by 1950 civil defense concerns pervaded American culture as the newly created Federal Civil Defense Administration (FCDA) took charge in preparing for the inevitable but potentially survivable nuclear attack. Meanwhile, the Subversive Activities Control Board ensured that concerns about security and the communist threat remained in the forefront as plans for creating the more powerful hydrogen bomb were publicly discussed. A growing group of atomic scientists came out against the further use and development of atomic weaponry, questioning the ethical implications and wisdom of the government's proposed course. By 1952, a large percentage of Americans believed that the Soviet Union would inevitably bomb the United States, and in this developing Cold War environment they placed their trust in the competence of the military and government nuclear research and development program to stave off destruction.[7]

In this historically unique context, it is clearly evident how contemporary events are continually used by Hollywood filmmakers in an effort to exploit perceived audience interest in specific topics. Immediately after the public was made aware of the existence of the atomic bomb, Hollywood rushed to exploit its novelty by merely writing atomic bomb elements into the script of a film just completed. *The House on 92nd Street* (1945) had dialogue added to its post-Hiroshima print to relate the plot to the "secret ingredient of the atomic bomb."[8] Plot gimmicks incorporating the atomic bomb were novel, and the use of stock footage of bomb tests and military maneuvers at test sites was inexpensive and rather impressive with scenes featuring technological gizmos and masses of regimented troops.

As Hollywood filmmakers take advantage of the publicity surrounding a recent event by incorporating that event into a film script, they also make use of the dialogue taking place in public forums, appropriating rhetoric and representations from these dialogues in the scripts. In the process, the ideological tone and mode of representation found in other media are replicated in film content. This can been seen in the plethora of films produced after the development of the atomic bomb, many of which incorporated or in some way attempted to draw upon contemporary interest in issues arising from atomic technology and its use.

For example, early films like *The Beginning or the End?* (1947) echo the religious imagery associated with atomic development as presented by government officials, scientists, and the media of the time. Dialogue from the film describing atomic technology as "all the energy of the universe" and "a hand God has extended" reflect rhetoric used to describe the bomb's first use. President Harry Truman himself repeatedly described atomic technology as "the force from which the sun draws its power" and as "the harnessing of the basic power of the universe."[9]

With such neat correspondences between contemporary events and film texts, it is easy to see why the creation of film content appears to be simply a reflection of society's interests and concerns at the time a film is produced. To a certain extent, this is true—films do express cultural norms and social trends; they do portray contemporary events. However, a wide variety of other pressures and influences upon film production are equally as important in the selection of film content, although not as clearly evident as the "reflection" of current events and interests. The economic pressures inherent in Hollywood's industrial mode of production, and the personal ideologies of individual filmmakers, may privilege the production of certain film texts over others. At varying times and with changing emphasis, the effects of direct public and government intervention also manifest themselves in the selective creation of film themes and images. Such interventions can take the form of subtle script changes in exchange for equipment and expertise from Pentagon officials, or the more overt pressure upon film content exerted in the 1950s by HUAC and public pressure groups such as the American Legion.

The House Un-American Activities Committee began in 1947 to criticize Hollywood films as containing communist propaganda and to target Hollywood personnel as Red conspirators. As the Hollywood Ten were tried and jailed, something of a witch hunt swept through the film industry. The threatened boycott of Hollywood products by the American Legion and other right-wing groups motivated the big film studios to attempt to restore their wartime patriotic image by approving a blacklist of suspected Hollywood personnel and by producing films that overtly conformed with the agenda of the political right. These films emphasized such Cold War concerns and fears as atomic attack from the Soviet Union, communist subversives thieving atomic secrets, and the need for a strong military defense program. Between 1947 and 1954, more than fifty anticommunist films were produced despite the fact that few proved profitable.[10]

Typically, such overt pressure on film production is unnecessary. Hollywood filmmakers on the whole seek to avoid controversy in order to please the largest audience, and if the predominant government and public agenda seem favorable to a specific set of values and ideas, filmmakers simply practice self-censorship in order to avoid criticism of their product and to attract the greatest number of viewers. In the "atomic age," the commercial nature of the Hollywood industry ensured that the elaboration of atomic themes would inevitably proceed according to specific ideological standards. Each film that experimented with atomic material could pose the issues in terms endorsed by the prevailing ideology—or refuse to acknowledge that ideological position at its own commercial risk.

And risk is not something that Hollywood as an institution happily embraces, particularly in periods of economic hardship. Hollywood's compliance with the government's agenda in producing these Cold War propaganda films and promoting them as entertainment can be seen as the industry's attempt to appease government criticism and fend off interference while it dealt with its internal economic troubles. Declining movie attendance was coupled with the structural reorganization made necessary by government antitrust action, mandating the separation of production and exhibition. This ruling destroyed the vertical integration that had allowed the five major studios to dominate the industry during the previous decade. Such monopolistic control, combining the production of motion pictures, the operation of worldwide distribution outlets, and the ownership of chains of theaters where the parent company's pictures were guaranteed a showing, was gradually destroyed. Between 1949 and 1953, theaters owned by producer-distributors were sold off to independent corporations.

The effects of such economic forces upon the selection of film content is not random; Hollywood must meet the needs of its audience while operating within the commercial margins of risk and investment. These imperatives dictate the conscious selection and standardization of genre and formula, the push for the development of new technology in the need to compete with other forms of entertainment, and the selection and appropriation of images that filmmakers believe their intended audience want to see. Changes in Hollywood's economic structure, based upon an industrial model for efficient production, also determine film content selection. For example, while the studios enjoyed their monopoly over production and distribution in the late 1940s, minor experimentation in film content was possible because of the guaranteed market for any studio product. The practice of block booking, in which the majors sold their pictures in blocks of various sizes, offering them to exhibitors on an all-or-none basis before the pictures had even been shot, enabled the studios to function at capacity with the assurance that even their poorest pictures would be bought. Thus, the studios could produce unappealing and unprofitable Cold War pictures at this time with little economic risk, while at the same time experimenting with various narrative formulas in relation to the atomic topic.

Although government pressure kept the studios producing fare that toed the government line and the Cold War agenda—movies that, for the most part, echoed the dominant government-sanctioned message about atomic development in realistic docudrama and dramatic form—the monopolistic trade practices that guaranteed Hollywood a venue for exhibition also allowed the studios to experiment with the representation of atomic technology. Early films offered novel imagery and variety in the atomic genre as the studios tried to find a profitable way to exploit the subject of the atomic bomb. Such experimentation took the form of science fiction, docudrama, and drama and involved paradoxical and contradictory representations of atomic development and use. These products allowed the studios to cater to public tastes as well as to appease Washington and avoid direct government scrutiny, while at the same time openly questioning the ethical implications of nuclear development in ways unheard of later in the 1950s.

The audience and their perceived interests and desires are always at the forefront in the creation of film content. Films are popular in part because they in some way reflect or cater to an audience's desires, wishes, and anxieties. Hollywood's experiments with blatant Cold War propaganda in entertainment form, meant to appease government pressures, were largely unpopular at the box office, proving that such offerings were unattractive and unpalatable to large audiences. Although the ideological atmosphere of these films was predominantly conservative, filmmakers attempted to capitalize on public anxiety over and interest in atomic issues by drawing upon a body of "residual" themes. Based on a complex tangle of contradictory images suffused with emotions and archetypes already existent within American culture, these themes form a body of residual cultural elements that can sometimes undermine the dominant culture and highlight its weaknesses, providing an avenue for critical expression limited in other channels of discourse.[11] In film scenarios, such elements, rather than being contained in the dominant ideology, often point to its inherent flaws and contradictions.

In the atomic era, these residual elements took the form of archetypal themes born out of older cultural practices that were intermingled and appropriated by filmmakers to help define, encapsulate, and convey an understanding of the emerging atomic technologies and their potential. Most film texts juxtaposed the contradictory nature of atomic development—visions of the good atom with its utopian promise and the bad atom unleashing its destructive force, of the transmutation of elements by a Magus, or alchemist, who often brings disaster upon himself and the society he lives in by rashly exploring and exploiting nature's mysteries. Transmutation became a key motif in nuclear films from 1950 onward; atomic technology was presented as transforming all it came into contact with—nuclear survivors, atomic spies, and alien invaders.

The notion that discovering nature's secrets could either transform civilization into a technological and social utopia or completely destroy it, along with the accompanying concept of the secrecy that surrounded these mysteries of nature, played a critical part in the genesis of the atomic discourse. Hollywood reconstructed these themes in order to profit from the atomic issue, in the process creating much film content that pointed to the weaknesses of the dominant ideology and thus presenting a potentially oppositional message.

As the 1950s progressed filmmakers became cautious of ideological scrutiny over atomic issues, audiences became weary of cold war diatribes, and atomic discourse gradually became veiled under the development of a new Hollywood genre—science fiction. Hence, whereas early attempts to exploit atomic issues in film involved a combination of elements that both reiterated official government policy and also questioned the ethical implications of bomb development, Cold War dictates overtly pressured Hollywood to discover more subtle ways to satisfy audience interest in imagining the consequences of the atomic program. Subtle criticism through the appropriation of residual meaning found expression in the creative freedom of the science fiction genre, through which speculation about the dangers and the possible drastic results of atomic development could be played out and recrimination even relegated to government policy. Hence, the emergence of the giant mutated creatures—giant ants in *Them!* (1954) to giant humans in *The Amazing Colossal Man* (1957)—all the unforeseen consequences of atomic development brought to the screen. The danger of the consequences of atomic development can be narratively resigned in the end of these film texts, yet the omnipresent specter of transmutation as retribution for invading nature's secrets offers an inherently critical message. Such potentially oppositional visions were repressed in official government discussions and the dictates of reality pressed upon wider public discussion.

Growing up in the western United States during this period, I can recall these contradictory and confusing themes of atomic weaponry and Cold War rhetoric that pervaded even the small world of my childhood. The terror that filled my heart when my first-grade teacher pontificated Cold War sentiments in suggesting: "What's the first thing American astronauts will find when they get to the Moon? Russians!" The weekly wailing of the air-raid sirens as we played outside and practiced a duck-and-cover maneuver under the pine tree in the front yard. Doubts about the survivability of nuclear war, and the fear of the deadly and possibly transmutational effects of radiation as we watched a bomb shelter being constructed in a neighbor's backyard. The awe and anticipation when presented with the marvels promised by the harnessing of the "good" atom, all neatly displayed in the form of atomic-powered dishwashers and kitchen ranges in the Monsanto "House of the Future" at Disneyland.

Such themes of the past remain part of American culture. This work is not meant to be a venture in nostalgia but an effort to deepen our understanding of the world in which we live. The topic of how nuclear images have been presented in popular culture is of such significance that it deserves its own extensive treatment, not left as a footnote in an overall cultural history of the development of the atomic bomb. Since the films produced by Hollywood display the extremes of anxiety, tension, hope, and fear found in American society at this time, and themselves participate in and further the process of social change, an understanding of the images and ideology expressed in these films is inseparable from the social history of the era. For it was during that era, which now seems so distant, that the fundamental perceptions that continue to influence Americans' responses to the nuclear menace were first articulated, discussed, and absorbed into the culture.

A Theoretical Perspective

Cinematic films have a complex, multifaceted nature as commercial products, art forms, and ideological constructs.[12] In analyzing films that incorporate atomic images, this book attempts to understand film texts in relation to the industry that has produced them. This industry-focused approach views cultural production as a material process unfolding under specific economic, political, and cultural conditions and offers insight into how the cinematic texts negotiated by audiences are produced in highly concentrated industries, constructed as a result of often contradictory determinants. These determinants work to shape the texts by encouraging, for instance, the production of particular genres and by privileging one specific set of images over others, ultimately restricting the discursive means available for defining atomic issues and imagery.

Since this research is concerned with how the economic dynamics of production and specific historical contexts structure film content, I seek to avoid presenting film as a mere reflection of society's norms and values, or as the purveyor of a monolithic dominant ideology generated by Hollywood's institutional framework and the interests of ownership. In investigating film content and its determining factors, this research draws upon the methodology and informing theoretical basis of the critical political economy perspective elaborated by Peter Golding and Graham Murdock. This perspective, with its emphasis upon the mediating role of cultural forms, focuses upon the connections between the organization of cultural production and changes in the field of public discourse and representation, pointing to "the interplay between symbolic, institutional and economic dimensions of public communication, the organization of cultural production and its traceable consequences for the range of discourses and representations in the public sphere."[13] This concern with the way cultural goods are produced, seeing the impact of the institution of production on the goods it produces as limiting but not absolutely determining, promotes the analysis of texts of popular culture in order to illustrate ways in which the representations they contain are related to the material realities of their production and consumption.

The emphasis upon the production of meaning places the critical political economy perspective within the field of cultural studies, which is centrally concerned "with the construction of meaning—how it is produced in and through particular expressive forms and how it is continually negotiated and deconstructed through the practices of everyday life."[14] The largest area of cultural studies concentrates upon the analysis of cultural texts in tracing their role in sustaining systems of domination. The theory argues that there are powerful ideological forces at work within institutions in society, such as the film industry, which work to inculcate the dominant viewpoint. However, individuals and groups are capable of resistance and the formulation of alternative conceptions, some oppositional to the dominant ideology.

Cultural studies rejects the notion that the media simply transmit a dominant ideology, seeing instead the communications system as a field or space in which contending discourses, differing ways of looking and speaking, struggle for visibility. In contrast to transportation models, which present the media as transmitting "messages" to consumers, the cultural studies approach sees them as mechanisms for ordering meaning in particular ways. Cultural forms are seen as mechanisms for regulating public discourse, and a cultural studies methodology analyzes the way in which discourses are handled within a text, whether they are arranged in a clearly marked hierarchy of credibility that urges the audience to prefer one over the others or whether they are treated in a more even-handed and indeterminate way that leaves the audience with a more open choice.

Critical political economy is interested in the interplay between economic organization and the political, cultural, and social life; it is particularly interested in tracing the impact of the economic structure of institutions on the range and diversity of cultural expression. It sees economic dynamics as defining the key features of the general environment within which cultural production takes places, but not as a complete explanation of that activity.[15]

This perspective also attempts to avoid instrumentalism's unwavering focus upon the media as instruments of class domination and the methods by which capitalists use their economic power within a commercial market system to ensure that the flow of public information is consonant with their interests. Individuals in positions of media ownership and control are capable of making operating decisions that work to fix the premises of discourse, and government elites are allowed privileged access to media productions that directly determine what the populace is allowed to see and hear. However, instrumentalism's focus upon direct intervention tends to overlook the contradictions within cultural production. The powerful operate within structures that contain as well as facilitate, institutions that impose limits as well as offer flexibility. Individuals in the media work with a range of codes and professional ideologies, with an array of aspirations, both personal and social, and with varying degrees of autonomy. The boundaries of this autonomy, given the economic structure of the industry, inhibit the production of some forms of meaning and allow others to find an outlet.

Fundamentally, the reproduction and dissemination of the images, symbols, and vocabulary with which people respond to their social environment occur in an industry motivated by economic priorities. It is crucial that any analysis of film content consider how this economic organization impinges upon the production and circulation of meaning. The critical political economic perspective attempts to address the complex field of factors that determine the selection of content—the connections between the production of selected systems of representations and economic priorities, routines of industrial production, interventions by other institutions, and wider historical context. For Hollywood film, these considerations point to the analysis of Hollywood industrial production and the changing economic pressures that help determine the selection of film content.

Hollywood Moviemaking

The goal of Hollywood film production is to create a product that will make a profit, or at least have the opportunity for an adequate return on one's investment. To do this, films are produced to attract audiences by responding to and exploiting perceived audience interests and tastes while providing diversion and escape in the most economical fashion.[16] The conception of the role of the audience in the production of media content has varied from the insistence that consumers vote with their dollars and have tremendous power over what is produced, to the argument that audiences have become so accustomed to a certain type of material that the same formulas can be used over and over in updated versions to sell products and the lifestyle of consumption.[17] To a certain extent, both these views of the audience are accommodated when the analysis of the process of Hollywood film production takes into account the negotiation between standardized production practices and the need for innovation in product creation.

The concern with economic viability places the industrial production of film products at the forefront. As an industry, Hollywood film is primarily based upon an industrial model composed of the three basic components of production, distribution, and exhibition. The organization and operation of the Hollywood film industry characterize it as an oligopolistic industry with few producer-distributors who create and control the supply of movies.[18] The routines of production limit what can be created and released, and predictable patterns of content result from these limits. However, although mass-produced, each film is a unique commodity. Film production defies order and demands risk taking in order to address demand uncertainty. Therefore, a constant tension exists between two major tendencies inherent in Hollywood film production—the standardization of the product for efficient and economical mass production and the simultaneous movement toward differentiation of the product in competition for the audience's income. These two factors have profound implications for the process of content selection in film production and help explain the similarities and variations among individual films as well as wider changes in subject matter, genres, and styles.[19]

The commercial nature of Hollywood film production compels its products to cater to the widest possible audience. The primary concern of the organization releasing the product (though not necessarily of the individual writers and directors) is the economic viability, audience acceptance, and technical quality of the work itself.[20] Thus, there is a definite tendency to create a standardized product that relies on familiar themes, clearly identifiable characters, and understandable resolutions. It is for this reason that films weave old, familiar plot elements, a dominant narrative, clarity, verisimilitude, and continuity in order to create a product quickly and simply.[21] The closed, fictional narrative, in which all narrative elements have been drawn together and all questions arising from the film have been answered, is the standard Hollywood film style, which has been adopted because of audience acceptance and cost-effective production.

The underlying themes and values that entertainment companies allow in their output are typically those that industry executives believe would not be objectionable to most people in their target audience. The entertainment industry is involved in the organizational creation and release of products to attract audiences for financial profit and not in explicitly educational, journalistic, political, or advertising endeavors; and as such the industry is not interested in any educational, commercial, or political messages that happen to be attached to its products. The media, on the other hand, operate within a culture and are obliged to use cultural symbols, the "cultural air we breathe, the whole ideological atmosphere of society, which tells us that some things can be said and that others had best not be said."[22]

To appeal to large groups of people, Hollywood filmmakers work to legitimate dominant institutions and traditional values, and their representational and stylistic conventions help instill ideology. These representational conventions include form as well as subject matter, such as narrative closure, character identification, sequential editing, and dramatic motivation. The thematic conventions that film incorporates, such as heroic male adventures and romantic quests, promote ideology by linking the effect of reality to social values and institutions in such a way that the latter come to seem the natural or self-evident attributes of an unchanging world. The focus upon individualism in privileging personal life stories over structural social issues of war and crime tend to make the existing order seem moral and good; the conventions utilized by filmmakers habituate the audience into accepting the basic premises of the social order.

The measure of success in moviemaking is attendance, either in terms of the number of theater admissions, the dollar value of box-office receipts, or the dollar value of rental fees returned to distributors. There is no proven simple and consistent relationship between film themes, costs of production, and box-office receipts.[23] Box-office receipts do not explain why people attend movies; they lack any predictive value. Therefore, movie executives are reduced to "reading tea leaves," to developing a mental "audience image" of the anticipated or desired audience as a mechanism of anticipatory feedback, in the process of script creation and filming. The various audience images of scriptwriter, director, and producer vie for dominance, their status based upon the success of their previous decisions.[24] The fact that the competing audience images cannot be tested before a movie is released means that "decisions may be made on the basis of irrelevant criteria."[25]

The creative process in the selection of film content also involves a form of "ritualism" that works to establish parameters of choice conditioned by the studios' perception of audience preferences. This routinized action on the part of filmmakers operates as a device to allay anxieties by clinging to tried-and-true formulas with known audience appeal, to minimize risks, and to perpetuate genres as imitations of successful themes and formats.[26] The division of the Hollywood industry into production, distribution, and exhibition segments also tends to further distance creative personnel from the audience.[27] Therefore, the audience has only a phantom existence; filmmakers anticipate audience preferences through public dialogue, perceived interest in specific contemporary events, and the success of previous genres and styles.

The need to address unpredictable, constantly changing audience interests and desires while remaining competitive necessitates innovative processes in film production, inhibiting assembly-line uniformity. The industry requires novelty, and within circumscribed limits, Hollywood has attempted innovations and standardized successes. This incorporation of novelty into standardized content causes Hollywood to operate in cycles: One successful film spawns a host of imitators. If an innovative genre or style produces positive results, usually measured in terms of box-office receipts, other studios try to duplicate that success. Such innovations can be generated by personalities and personal interests, and individuals who work in the film industry can "make a difference" in the creation of film content, under certain conditions and within the limits of the organizational and industrial structures. What the boundaries of freedom are can be determined by a combination of personal factors and the structural aspects of the organizational environment.[28]

The process of Hollywood film production involves a negotiation between innovation and standardization in an effort to cater to audience desires and interests. This process of negotiation operates in an institutional framework, in the political cultural field, with shifting direct and indirect pressures upon film production. In analyzing the development and proliferation of Hollywood-generated nuclear images, it is clear that these factors influenced content selection to varying degrees. Sometimes direct government pressure works to suppress and dictate content selection, and at others times the changing economic structure of the Hollywood industry and varying audience demands motivate innovation in genre, technology, and style, even to the point of incorporating and accommodating individual interests.

An Analysis of Atomic Films

This analysis is unique to research on nuclear culture in that it confines its scope to depictions of the use of nuclear power and its consequences in Hollywood fictional film.[29] There is a growing literature on atomic development and American culture, but no works specifically address the process of and determinants upon the creation and selection of images of atomic technology and related issues in film production over an extended period of time. Paul Boyer's *By the Bomb's Early Light* provides a detailed document of the impact of the atomic bomb on American discourse between 1945 and 1950, whereas Spencer Weart's *Nuclear Fear* offers an overview of the origins of nuclear images in their historical context. Similar cultural histories include Constantina Titus's *Bombs in the Backyard*, a history of the atomic testing program; and H. Bruce Franklin's *War Stars* and Ira Chernus's *Dr. Strangegod*, which both provide insight into the ideological development of atomic symbolism.[30]

An extensive literature exists on fiction and nuclear themes, such as David Dowling's *Fictions of Nuclear Disaster* and Paul Brians's *Nuclear Holocausts*. These books trace the development of nuclear themes particularly in science fiction literature, but they emphasize an analysis of formula over production and historical context. Research into film images that touch upon nuclear themes include Peter Biskind's ideological reading of films produced in the 1950s, *Seeing Is Believing*. His analysis presents these films as "conscious anti-Communist propaganda, and as an unintentional register of anxiety," reflecting, shaping, and expressing the dynamics of political consciousness.[31] Biskind's essay "Pods, Blobs, and Ideology in American Films of the Fifties" offers another ideological reading of science fiction film of the 1950s, grouping them by latent structure and manifest narrative into conservative and liberal categories.[32] The factors influencing the production of films such as *The Beginning or the End?* (1947) and *Fat Man and Little Boy* (1989) are briefly but insightfully addressed in Robert J. Lifton and Greg Mitchell's *Hiroshima in America*.[33]

Finally, there are film studies that pose film as a simplistic reflection of national mood or contemporary events. Jack Shaheen's compilation *Nuclear War Films* stands as such an example, in which nuclear images are seen, for the most part, as mere registers of current social and political events.[34] Methodologically, it is easy to view film as a "mirror of society," to document a correspondence between contemporary social issues and film content. But this view ignores the fact that the development and perpetuation of a specific set of representations take place in a complex, shifting network of determinants. Robert Sklar's cultural history of the development of the American film industry, *Movie-Made America*, is an example of film research that incorporates the influences of changing technology, the nature of movie audiences, the factor of government policy, and the institutional framework of Hollywood production on film content. Andrew Tudor's *Monsters and Mad Scientists* attempts to incorporate such factors into a specific genre analysis.[35]

In a similar vein, this research examines the array of factors that work to determine the selection and production of film content. However, the methodology that informs this analysis incorporates both quantitative and qualitative methods in addressing nuclear images in film content. The basis for this research consists of ninety representative fictional films produced and disseminated by Hollywood between 1947 and 1965. The quantitative analysis identifies key categories of content within each text and the representation of nuclear weapons, war, nuclear use, and the possible ramifications of nuclear use. A list of films containing references or depictions of nuclear energy or its use was compiled by searching motion picture trade literature. To be included in the sample, the film had to meet the following requirements:

1. The film text had to make specific reference to atomic war or its aftermath, atomic testing and its effects, radiation, atomic technology, postatomic holocaust societies on earth or imagined planets, or atomic scientists.
2. The film had to be a feature-length fictional drama. This requirement excluded documentaries, short-subject films, and cartoons from consideration, but included dramatizations of real events, or docudramas.
3. The film had to be produced and released by the U.S. commercial motion picture industry between January 1, 1949, and December 31, 1964. It had to be distributed in commercial theaters.

Using content analysis techniques, I generated a quantitative database to track the frequency and evolution of these representations throughout the sample period. The analysis consists of logging time spent, in seconds, on the representation or discussion of nuclear issues or images, and graphing them by year. Specifically, only units of content that could be counted were included such as atomic explosions (whether actual footage or artificial), depictions of technology, images of the atomic bomb or the mushroom-cloud explosion itself, portrayals of arming the bomb, images of radiation and its effects, and so on. Charts were generated from the content analysis to illustrate the time and attention devoted to specific images of nuclear use, and how the emphasis on these images changed and corresponded to events and discussions in American society. The quantitative data pointed to content changes in years that defined the three major periods of the development of nuclear images in Hollywood, which lend structure to this book.

16

TABLE I.1   Time Line

1945

"Trinity," the first atomic explosion,
   successfully detonated at Alamogordo,
   New Mexico, July 16
U.S. bombs Hiroshima, Aug. 6,
   and Nagasaki, Aug. 9

House on 92nd Street
First Yank in Tokyo

1946

Atomic Energy Commission (AEC)
   established
Operation Crossroads—A-bomb tests
   at Bikini Atoll
Federation of Atomic Scientists
   publishes *One World or None*

Cloak and Dagger
Lady from Shanghai
Notorious

1947

Containment policy initiated
HUAC hearings
First flying saucers spotted
   in Washington State

Sombra, the Spider Woman
The Beginning or the End?

1948

U.S. introduces long-range
   aircraft for intercontinental bombing
Inauguration of Strategic Air Command

The Iron Curtain
Walk a Crooked Mile
Sofia

1949

China becomes communist republic
Soviets explode first atomic bomb

White Heat

1950

Truman instructs AEC to produce
   H-bomb
Korean War begins
Rosenberg Trial

Rocketship XM
The Flying Missile
Destination Moon
Captain Video
The Flying Saucer
DOA

1951

U.S. begins A-bomb tests
   in Nevada
NATO agrees to station U.S. nuclear
   weapons in Europe
First atomic-powered
   generator produces electricity
Second round of HUAC hearings

Five
The Day the Earth Stood Still
I Was a Communist for the FBI
The Thing
Unknown World
The Whip Hand
The Lost Continent
Ma and Pa Kettle Back on the Farm

(continued)

TABLE I.1   *(continued)*

1952

Operation Ivy-First
H-bomb test in Marshall Islands
Britain tests atomic weapon in
  Australia

Above and Beyond
Retik, The Moon Menace
Invasion U.S.A.
The Atomic City
The Thief
Red Planet Mars
Captive Women
Zombies of the Stratosphere

1953

USSR explodes H-bomb
Eisenhower's "Atoms for Peace"
  program launched
Rosenbergs put to death

The Beast from 20,000 Fathoms
Pickup on South Street
It Came from Outer Space
Robot Monster
The 49th Man
Invaders from Mars
Run for the Hills
Split Second

1954

BRAVO test at Bikini Atoll
First atomic-powered submarine
Oppenheimer investigation
U.S. adopts policy of "massive retaliation"

Atomic Attack
Living It Up
Them!
Tangier Incident
Killers from Space
The Atomic Kid
World for Ransom
Hell and High Water
Monster from the Ocean Floor
Operation Manhunt
The Stranger from Venus
20,000 Leagues Under the Sea
Paris Playboys
This Island Earth

1955

Soviets unveil intercontinental bombers
  and start new atomic testing
Accord signed between U.S.
  and Britain on peaceful
  uses of atomic power
Disarmament discussed
  at Geneva summit

Kiss Me Deadly
Strategic Air Command
Medic
It Came from Beneath the Sea
Creature with the Atomic Brain
Tarantula
Port of Hell
A Bullet for Joey

1956

First airborne H-bomb test
U.S. starts new H-bomb tests
  in Pacific

The Day the World Ended
The Day North America
  Is Attacked

(continued)

18

TABLE I.1   *(continued)*

Fallout blows across Australia	*First Man in Space*
Private atomic energy plants	*Bride of the Atom*
authorized by AEC	*Phantom from 10,000 Leagues*
	World Without End
	Attack of the Crab Monsters
	The Werewolf

1957

Soviets deploy first intercontinental	*The Monster That Challenged the World*
ballistic missiles	*The Black Scorpion*
Sputnik I launched	*The Incredible Shrinking Man*
"Project Plowshares" inaugurated	*The Amazing Colossal Man*
SANE formed	*Jet Pilot*
First U.S. underground	*Bombers B-52*
nuclear test in Nevada	*Strategic Air Command*
	The Beginning of the End
	The Story of Mankind
	Five Steps to Danger
	Not of This Earth
	The Giant Claw
	The Deadly Mantis
	The Cyclops
	From Hell It Came
	Kronos
	The Invisible Boy

1958

U.S. deploys ICBMs,	*Missile Monster*
launches space satellite	*Satan's Satellites*
SANE ad to halt nuclear testing aired	*The Monster from Green Hell*
Campaign for Nuclear Disarmament	*The Lost Missile*
holds first meeting in London	*Night of the Blood Beast*
	Terror from the Year 5,000
	It—The Terror from Beyond Space
	War of the Satellites
	The Space Children
	War of the Colossal Beast
	The Astounding She Monster
	Fiend Without a Face
	Earth vs. the Spider
	Attack of the 50 Foot Woman

1959

Fallout rise alarms world:	*The World, the Flesh and the Devil*
300% increase in atmospheric	*On the Beach*
radioactivity in eastern U.S.	*The Giant Behemoth*
Two nuclear accidents occur in U.S.	*Invisible Invaders*
	Island of Lost Women
	City of Fear
	The Hideous Sun Demon

(continued)

TABLE I.1   *(continued)*

	The Cosmic Man
	The Black Scorpion
	Alligator People
	4-D Man

1947-1962
106 nuclear tests in Pacific

1960
U.S. develops first nuclear-powered
  submarine
Partial test-ban treaty
France explodes atomic bomb

Twelve to the Moon
Amazing Transparent Man
The Time Machine
Beyond the Time Barrier
The Last Woman on Earth
Atomic Submarine
Beast of Yucca Flats

1961
U.S. Civil Defense Program begins
Soviets detonate largest bomb to date:
 50 megatons
Treaty of Antarctica proclaims
 continent nuclear free

Rocket Attack U.S.A.
Master of the World
Voyage to the Bottom of the Sea
The Flight That Disappeared
Atlantis, the Lost Continent

1962
October Cuban Missile Crisis
U.S. resumes nuclear testing after
  3-year moratorium

Panic in Year Zero
The Day Mars Invaded Earth
Underwater City
Creation of the Humanoids
This Is Not a Test
Hand of Death

1963
U.S., Britain, and USSR sign
  limited test-ban treaty
U.S. and USSR agree to establish hotline
  link to minimize risk of accidental war

A Gathering of Eagles
Ladybug, Ladybug
Slime People

1964
China detonates atomic bomb
American military intervention
  in Vietnam escalates

Dr. Strangelove
Failsafe
The Time Travelers
Monstrosity, the Atomic Brain
Demon from Devil's Lake
The Horror of Party Beach
Seven Days in May

1965
U.S. combat troops arrive in Vietnam

Die, Monster, Die!
Crack in the World
Mirage
The Bedford Incident

1

Hollywood After the Bomb, 1946–1953

Fictitious scientist Matt receives a fatal dose of radiation while working on the A-bomb in *The Beginning or the End?* (1947)

By 1946, only one year after the atomic bombs had been dropped on Japan, Hollywood studios were anxious to capitalize upon the public interest in what *Life* magazine called the "biggest event since the birth of Christ."[1] In the aftermath of the military use of this new technology, an urgent public discussion arose via newspapers, magazines, and radio broadcasts. Rhetoric postulating upon the potential danger of atomic power pervaded American culture at this time. For example, dialogue from a 1946 public-affairs program from the University of Denver explained: "A time bomb is under your home. It is ticking slowly away. Even while I talk, even while you listen, time is running out. America must act, if we are to choose the road of atomic peace rather than atomic war."[2]

The American media began devoting massive and direct attention to atomic issues; over three hundred articles on the topic of the atomic bomb were published in major popular periodicals such as *Time, Life,* and *Reader's Digest* in 1946 alone.[3] American society at this time was certainly relieved by the war's end, but with the euphoria brought about by Japan's surrender came a gradually growing anxiety and uneasiness about the atomic future.

Commercial entertainment films produced during this period provide insight into Hollywood's initial attempts to frame and present atomic topics while still realizing their main goal in film production—profit. The antitrust measures, economic troubles, and direct government pressure on film content had not yet taken full effect, and Hollywood studios felt some freedom of experimentation with genre and style in exploiting nuclear themes. Although pressure from exhibitors exerted a fundamentally conservative influence that encouraged the production of standard formulaic fare imbued with the country's dominant ideological stance, topics that overtly questioned the government's atomic weapons policy and atomic testing program did appear to a limited extent in Hollywood products.

Such experimentation took the form of various science fiction and dramatic fare presenting paradoxical and contradictory representations of atomic development and use. Early films that portrayed attempts to justify the bomb's recent use (*The Beginning or the End?* 1947) were mixed with comic portrayals of atomic tests (*The Atomic Kid,* 1954). A variety of science fiction scenarios were developed in this new Hollywood genre, including narratives presenting the use of atomic power as weaponry (*Sombra, the Spider Woman,* 1947; *The Flying Missile,* 1950) and survival adventures in postholocaust environments, both on Earth and on other planets (*Red Planet Mars,* 1952; *Rocketship XM,* 1950). Such products allowed the studios to cater to public tastes and direct government scrutiny, while questioning the ethical implications of nuclear development in ways unheard of later in the 1950s. A few independently produced films promoted a view of atomic technology that was overtly against atomic proliferation and the official government nuclear agenda (*Five,* 1951; *The Day the Earth Stood Still,* 1951).

Initially, most Hollywood films that addressed atomic issues merely incorporated the new public interest in all things atomic into scripts already under production, or as a plot element in a formulaic spy thriller. Immediately after the bomb's military use, an atomic element was added in postproduction to the plot of *The House on 92nd Street* (1945). *First Yank in Tokyo* (1945) worked military footage of the devastation in Hiroshima into its low-budget production in an attempt to be the first to capitalize upon the recent event. Noted directors such as Alfred Hitchcock, Orson Welles, and Fritz Lang didn't hesitate to hint at atomic substances and secret atomic plans in their otherwise standard dramatic mysteries in films such as *Cloak and Dagger* (1946), *Lady from Shanghai* (1948), and *Notorious* (1946).

In their attempts to reap profit from public interest in atomic technology, Hollywood producers devoted much film time to describing and presenting mysterious atomic substances, military technologies, and depictions of atomic explosions. Films like *White Heat* (1948) and *The Beginning or the End?* (1947) are exemplary in their emphasis upon the image of the explosion. The initial fascination with these relatively realistic images gradually waned as they became a common, familiar film image; the explosions were replaced by more bizarre and imaginative technological creations in the science fiction films of the 1950s.[4]

Hollywood Production Contexts: 1945–1953

What type of film was actually made, and how atomic-related content was selected and constructed, depended to a large extent on the specific context of production. Although 1949 marked the time when the old style of production was slowly being undermined by government antitrust cases, this traditional Hollywood mode of production, developed in the early years of the industry, remained for the moment unchanged. During this period, five major film companies dominated the screen in the United States. The largest was Warner Brothers, followed by Metro-Goldwyn-Mayer (MGM), Paramount, RKO, and Twentieth Century Fox. With stables of in-house stars, writers, directors, producers, and technicians, each of the majors produced from forty to sixty films per year. In 1945, these majors owned most aspects of production, distribution, and exhibition, enjoying almost complete vertical integration of the industry.

These studios produced practically all the class-A features, the films that were played in the best theaters and generated the most revenue. However, a large market existed for "B" class movies as well, produced for release in the second segment of a double-feature program. This tradition of presenting two-for-one double bills was originally created to lure back shrinking movie audiences in the 1930s. The practice of block-booking marketing, in which a distributor was forced to purchase an entire package of pictures, both A and B class, ensured a financial return on any product a studio produced. B movies, which were produced inexpensively and quickly, were often a testing ground for new writers, directors, and producers, and for experimentation with new topics. The amount of money spent on a given picture was presumably related to the anticipated drawing power of its combination of talent and production values.[5]

Until the early 1950s, most Hollywood film production was characterized by the "studio system" developed during the initial development of the feature film. The major studios were organized by hierarchical departments, with work allocated to centrally organized departments, all under the control of the studio head. For example, MGM boasted a workforce of six thousand, who were distributed into twenty-six departments involving all aspects of filmmaking. The studio head was primarily concerned with business affairs, negotiating contracts with stars and ensuring that the studio operated efficiently. After the story idea, or property, was selected, it was then assigned to an associate producer, who saw the project through to completion. MGM employed one head of production and ten subordinate associate producers, each specializing in a particular genre of film such as action, comedy, or western.

The relationships within a major studio among the various departments handling production, distribution, and exhibition were most important in respect to determining the type of film made. Enjoying the most advantageous positions by virtue of the division of labor in the industry, film distributors and exhibitors were more closely in touch with the moviegoing public than were the in-house producers. They helped determine the genre of picture to be made, the number of pictures in each cost class, and the type of story. Generally, the studio's head of distribution announced the number of films desired for the upcoming season based upon an estimate of what could be profitably sold, and the chief executive announced the amount of money available for the season's production schedule.[6]

Therefore, company executives and exhibitors, together with sales estimates, determined the total amount of money to be spent, how funds would be distributed among various classes of pictures, and the deadlines for completion and distribution. The exhibitor group controlled the purse strings and accounted for more than nine-tenths of the studio's invested capital and two-thirds of the industry's income. Distributors also exerted a conservative influence upon film content, tending to promote previously profitable formulas over the experimental or untried. In the early 1950s, the government mandated the breakup of the studio oligopoly, and the subsequent rise of independent production and exhibition industries eventually altered film content.

Most films with nuclear themes were B movies, produced on a low budget for exhibition on the back end of a double feature; they were not meant to showcase stars or directors. Because of the low priority and limited investment the studio allotted to these products, more experimentation was allowed in testing new ideas for film formulas. The monopoly that the major studios enjoyed over film production and distribution, which ensured a market for any studio product, also contributed to the flexibility that in-house producers were allowed in experimenting with nuclear images. However, by the early 1950s, the effects of the economic restructuring of the film industry, the changing government agenda, and the developing Cold War ideology would drastically inhibit the portrayal of this specific issue in film content.

The differences in the presentation and emphasis of atomic issues in Hollywood film between the late 1940s and early 1950s can be illustrated by comparing two major motion pictures produced in the docudrama genre by one of the largest film studios, MGM. The variations between the two docudramas embody the political concerns of the American public and the economic pressures on the Hollywood industry at the time of each film's production. Produced immediately after the war, *The Beginning or the End?* (1947) typifies the view of the atomic bombing of Japan presented to the American public immediately after World War II by the media and official government channels.[7] The film captures the ambivalence and contradictory nature of the moral implications of the atomic bomb that was then being expressed in public dialogue. Its narrative overtly questions the ethical nature of the bomb's development while adopting official government rhetoric to justify its recent use. The film's producer also appropriated residual cultural elements to link the atomic discovery to contradictory metaphors of its destructive and constructive potential.

In comparison, *Above and Beyond,* produced only five years later in 1952, illustrates how the themes and images concerning the development and use of the atomic bomb evolved from the seminal depictions that expressed the controversial and contradictory nature of atomic technology to more Hollywoodesque presentations embodying Cold War ideology and promoting government interests. Both films deal with the same historical period and the same sequence of factual material, that of the Manhattan Project and the bombing of Hiroshima and Nagasaki, but each selectively emphasizes different historical aspects of those facts. It is these differences that reveal the changing historical context—the evolving transformations of the film industry and their influence upon the appropriation and construction of nuclear themes.

MGM and the Atomic Bomb: *The Beginning or the End?* (1947)

> *The people of our century unleashed the power which might, for all we know, destroy human life on this Earth. . . . We know the beginning, only you of tomorrow, if there is a tomorrow, know the end.*
>
> (*The Beginning or the End?*)

Louis B. Mayer, chief executive of the second-largest Hollywood film studio, Metro-Goldwyn-Mayer, was anxious to produce the first film documenting the development of the atomic bomb. He was interested in capitalizing upon the anticipated prestige the studio would attain in explaining the history of atomic de velopment to curious audiences, while placing itself at the forefront of the public debate concerning the potential future use of the technology.

After buying the story from Hal Wallis of Paramount, who owned the rights, the studio jumped into the production of a fabricated account of the Manhattan Project, proposing to create an in-depth presentation of the implications of the bombing of Hiroshima and Nagasaki.[8] Titled *The Beginning or the End?* the film took its name from a quotation by President Truman about nuclear development. The script consisted of a fictional framework presented in a pseudodocumentary style, it went on to become a seminal example of the docudrama genre. The story of the development of the atomic bomb was presented against a romantic subplot involving a fictitious young scientist, Matt, and his bride.

MGM planned to adapt the atomic bomb issue to the previously successful documentary-style format. Norman Taurog was selected to direct the film, largely because of the success of his past work, particularly the documentary film *Young Tom Edison* (1940). The producer, Sam Marx, hoped *The Beginning or the End?* could be made in a similar style and tone and garner the same box-office success. Unfortunately for MGM, however, the ethical implications and the competing ideological interests surrounding the atomic issue were not as easy to manipulate into a simple entertainment format, as the more hygienic scientific discovery of electricity had been. The potential benefits to humanity of the atomic bomb were dubious, and although the dominant consensus embraced the idea that the use of the weapon had helped shorten the war and save thousands of American lives, a myriad of unanswered questions as to the morality and future direction of atomic technology were being debated within American society.

MGM promoters focused upon the controversial nature of the subject as a viable selling point. Offered as adult entertainment that questioned the morality of the bomb and provided justification for its use, *The Beginning or the End?* was advertised as a film of "unique value to all humanity." Since many facts concerning the bomb's development had yet to be publicized, the producer sought to capture a large audience by emphasizing that the film would reveal new information. Publicity posters promised to present the "true story of the A-bomb, the story of the most Hush-hush secret of all time."[9] This strategy of presenting in a docudrama format a transparent document of historical fact is evident in the film's opening sequence. In the first few scenes, the audience is presented with an explanation of the film's intended purpose. It was produced, according to the narration, for the sole purpose of being placed in a time capsule, not to be opened for five hundred years. Canisters of film, supposedly copies of the film the audience is about to see, are shown being buried in a grove of California redwoods. Replicating common newsreel style, the voice-over proclaims: "A message to future generations! Come what may, our civilization will have left an enduring record behind it. Ours will be no lost race."

Sam Marx ambitiously intended to present the facts concerning the entire course of the development of the atomic bomb in entertaining fashion. In doing so, the film narrative selectively emphasizes historical aspects deemed "entertaining," from Enrico Fermi's initial Chicago experiments to the destruction of Hiroshima, while providing a simplified explanation of atomic fission and the history of atomic research.

The conception of a Hollywood film that would ponder a serious threat to the continuance of American society, a threat born out of the government's own weapons research program, posed a message that was potentially oppositional to Washington's official nuclear policy. Early film scenes present Hume Cronyn portraying J. Robert Oppenheimer gravely questioning whether the birth of the "atomic age" represents "the beginning or the end" of civilization and "life, as we know it." Hence, the very title of the film conveyed the controversial and contradictory images involving the atomic subject found in American society at the time. Although the film narrative ultimately justifies the development of the atomic bomb, the negative ethical implications of its use as a weapon are openly debated throughout the film. This was the first such questioning of nuclear morality to be found in an entertainment format in Hollywood film. Although such questioning can be found in early science fiction productions (*Five*, *The Day the Earth Stood Still*, *Unknown World*, *Lost Continent*), such straightforward criticism of the bomb's morality is not to be found again until the early 1960s.

The elaboration of such potentially controversial content was not due to the producer's personal mandate or to any moral obligation he may have felt to present all sides of the issue. The content represents the complex negotiations between director Norman Taurog, government officials such as General Leslie Groves, and activist scientists Oppenheimer and Leo Szilard, all of whom had an interest in seeing their view of the issue sympathetically promoted. Such consideration of various interested parties was mandatory on the part of MGM. The film's docudrama format forced the studio to adhere to a legal requirement that no longer exists: In order to depict living, well-known public figures, film studios had to secure their permission in writing. Some individuals expected large fees and usually demanded the right to review and alter the script. Hence Taurog was forced to negotiate script approval from Pentagon officials and dissident Manhattan Project scientists, while still managing to imaginatively depict events that appealed to perceived audience tastes.[10]

The development of the initial script grew out of contacts between Sam Marx and members of the newly formed Atomic Scientists' Movement, a group of young, antimilitary Manhattan Project alumni who hoped to educate the public about the true nature of atomic weapons. (The movement soon developed into the Federation of Atomic Scientists.) Of utmost importance to the studio, however, was dramatic license in the depiction of events for maximum box-office draw. Certain convolutions in factual events were improvised in order to build dramatic tension. Specifically, the Manhattan Project and its research efforts were falsely presented as a race against both the Japanese and the Germans, who were portrayed as nearing completion of their own atomic bombs. This emphasis ig nited heated criticism from the scientists involved in the production, although MGM insisted that the changes were a commercial and artistic necessity. Words to this effect are found in a 1946 memo sent to Albert Einstein by Mayer himself: "It must be realized that dramatic truth is just as compelling a requirement on us as veritable truth is on a scientist." The license that MGM felt it had to falsify history for the sake of dramatics and box-office draw was simply excused in the opening credits: "This is basically a true story. However, for dramatic license and security purposes, some rearrangement of chronology and fictionalization was necessary."

This insistence upon "dramatic truth" caused the Atomic Scientists' Movement to withdraw their support and involvement from the project. They had hoped to determine the script's point of view and had received contributions from MGM for their assistance in early script development. When Marx refused to change the emphasis, the scientists withdrew their support with the expectation that senior scientists and military officials would likewise withhold their endorsements.[11]

Although they openly protested the direction the film seemed to be taking, the principal participants in the Manhattan Project continued to support the film's production. Robert Oppenheimer, Leo Szilard, Leslie Groves, and Vannevar Bush had already accepted fees from MGM, some as high as $10,000, in return for their permission to be depicted in the film. However, senior Manhattan Project personnel protested the original propagandistic tone of the screenplay, and MGM was forced to make some changes in the script to allow moral soul-searching on the part of the fictional scientist Matt and to adhere more closely with historical events. Hence, through negotiations between these individuals, the interests of the dissident scientists were at least partially served.

On the other hand, the film was created with the complete approval of both the White House and the War Department. General Groves and Vannevar Bush assisted MGM throughout production, concerned primarily that the movie not violate national security or discredit anyone involved in the Manhattan Project. A long-standing War Department policy stipulated that the Pentagon could help on a movie only when it benefited the services being portrayed or when cooperation was in the best interest of the military.[12] Explicit Pentagon regulations required that military procedures and personnel be pictured authentically and that the events portrayed be historically and technically accurate, or at least plausible. In this specific movie there were also security and political considerations, because not all of the information about the Manhattan Project had been made public by 1946. Military leaders voiced concern over certain scenes because the atomic bomb remained a high-priority security risk.[13]

The script was reviewed by William S. Parsons, the naval officer who completed the final assembly of the atomic bomb aboard the Enola Gay and who now served as assistant chief of naval operations for the Pentagon. His only critical hesitation was with the moral reservations and worries about the bomb expressed by the main character, Matt, the very emphasis insisted upon by the scientists involved.[14]

However, MGM stuck with the script as modified to suit the scientists and still received assistance from the War Department.

Creative License and Historic Fact

After trying to appease all these disparate elements, the completed film loosely presented historic events with some accuracy. Film scholars often cite *The Beginning or the End?* and its imaginative manipulation of historic fact as a seminal example of the development of the docudrama genre. For example, an early scene shows the fictitious character Matt convincing Albert Einstein that he should write to President Roosevelt and explain the necessity of atomic development in the race to outperform Germany's advancing atomic program. This has often been criticized as a falsification: "Einstein's letter is depicted as the sole reason for the Manhattan Project."[15] However, a deeper examination of the film narrative reveals that Einstein's letter as depicted by the movie was much closer to the truth than these scholars admit. After all, Einstein had complete script approval. Having been warned by members of the Atomic Scientists' Movement that the film would reflect the Pentagon's viewpoint, he twice refused his consent to be portrayed, only reluctantly approving after insisting upon script alterations that would ensure a factual presentation of his involvement with atomic development.[16]

In reality, Einstein did agree to lend his support to the efforts of many American and European scientists led by Leo Szilard, Eugene Wigner, and Edward Teller to develop atomic power. News of a full-scale uranium project being conducted by the German army's Weapons Department had persuaded the scientists to bring their fears to the attention of President Roosevelt. On August 2, 1939, Einstein signed a letter to the president emphasizing that studies of uranium fission foreshadowed the development of weaponry incorporating atomic power. The letter stated that the Germans were aware of and were actively working toward the development of these possibilities.[17] Einstein's message did not reach the president until ten weeks later, after the war in Europe had begun.

The Beginning or the End? presents its version of Einstein's collaboration with other atomic scientists as a meeting with the fictitious Matt, along with the other scientists working on bomb development. Here, presented as "the world's greatest living scientist," the Einstein character voices his concerns over Germany's motives in stopping all exports of uranium, even referring to his letter warning about German atomic development. Einstein then begins, along with the other scientists, to draft a letter to Roosevelt concerning Germany's potential development of atomic weapons.

Einstein's letter was not the sole motivation behind Roosevelt's condoning atomic bomb development. In the summer of 1941, the Military Application of Uranium Development (MAUD) Committee of Great Britain reported that an atomic bomb was possible, and Emilio Segre and Glenn Seaborg, working at Berkeley, made discoveries that solved the problem of creating a chain reaction.

On December 6, the day before the attack on Pearl Harbor, Roosevelt made the decision to provide resources for the construction of the atomic bomb.[18] The film narrative does attempt to fully illustrate the myriad of factors involved in the bomb's development. Through the use of newsreel footage and reenactments, it displays a montage of images of Hitler's invasion of Czechoslovakia, British and American scientists at various universities involved in atomic research, and the bombing of Pearl Harbor. The explanatory narration, in the newsreel style typical of the period, explains: "Universities and Colleges throughout the nation steeped themselves in atomic research. . . . Our scientists pushed forward in the race for knowledge . . . in the gigantic battle to conquer the atom."

This point is crucial—the script had no need to fabricate facts or events that at the time of its production were prevalent in the media and enjoyed much public exposure. To fabricate such simple chronological events of which the public was well aware would make the film appear false and foolish, thus working against the studio's wish to create a true document of the period.

The script is flexible in the retelling of factual events in the small but significant nuances of history. For example, in the movie, Matt contracts a lethal dose of radiation while arming the bomb all by himself on the airstrip where the Enola Gay awaits. In reality, the bomb's first fatality due to radiation occurred in Los Alamos in August 1945. Also, the petition that was circulated against the bomb's use by many scientists working on its development is not depicted, and there is no mention of Leo Szilard's attempts to prevent the bomb from being used against Japan. The movie does contain a scene showing a group of scientists who choose to stop participating in the bomb's development. They are shown from a sympathetic point of view telling the military that "this has now become a munitions project, hence we, as scientists, must resign." However, the Matt is the only scientist who explicitly questions the use of the bomb as a weapon, whereas in reality sixty atomic scientists signed a petition urging that the bomb not be used against Japan without a convincing warning.[19]

It is in the justification for the bomb's use that the film blatantly fabricates historical fact. In the film, leaflets warning the people of Hiroshima of the coming catastrophe are dropped ten days before the bombing: "We'll shower the cities for ten days, telling the population to leave." In fact, no such leafleting occurred. The Japanese were warned in an ultimatum on the evening of July 26 by the United States, Great Britain, and China to give up immediately or suffer annihilation. The ultimatum called upon the government of Japan to "proclaim now the unconditional surrender of all Japanese armed forces, and to provide proper and adequate assurances of their good faith in such action, or suffer prompt and utter destruction."[20] There was no specific mention of the atomic bomb, and Japanese Prime Minister Kantarō Suzuki told a group of reporters at a press conference two days later that they planned to ignore the ultimatum and "carry the war to a successful conclusion."[21] One can only speculate that the imaginative element of advanced warning was a move on MGM's part to help alleviate American guilt for destroying a target composed mainly of civilians, so that this "entertainment film" would not oppressively burden and alienate the audience it hoped to attract.

The Beginning or the End? for the most part portrays atomic weaponry and its technology as an instrument of peace. Statements in the dialogue justify the use of the atomic bomb in the context of World War II propaganda, which explicitly presents the bombing of Japan as a "necessary evil, less destructive than the prolongation of the war." Truman states in the film that the "consensus of opinion is that the bomb will shorten the war by approximately one year." In this, the film directly reiterates the Pentagon's and the Truman administration's official position that using the bomb would prevent the necessity to invade Japan, which by all estimates would prolong the fighting for another year and result in thousands of additional deaths.[22] Despite such justification, moral questions are nevertheless raised by the dialogue, which is prevented from being completely subsumed by pro-government ideology.

For example, throughout the script there is constant discussion of the ethics of developing atomic energy as a weapon, justified continually in post–World War II terms by the alleged race to develop the bomb before Germany does. Typical of such questioning and immediate justification is the following:

Must it end up as a bomb?
It's inevitable, so which end of the bomb do you want to be on?
Get it done before the Germans and Japs, then worry about the bomb.

Also typical is this exchange between President Roosevelt and Vannevar Bush, a representative of the scientists working on the Manhattan Project:

ROOSEVELT: Atomic energy on the loose could open the way for the destruction of all civilization.
BUSH: The development of atomic weaponry is inevitable, if not by this country, then by some other.
ROOSEVELT: Do you have any idea how far Hitler's scientists have progressed?
BUSH: They're probably ahead of us.

Toward the end of the film, further justification for using the bomb centers around the argument that it will shorten the war, especially given the prevalent idea that the Japanese would fight "to the last man, woman and child": "Thank God we've got the bomb and not the Japanese. If they had it, they would surely use it on us." After the bomb's successful test, one film character comments: "Now it seems certain we can hurry the end of the war. . . . A year less of war will save thousands of lives."

In promoting this rationale for dropping the bomb, the film was at least partially successful. Even trade magazine reviews echoed this emphasis in speculating that: "The onlooker absorbs the idea that if it weren't for the real life counterparts of all the characters unfolded on the screen they might very well not be here to view this film as an American film company produced it; in truth, had the Germans won the race for the secret weapon we might have been Hiroshimated instead."[23]

Whatever liberties the studio took in the imaginative alteration of events, its main motivation was purely commercial and not propagandistic. MGM needed to appease all interests involved in the film's production and at the same time create a profitable commodity. Fundamentally, an interesting dramatic story with the necessary, however fictitious, romantic elements was deemed necessary to attract the female audience that was so crucial in maximizing a film's commercial value. This necessitated portraying historical global events in a manner that the producer and director imagined would interest audiences. The incorporation of moral questions regarding the future use of this technology, and the future itself in the new nuclear world, were added as plot elements for the most part to appease the interests of the scientists involved in the project. The justification for the bomb's use and further military development promoted the interests of the military while echoing the dominant ideological stance of the time. Hence, the completed film embodied an uneasy and ambivalent attitude toward atomic technology. The strong ideological line of the Cold War touted by Hollywood screenplays had yet to be realized. Later, in the early 1950s, the justification for the initial use and continued development of atomic weaponry would be provided in terms of national security and broad suggestions of outside aggression. Few film narratives would leave an opening for such potentially critical speculation.

The Image of the Scientist

An important aspect of *The Beginning or the End?* is its emphasis upon the scientist as a main character in the action, as the "hero" of the war. The atomic scientists are repeatedly spotlighted as the individuals most in control while military characters play secondary parts, acting almost as light comic relief. The military characters appear simpleminded and even silly when compared to their more serious scientist counterparts. For example, a fictional subordinate of General Groves is presented as a womanizer and an opportunistic wise guy, someone who according to the actual General Groves "would not have been tolerated in the corps of engineers."[24]

This difference in characterization is largely due to the specific direct control over production employed by Oppenheimer, Einstein, and other participating atomic scientists. Negotiations between Oppenheimer and Sam Marx ensured that the film would designate the Oppenheimer character as the center of the action, the person in sole command of the Alamogordo test. Marx assured the scientist: "We have changed all the lines at the New Mexico test so that General Groves is merely a guest and you give all the orders." Furthermore, Oppenheimer insisted that his character be "an extremely pleasant one with a love of mankind, humility, and a fair knack of cooking."[25] Oppenheimer even visited during filming and was assured that his character would display "humility" and "a love of mankind."[26] Such concessions were necessary to appease the script interventions of the scientists, while Groves and other military leaders depicted in the film made surprisingly fewer demands upon characterization.

Despite such conscious emphasis on the positive nature of scientists and their role in atomic development, contradictory notions about the future benefits of atomic development and the scientists' role in the process are evident in the film's narrative. The atomic scientists are depicted as kindly, heroic figures, yet Matt, the character who expresses the most reservations about the ethics of the bomb, is killed by a radiation leak. The film's concluding sequence presents Matt's pregnant widow standing before the Lincoln Memorial in Washington, inspirationally explaining to the film audience that "the world will be a better place because of Matt's sacrifice." The choice of the Lincoln Memorial as the setting for this speech may suggest that the scientist is a martyr-hero. However, Matt's dying words, "That's what I get for building this thing," appropriate residual concepts from an earlier period in cultural history, that of the alchemist who, in delving into the secrets of nature, is destroyed by his own foolish, misguided research. The contradictory view toward atomic technology that the film also presents, juxtaposing atomic energy's terrifying potential for destruction and its more positive utopian promises, are also appropriations of residual themes of earlier scientific technologies already existent in American culture before the advent of the atomic bomb.

This ambiguous image of the scientist and his potential for creating both destructive and beneficial technology corresponds to the public dialogue prevalent during this period, which drew to a large extent from these residual themes. Immediately following the war, the participants in the Manhattan Project were honored and hailed as heroes, and their efforts were praised by Truman as "the greatest achievement of organized science in history."[27] The stature of the "atomic scientists" at this time grew to near-veneration because they were believed to understand the marvels of atomic technology and what part this technology could play in the future.[28] The atomic scientist was seen as having the ability to explore, understand, and manipulate the power of the universe, the power of creation that had previously been the domain of God alone. "In the public mind, these men had something of the aura of magicians; they seemed to possess ultimate power."[29]

Atomic scientists, with their newfound prestige after the bombing of Hiroshima, joined together to convey their anxiety about the atomic bomb and its darker potential. The ethical implications of developing and deploying the bomb had begun to concern the scientists involved in its construction even before the weapon was tested. A number of Chicago scientists, including Leo Szilard, had petitioned the U.S. government to detonate an atomic bomb on a deserted island as a demonstration, rather than dropping it right away on a civilian target. They worried about a postwar world in which there would be no safety from atomic bombs without drastic changes in the mechanisms of the world order, including the establishment of an international peace force. After the war, many Manhattan Project scientists worked to promote the concept of a world government.

The Atomic Scientists' Movement, which openly opposed further U.S. atomic weaponry development, enjoyed public respect for a time and was widely praised for the responsible way in which it investigated the social and cultural impact of the bomb. Articles began to be published describing the potential risks to civilization posed by the bomb, explaining in detail the damage such bombs could cause and exploiting public apprehensions about atomic technology. New forms of governing this technology were encouraged in order to safeguard against world destruction. In 1946, Albert Einstein expressed such sentiments: "Our world faces a crisis as yet unperceived by those possessing the power to make great decisions for good or evil. The unleashed power of the atom has changed everything save our modes of thinking, and thus we drift toward unparalleled catastrophe."[30]

The Federation of Atomic Scientists was formed largely from the Atomic Scientists' Movement in order to help move society toward specific goals. "Our first objective," the federation's members reported, "must be to mobilize a healthy, action-goading fear for effective measures against the real danger—war."[31] The group promoted the need for international control to avoid an otherwise inevitable doom. All nations were pressed to place their planned nuclear energy projects under one world government. The scientists consciously constructed an image of a utopian world of a millennial age of peace, adopting such conceptions as the atomically powered city first envisioned with the discovery of radium itself, and H. G. Wells's vision of a "Golden Age."

This "world government plan" for the international control of atomic energy was devised in part by Robert Oppenheimer and positioned scientists in the crucial role of controlling worldwide atomic development and use. The plan, which was accepted in principle by a large majority of United Nations members, generally proposed to allow selected atomic scientists to police the free exchange of information among international teams that would inspect nuclear facilities. The international agency would also employ scientists to develop new, peaceful uses for atomic technology. The National Committee on Atomic Information, which brought together the National Farmers' Union, the American Federation of Labor, and the League of Women Voters, promoted the idea that only international controls could provide safety.

By 1950, however, the Federation of Atomic Scientists, with its goal of an international scientific world order, had been reduced to a small and powerless organization. There has been much speculation on the reason for this failure. Paul Boyer, in his cultural history of the years immediately following World War II, reasons that as the atomic scientists worked to intensify public emotions, they unknowingly "created fertile psychological soil for the ideology of American nuclear superiority and an all out crusade against Communism."[32] Spencer Weart's history of the same period offers a similar conclusion; it presents atomic energy as an extremely powerful and destructive technology that was being developed at a time when the government was promoting anticommunism and fear of subversive infiltration and foreign intervention. Under these circumstances, Americans were reluctant to seek assistance from an international agency made up of mostly foreign-born scientists.[33]

The ultimate failure of the Federation of Atomic Scientists can also be linked to the powerful negative image of the scientist prevalent in American culture, an image that was too deeply rooted to be dispelled by recent historical events, public relations, or goodwill. The public mood at this time was complex and ambivalent, and along with a desperate faith in scientists and their developing technology were concerns of mistrust and feelings of fear and disillusionment related to a more negative view of scientific discovery already existent within the culture.[34] As general speculation concerning nature's secrets and God's mysterious beams became associated with atomic energy, many became nervous about the growing power of science, particularly as scientists were described by the media as "playing with bombs like toys" and "playing God."

Debates over the role that science should play in American society led many people to conclude that scientists were delving into mysteries of the universe that were better left alone. The image of the scientist as a single-minded, powerful, and antisocial individual, excessively inclined to inflict violent change on society, was perhaps too strong a notion for the public to fully place its trust in. Whatever the factors contributing to the demise of the Federation of Atomic Scientists, scientists were to enjoy their elevated stature in film for only a short time. Soon, the Hollywood studios would replace the image of the competent scientist with an emotionless and self-serving Dr. Frankenstein, while the military hero emerged as the more admirable character.

Images of Atomic Technology

The descriptions of the technology and effects of the atomic bomb in *The Beginning or the End?* were appropriated from the rhetoric found in the popular media, government speeches, and public claims made by atomic scientists, which described atomic development in terms of natural phenomena and religious imagery. Scientists had consciously evoked themes relating this technology to the "unlocking of the mysteries of nature," while debate over the contradictory character of atomic energy as utopian power and death force had evolved from the seminal discovery of radium. Traditional themes dealing with nature's forbidden secrets and the Earth's untapped potential were employed by the media to encapsulate and make understandable the phenomenon of nuclear fission. The language and images used to discuss this new phenomena were partly a reflection of the attempt to slot the new reality into the older existing themes of American culture, and in so doing to delineate the "bounds for possible thought" about nuclear technology.[35] The use of specific imagery to convey certain notions about this technology, making it familiar and acceptable, was also no doubt meant to serve the purposes of those who were concerned with perpetuating its development and deployment.

But in drawing upon traditional themes to partially embody the image of nuclear technology, the media, politicians, and Hollywood producers participated in a process that involved the resurrection and selection of residual cultural elements. Every society relies on a central system of practices, meanings, and values that is dominant and that contributes to an understanding of the nature of the world, constituting a sense of reality for the majority in that society. This central system is absolute in the sense that it is difficult for most people to move beyond it, but it is not static. A process of incorporation is always at work, constructed by agencies that transmit dominant culture, such as educational institutions and the Hollywood film industry.

These agencies work in a "selective tradition," a process by which the terms of the dominant culture are passed off as society's genuine past and sole legitimate tradition, and by which other areas of meaning and practice are excluded or interpreted into forms that support elements of the dominant culture. However, some meanings exist in society that are based upon older forms of culture, meanings that form a body of residual cultural elements. For example, religious values are one aspect of the past that must be incorporated into the dominant culture if it is to make sense. These residual cultural elements can be appropriated by the dominant culture to interpret and give meaning to new events or phenomena. However, such incorporated residual meanings can also challenge the dominant system by highlighting its contradictions, its weaknesses and flaws.[36]

Such is the case with the emerging technology of the atom. Residual themes deeply embedded within American culture concerning nature's secrets and the role of the scientist were intermingled and appropriated by social agencies to help define and convey a specific understanding of the issue and its potential ramifications. The themes that gradually became linked with atomic energy usually involved two sides, often polar opposites. For example, along with the healing capabilities of radiation came the potential for death and destruction. These images were sometimes evoked by the scientists working with radium or were used by government officials and the media to convey the drama and significance of each new atomic discovery. Later, members of the Hollywood industry sought to find the most profitable ways to incorporate these two-sided themes, further linking specific meanings to atomic development in their quest for box-office dollars.

In selecting these residual cultural meanings to frame the new technology, Hollywood in effect worked to incorporate such meanings into the dominant culture. However, the atom's potential to destroy civilization, or even the entire planet, makes it unique. Nuclear development was so tied to questions of morality and human existence, so emotionally charged, that the use of these older cultural themes to interpret the phenomenon also pointed out contradictions within the dominant ideology. Such contradictions raised the idea that the consequences of nuclear development could never be completely predictable or containable, even under the federal jurisdiction that was so respected in Cold War America.

Before the end of World War II, knowledge about the atomic bomb was confined to high-level government politicians and multinational scientists administering and working on the Manhattan Project. The only information that was initially publicized was simply that the United States had developed a bomb that could destroy an entire city. The public, however, could only comprehend such news in terms of familiar images—namely, conventional explosives and bombs. Very little concrete information was freely circulated about the bomb's full destructive power, and the public and press came to depend upon censored government reports for descriptions of nuclear energy and its myriad consequences.

After the public became aware of the existence of this technology, it became necessary for the media to cover the issue. It is precisely during this process that certain residual cultural elements were adopted by various individuals in order to promote a selective view of nuclear technology.[37] Specifically, the technology was imbued with a religious meaning in an attempt to provide safe and familiar metaphors for what could have been perceived as "unnatural" or "unworldly." Joseph Rotblatt, a physicist who pulled out of the atom bomb project, commented upon the "naturalization" of the bomb: "While everybody agrees that a nuclear war would be an unmitigated catastrophe, the attitude towards it is becoming similar to that of potential natural disasters, earthquakes, tornadoes, and other acts of God."[38]

Religious rhetoric was immediately linked to atomic technology as the Trinity test in 1945 gave scientists and the military their first look at the results of their labors. From the experience of the image of the bomb's explosion came Oppenheimer's much quoted phrase from the Bhagavad Gita: "I am become Death, the shatterer of worlds." Perhaps more pertinent was the conscious connection of Christian religious imagery to atomic technology, particularly in the choice of the name "Trinity" itself and in the language of birth and apocalypse in the description of the bomb's effects. The sound of the explosion was equated to the "warning of doomsday . . . making us feel that we puny things were blasphemous to dare tamper with the forces heretofore reserved to the Almighty." The spectacle was described as "the first cry of a newborn world," "like being present at the moment God said 'Let there be light.'"[39] The official War Department report on the Trinity test incorporated biblical phrases such as "the darkening heavens poured forth rain and lightning" and "the witnessing of the ultimate creative force."[40]

Describing the atomic bomb in terms of religious awe was useful not so much to describe the new concept but to diminish human control over and political responsibility for its use. This language worked to conceal the horror of the consequences of the bomb, which was largely ignored by politicians and the press. A set of positively valued words for describing the bomb and its effects also emerged, which were adopted particularly by official government spokespeople. Linking the weapon to natural elements was a common tactic immediately following the Hiroshima bombing. In his speeches, President Truman repeatedly described atomic technology as a natural phenomenon with such rhetoric as: "It is an atomic bomb. It is the harnessing of the basic power of the universe" and "The force from which the sun draws its power has been loosed against those who brought war to the Far East."[41] A typical American newsreel explained that the bomb had destroyed Hiroshima by a "cosmic power . . . described by eyewitnesses as doomsday itself."[42] Soon, it became commonplace for the media to describe the development and the dropping of the bomb as somehow outside of human control, a natural process.

In drawing upon popular descriptions to give meaning to the atomic spectacle, Hollywood film furthers the link between religion, natural phenomena, and atomic technology. The creators of *The Beginning or the End?* employed these descriptions in the film's narrative. For example, after the first atomic pile experiment, Enrico Fermi is portrayed as commenting: "We have unleashed a force that can be very good—all the energy of the universe, locked up since the beginning of time, now we've finally turned the key."

The dialogue also reverberates with the rhetoric associated with atomic energy since its inception, the potential for good and for the creation of utopian civilization evoked by the media and government officials. For example, Matt comments upon the future of this technology: "It's a harnessing of the basic power of the universe. . . . In peacetime, atomic energy could be used to bring about a golden age, such an age of prosperity and well-being the world has never known."

The film's final scene reaffirms the justification for the bomb's development in the glowing terms of a future atomic utopia in which atomic energy is used for the betterment of mankind: "Atomic energy is a hand God has extended. . . . Someday the atoms in a cup of water will heat a home, the energy in a blade of grass will send planes to distant lands. . . . Everything that went before atomic energy was the dark ages. . . . We have found the secret of the power of the universe, and men will use this knowledge well."

The utopian promise of atomic energy has had a long history. By the 1920s, the idea that radium held the secret that could revolutionize civilization was a widely familiar theme with the American public. After Ernest Rutherford and Frederick Soddy's discovery of transmutation, every voice from newspaper writers to public lecturers presented euphoric visions of atomic technologies and exclaimed that the new power gave scientists a tool with which to revolutionize civilization. Radium might be harnessed to illuminate cities, propel vehicles, create new metals—to do almost anything imaginable.[43]

Gradually, the media began to elaborate upon the coming "golden age" with descriptions of a future world, a technological garden of Eden, to be built anew, perhaps on a clean slate once an atomic war was over. Some scientists depicted an underground civilization, with the surface of the earth given over to parks and wilderness. This vision of utopia, the media stated, was not a promise centuries away but was already being created in scientific laboratories. "It is a new form of power—atomic power."[44] Experts continued to predict that new energy sources would resolve every difficulty and that science would lead to inevitable progress.

The first individuals to have knowledge about atomic energy nearly always connected it with ancient myths, using the concepts of transmutation and a utopian future to publicize their findings. Science journalists usually joined in the scientists' enthusiasm about the new discoveries and further emphasized traditional images in association with the new technological developments.[45] For example, the transmutational properties of radiation were immediately associated with the "hidden power of the universe," as radioactivity was shown to release more energy, atom for atom, than any other process known. This discovery was relayed to the public by the press in May 1903 in a British magazine. In his 1908 book *The Interpretation of Radium and the Structure of the Atom,* Frederick Soddy further explained the "inexhaustible" power of radioactivity as having the potential to "transform a desert continent, thaw the frozen poles, and make the world one smiling Garden of Eden."

> Looking backwards at the great things science has already accomplished, and at the steady growth in power and fruitfulness of scientific method, it can scarcely be doubted that one day we shall come to break down and build up compounds, and the pulses of the world will then throb with a new source of strength as immeasurably removed from any we at present control as they in turn are from the natural resources of the human savage.[46]

The idea that science and technology would lead to the betterment of society was, of course, already existent within the culture at the time of the discovery of X rays and radium. A utopian "white city," a model of a future metropolis, was constructed for the Chicago International Exposition of 1893. The planet Mars had recently been described as being covered with aqueducts, remnants of a superior utopian civilization constructed by technologically advanced Martians engineers. Scientists themselves forwarded the idea that eventually scientific discoveries would lead to a utopian future by, for example, providing a limitless source of energy.

But with such glorious praise of technology came the fear of delving into "God's secrets," which were better left untouched—the idea of opening a Pandora's box that had the potential to destroy the world. Frederick Soddy had emphasized the disturbing idea that the Earth was "a storehouse stuffed with explosives, inconceivably more powerful than any we know of, and possibly only awaiting a suitable detonator to cause the earth to revert to chaos."[47] Hand in hand with the goodness of creative and healing atomic rays came their polar opposite—the destructive "death ray."

The idea of a malevolent radiated force can be linked to a wealth of death-ray mythology. Ideas that were common folklore in many cultures, ideas that rays represented illumination or blazing thunderbolts from God, that rays altered minds or peered into secrets, were concepts that became linked to radiation. And the potential use of such a ray as a weapon, against one's enemies, was also nothing new. The Romans perpetuated the legend of Archimedes blasting an invading fleet with giant mirrors that concentrated the rays of the sun, while talk of a philosopher's giant burning glass destroying armies has continued down through the centuries. As soon as Wilhelm Conrad Röntgen announced his discovery of X rays, some people wrote to him to express their fears of his "death rays."[48]

Not surprisingly, *The Beginning or the End?* mentions this destructive potential of atomic technology only briefly, for example in the comment from the bombers in the Enola Gay as they witness the destruction of Hiroshima: "If there ever is another war, it won't be cities burning each other, it will be the whole world on fire, eating itself to ashes."

Hollywood Film Style and Atomic Images

In blending together popular imagery and government rhetoric into the narrative of *The Beginning or the End?* MGM adopted a proven stylistic form in order to convey the timely significance of the events surrounding the atomic bomb. In proposing to present the "true story" of the development of the atomic bomb, director Norman Taurog chose to construct the narrative in a "march of time" style currently fashionable for depicting important historical events. This docudrama style allowed for the exploitation of factual material while permitting artistic license in developing fictional subplots. The format also promised more commercial viability, appealing to a larger audience than pure documentary while "imparting a sense of realism beyond average."[49]

The Beginning or the End? depends to a large extent upon stock and newsreel footage for the development of its narrative. This technique ties the film and the events depicted to reality, where they are afforded more credibility. This use of newsreel footage as a reference point for the real world was a popular style in the late 1940s, particularly in docudramas of this type. Because of the reliance upon stock footage of, for example, the mushroom cloud of the detonated atomic bomb, the same scenes were found in many different movies and soon became familiar referents to nuclear development. Later in the decade, stock footage was incorporated more and more into science fiction films that dealt with the manifestation of imaginary beings, to provide a basis in reality for such creatures as the radiation-produced monster.

Largely because of the novelty of the image, *The Beginning or the End?* is typical of early films involving atomic themes in that it devotes much film time to showing bomb explosions and scientific technology. The camera lingers upon the fabricated atomic explosion, for example, and presents an abundance of rapid cuts between explosions and the awestruck faces of spectators. This repeated image emphasizes the powerful force and unbelievable potential of the technology, a moving spectacle only available in theaters to pretelevision audiences.

However, actual footage of atomic explosions was unavailable to Hollywood at that time. The awe-inspiring explosions presented by the film were in reality complete Hollywood constructions—they were fabricated by the cinematographer A. Arnold Gillespie, who won an Oscar for his effects. By devising a miniature fake atomic explosion using an underwater camera and exploding sacks of dye, Gillespie created a plausible image of what he thought an atomic explosion should look like. The simulated blast was so impressive that the U.S. Air Force used it in a training film, and the same scene went on to be used as an authentic document of an atomic explosion in many other documentary and Hollywood productions.[50]

In exploiting the general fascination with atomic technology prevalent at this time, MGM drew upon another stylistic mode of presentation. Relating atomic technology to science fiction foreshadows the popularity of that genre, in which the majority of future Hollywood films with atomic themes would occur. For example, throughout the film's dialogue there are direct references linking atomic technology to popular science fiction. As Matt is introduced to an army observer, this dialogue ensues:

MILITARY OBSERVER: I'm a little behind on Flash Gordon's latest.
MATT: Compared to what we're trying to do, Flash Gordon is a boy from the stone age.
MILITARY OBSERVER: Oh, then I'm a prehistoric ape.

The appearance of the bomb itself, far from the traditional cylindrical bomb shape we are now familiar with, is something out of the Flash Gordon serial popular during this time. Its shiny, painted, and finned "rocket ship" attributes are borrowed from science fiction props.

The further linking of atomic development to the futuristic marvels of science fiction is evident in the dramatization of scientific technology and technique. The initial Hollywood scenarios portraying atomic experimentation emphasized sensational technological spectacle at the expense of historical accuracy. Much film time was devoted to presenting devoted scientists hovering over elaborate electronic constructions or vigorously scribbling notes as imposing instrument panels furiously beeped and buzzed. Rather than depicting the carefully documented and visually dull routines involved in most actual scientific procedure, Hollywood chose to concoct imaginative scientific procedures replicated from the early science fiction serials, even in the portrayal of actual experiments. Producer Marx was interested not in how science was actually conducted but in how the public thought it was.[31] MGM's version of the Chicago atomic pile experiment takes place in a contrived and purely imaginative electronic laboratory, which featured the loud buzzing sounds of "the splitting of uranium atoms" and an abundance of mysteriously flashing gizmos. The atomic pile is also misrepresented as an imposing pyramid composed of various rods and batteries of blinking lights. The actual pile was covered with balloon cloth and was visually unimpressive.[32]

Such construction of sensational images to attract audience interest in one sense glorified the atomic scientists and the specialized knowledge at their command, their ability to work in a realm few have access to. This focus upon the selective, mysterious, and unearthly work of science resonates with the alien nature of the scientist figure, a theme that would eventually overtake the more positive portrayal of scientists created by Hollywood immediately after Hiroshima.

Before the premier of *The Beginning or the End?* MGM expected that they had produced a "daringly strong audience picture." Although promoted by *Variety* as having "authenticity and a special historical significance," the film did not enjoy much critical or financial success. At least seventy-five films grossed more at the box office in 1947.[53] The film was widely criticized as a piece of "cheery imbecil-ity," and critics worried that its poor success and "thin showmanship" would "dis-courage the making of better pictures on the subject." Scolding Hollywood "for treating cinema goers as if they were spoiled children," few reviewers questioned the historical accuracy of the narrative or the dubious stance for the justification of atomic development.[54]

The need to negotiate with so many diverse interests in the production of the film was offered by Marx as rationale for its dismal box-office draw. Dramatic li-cense had to be subordinated to the general depiction of historic fact; the film-makers had been forced to rewrite or delete many scenes to please particular in-dividuals. The dubious interest of a large audience in a film that presented the serious implications of atomic development was also offered as an excuse. To counteract the drab nature of the topic itself, MGM went on to release the film as the bottom half of a double bill with a Red Skelton comedy.

However, in the years since its release, *The Beginning or the End?* has reached a large audience, particularly as part of the MGM archive collection aired on Ted Turner's cable television movie channel. Due to its documentary style, this care-fully constructed film view of history has probably come to be accepted as an ac-curate version of the actual events for most viewers. Popular movie guides describe the film as "an engrossing account of atomic bomb development," recommending the film as a perfectly credible reflection of history. Few viewers question the de-liberate falsifications in the film or the motivations of the producers.[55]

2

MGM and the Cold War

Above and Beyond (1952)

Military personnel display knowledge of atomic technology in *Above and Beyond* (1952)

FIVE YEARS AFTER RELEASING *The Beginning or the End?* MGM again chose to produce a film that presented the development of the atomic bomb with *Above and Beyond* (1952). However, the studio's motivation was not entirely success at the box office. Rather, the film represents an attempt to appease public concern and government scrutiny into the suspected subversive nature of Hollywood and its products. MGM also chose to frame this new version of the development of the atomic bomb in a standardized dramatic formula, focusing plot development entirely upon the actions of one individual—Colonel Paul Tibbets, whose mission was to drop the atomic bomb on Hiroshima.

Many factors helped determine this change in emphasis and tone in a film that depicted largely the same historical time period and events as *The Beginning or the End?* Increasing financial troubles were affecting the major studios due to economic restructuring and decreasing film attendance. Direct governmental scrutiny into film content by the House Un-American Activities Committee (HUAC) placed a censorial pressure upon film producers. Although the war with Germany and Japan had ended, greater resources were being devoted to the development of larger atomic bombs—the United States was well under way in construction of the hydrogen bomb—and an expanding defense institution. The United States no longer enjoyed exclusive ownership of the bomb, as it had in 1947—the Soviet Union demonstrated its atomic technology in 1949. A full-scale nuclear arms race was escalating and the Korean War had begun. These events all took place in the period between the production of *The Beginning or the End?* and *Above and Beyond*. Consequently, the latter movie justifies the activities of the Manhattan Project not in terms pertinent to the historic context in which the events took place but in terms of the cultural atmosphere of 1954.

Above and Beyond was the forerunner of a series of air force movies made later in the 1950s, all which portrayed the atomic bomb as a deterrent to war and an indispensable weapon for national defense. Films replicating this agenda include *Strategic Air Command* (1955), which showcased Curtis LeMay's bomber force as the major deterrent to communist domination of the world, and *Bombers B-52* (1957), which presented the Strategic Air Command (SAC) and the bomb as tools for maintaining peace. Almost formulaic in their characterization and emphasis, these films were later labeled "Cold War propaganda tracts" because of their glorification of the competence of the military as an organization and their portrayal of individual military heroes. Also common to such films' narratives is their open justification of defense industry expenditures in terms of the war against communism abroad and against subversion within the United States[1]

This emphasis upon military efficiency as the guarantor of the American way of life is evident from the film title itself. *Above and Beyond* centers upon a military hero whose devotion to job and country require him to sacrifice "above and beyond the call of duty," rather than questioning the future of humanity in the atomic age as did *The Beginning or the End?* The focus upon the military character as a competent protector of the country's interests and very survival, along with a growing emphasis upon national security, opens a period in which the military and the military hero is paramount in film narratives. In the 1950s, Hollywood products began to promote the importance of the military in sustaining the nation's well-being while urging civilians to accept secrecy, avoid meddling with military concerns, and be grateful that the United States had an atomic arsenal.

Of course, existing atomic technology and future research was now inescapably tied to military interests. Much rhetoric about national security achieved through military power appeared after 1945, and from 1946 to 1953 the United States's atomic program concentrated almost exclusively on expanding the country's nuclear arsenal. The growing Cold War between the United States and the Soviet Union halted all attempts to establish international control over atomic energy and weaponry. During the next decade, the United States would devote vast sums of money to defense. In the effort to develop scientific research and technology to keep the United States ahead of its rivals in weaponry, and hence to ensure American security, the government mobilized large numbers of citizens as well as monetary resources in national defense programs.

After the Soviet atomic bomb test in 1949, President Truman approved a crash program to begin developing a hydrogen bomb, or "super" as it was known at the time. The concept of using an atomic bomb to initiate a fusion reaction in hydrogen, thus releasing huge amounts of energy, was conceived by Edward Teller during the Manhattan Project. The "super" was expected to be a thousand times more powerful than the atomic bomb, a weapon of mass destruction that administration officials hoped would put the United States back in the lead over the Soviet Union in nuclear weapon technology.[2]

In part to promote this new agenda, Hollywood studios and the Pentagon strengthened their links. Increasingly, military interests were served by Hollywood products, due to the military's direct involvement in script development and the government's pressure on Hollywood to create suitable content. In preparing the script and filming the story of the first atomic bombing for *Above and Beyond*, MGM hired General LeMay, creator and chief of the SAC, and Colonel Tibbets, pilot of the Enola Gay, as script consultants. Whereas MGM hoped that such a film justifying the development and use of the atomic bomb strictly from the Pentagon's point of view would help alleviate the political pressure of the HUAC investigations, LeMay hoped that such a movie would help boost the SAC's public image, which was also under scrutiny. The public complained of the SAC's heavy costs with little noticeable return, and LeMay wanted to convey the SAC as an indispensable organization for national security.[3]

The Strategic Air Command had been formed seven months after the end of World War II; it was assigned the mission of preparing to carry out nuclear attacks anywhere on the planet. By 1951, the atomic arsenal had become crucial to U.S. military strategy, and nuclear-capable B-29s were stationed at bases throughout the Northern Hemisphere. The number of radioactive cores for atomic bombs grew from thirteen in 1947 to nearly three hundred in 1950, with a corresponding increase in delivery capability.[4] The SAC wanted to project an image of itself as a deadly force, and the logic of deterrence entailed convincing the enemy that war would mean utter destruction. The American public not only had to see the SAC as crucial to its very survival, but to have respect and confidence in its bombers. And at the same time, the SAC had to appear imposing and formidable to foreign countries.

These factors largely dictated the tone and emphasis of *Above and Beyond*. Immediately evident is the justification of the bomb's development and use set in a Cold War agenda. In the film narrative, issues of the morality of the atomic weapon are explicitly linked to the continuance of the American system and way of life, directly echoing the reasoning behind the government's defense policy at the time. An example of this strategy occurs in a scene where Colonel Tibbets's wife comments that "somewhere at this very moment bombs are being dropped and children are being killed." This moment of moral questioning provokes an intense reaction from Tibbets, who espouses the justification not only for the use of the bomb but for its continued development:

> Look, let's clear up one little piece of morality right now. It's not bombs alone that are horrible, but war. War is what is wrong, not weapons. Sure innocent people are being killed, but to lose this war to the gang we're fighting would be one of the most immoral things we could do to those kids in there.

Or, as Tibbets ponders the implications of dropping the bomb the night before the event, he says: "I'm scared of what can happen if this thing we're unleashing doesn't stop the war—and all others."

The rationale of atomic weaponry development as a major deterrent to war was an idea officially promoted in 1954, and the script of *Above and Beyond* was a conscious strategy on the part of the Pentagon working with MGM to justify continued work on the bomb in the historic context of World War II. This reasoning marked a shift in the selling of atomic weaponry to the American public, from the immediate reason that the bomb was developed to end World War II to the interests of the military industrial complex in furthering weapons development in peacetime. There was scarce mention in the movie of the German or Japanese enemy, as in *The Beginning or the End?* In fact, if viewers were unfamiliar with the events of World War II, they might not even know with whom the Americans were fighting.

This direct military involvement in promoting a specific depiction of atomic technology served to repress the more contradictory images of nuclear development found in the late 1940s. Gone are the "hidden secrets of the universe" descriptions found in the early rhetoric of the atomic issue. The evocation of the positive and negative nature of bomb development and the religious imagery are replaced by straightforward, antiseptic dialogue. For example, a military spokesman in *Above and Beyond* explains the fundamentals of atomic technology:

"The right amount of atomic material has the explosive force of twenty tons of TNT . . . For maximum efficiency the bomb must be exploded in the air."

Basic questions and anxieties concerning atomic technology, and the contradictory residual images of the earlier debate, were displaced to another genre, science fiction, which allowed such potentially dissenting opinions to be presented without Pentagon scrutiny.

The Military and Scientists

The narrative of *Above and Beyond* portrays the main character, Tibbets, as a hero who places his duty to country over his own life and the well-being of his family. His unwavering devotion to his military superiors and to the task before him is constantly emphasized. There is no place for emotion or questions of morality in the military: "I've known a lot of men who have difficulty showing emotion—it's a quality which is sometimes indispensable."

Such stoicism is presented as a necessary characteristic of individuals who man the controls of the atomic arsenal. Rather than guiltily weighing the ethics of decisions, as the scientist Matt does in *The Beginning or the End?* Tibbets reports back stone-faced to headquarters after viewing the Hiroshima destruction: "Results good." No deep pondering about the fate of the world in the atomic age or about the next war. Another example of this emphasis upon duty and stoicism is a dialogue between Tibbets and his commanding general:

GENERAL: No one's ever dropped an atomic bomb before. I can't give you
    any guarantee you'll come back.
TIBBETS: A guarantee didn't come with the uniform.

The film's atomic scientists however, are depicted as weak and unable to come to concrete decisions. Tibbets must decide when the bomb is ready to be dropped because the scientists are uncertain and don't want to take the responsibility for a "decision of this magnitude." They also display a flippant attitude when the final decision must be made concerning the readiness of the atomic bomb for use. When a group of Manhattan Project scientists are asked when they will be certain the bomb is ready, this conversation ensues:

SCIENTIST: Hard to say, maybe months . . .
TIBBETS: A lot of men can die in a month.
SCIENTIST: Then the responsibility for its use must be completely and
    solely yours.

Not only do the civilian scientists appear weak, they seem to have lost their former credibility as purveyors of knowledge: It is a military character who explains atomic principles to high-level officials in a meeting, not the civilian scientists.

It was in the interest of the Pentagon, the Atomic Energy Commission, and MGM to portray the atomic scientists in this light. Atomic technology's immediate use had depended to a large extent upon the scientists who had developed the bomb in wartime, and further weaponry development depended upon scientific discovery. However, the interests of the military and the scientists had conflicted throughout World War II, and relations had been strained between the Manhattan Project scientists and the military personnel responsible for the project's security. The scientists blamed the military whenever they felt that their work was being impeded, and after the war, the two groups conflicted over how the development of nuclear power should be administered.[5]

This debate led to the McMahon Act of early 1946, which vested control over atomic research and production in a five-member civilian Atomic Energy Commission (AEC), giving the commission control over the production of fissionable material and all information concerning atomic energy. The bill also provided for the creation of a military liaison committee to cement relations between the AEC and the military and provided for creation of the General Advisory Committee (GAC), made up of a panel of scientists, to council the AEC. The act also subjected scientists to tight secrecy restrictions, reflecting the widespread hope that the bomb could be kept as an American monopoly.

By 1951, the American atomic bomb monopoly and the scientists' movement advocating world government and international control over atomic development had failed, while a mood of anti-intellectualism had arisen.[6] The prestige afforded scientists in the aftermath of the war had diminished, and their campaign for world government was being publicly criticized. Their motives in grouping together to offer social and political advice were being examined. Some saw their actions as motivated by unacknowledged guilt over Hiroshima and Nagasaki. Atomic scientists now were being presented as no more qualified than any other informed citizens to offer political and social guidance. Paul Boyer writes that from 1945 through 1947, the prevailing attitude toward members of the scientists' movement had been of approval and admiration, but that by the end of 1947 such admiration had faded. By 1949, opinion polls found growing public sentiment against atomic scientists. This decline in public favor is attributed to the conflict between what the scientists had to say about the hazards of bomb development and the AEC's positive portrayal of atomic energy.[7]

The AEC used scare tactics to garner support for weapons development and used the public's fear of communism to discredit its opponents, as in the case of Oppenheimer. The AEC's advisory committee, the GAC, which was headed by Oppenheimer, opposed the development of the hydrogen bomb, arguing that such a weapon should not be built before all arms control possibilities had been examined and explored. When Oppenheimer publicly came out against the development of the hydrogen bomb in 1953, the commission charged him with being a communist sympathizer. Such an accusation was at the time enough to end a government career, and it is ironic that the AEC chose this line to discredit Oppenheimer when his ties to the Communist Party were known years earlier when he was originally selected to head the Manhattan Project.

The official charge against Oppenheimer contained allegations of improper association with communist sympathizers and denounced the scientist for having opposed the development of the hydrogen bomb. A three-person review panel heard testimony on Oppenheimer, concluded that he posed a security risk, and forced him to leave government service. A "blank wall" was placed between Oppenheimer and all classified government information, which outraged the scientific community. Scientists began to feel themselves vulnerable to government scrutiny and repressed by the intense security measures surrounding all nuclear development.[8]

This emphasis upon security and the maintenance of military secrets is also stressed in *Above and Beyond*. Much film time is devoted to illustrating security measures during the Manhattan Project—the covert investigation and surveillance of individuals, procedures for securing building entrances, secret coded messages, and code names for secret projects. The need for extreme secrecy in the interest of military security is shown contributing to marital discord between Tibbets and his wife. She is portrayed as bitterly unhappy because the military insists that she "stay out of her husband's business." Eventually, she becomes so determined to discover the "secret" of her husband's work that she becomes a security risk and is forced to leave the training base and Tibbets's life, at least until the bomb is dropped and the nature of his mission can be revealed.

Such concern with security developed out of the history of the bomb's development. Wartime censorship of all published articles concerning atomic power, whether in professional publications or in the mass media, had begun in June 1940. Secrecy was a primary concern of the Manhattan Project; its research and testing sites were built covertly and its scientists traveled under assumed names. According to Leslie Groves, "security was not the primary object of the Manhattan Project. Our mission was to develop an atomic bomb of such power that it would bring the war to an end at the earliest possible date. Security was an essential element, but not all controlling."[9]

When the Manhattan Project was at last revealed to the general public after the war, its success in retaining its secrecy up to that point impressed many Americans. The project was described by the press as the "best kept secret of the war."[10] Debate concerning the secrets of the bomb itself and whether they should be released to the world were conducted in postwar cabinet meetings, and much discussion in newspapers as well as in popular fiction reflected such concerns.[11]

This linkage of secrecy and atomic technology continued after the war, becoming almost a mania, as the control of nuclear energy began to mean the control over secrets. Nuclear scientists now found that basic scientific information was secret government property, contradictory to their pre-1940 tradition of open publication on fission research. The AEC had sweeping powers over censorship of information and maintained the standards of security originally imposed upon the Manhattan Project. The concern about security leaks focused increasingly upon the scientists, who were scrutinized and even placed under surveillance. By the end of the 1950s, the government had investigated in detail some 150,000 people related to the nuclear industry.

The emphasis upon secrecy conveyed in the narrative of *Above and Beyond* continued to remain a central characteristic of Hollywood films involving nuclear imagery during the Cold War, when protection from alien ideologies and internal subversion became crucial. This pervasive theme represents part of an elaboration by Hollywood of the Cold War ideology manifesting itself in American culture.

Cold War Ideology

The Cold War as the generalized political, social, and military fearfulness that resulted from the international rivalry between the United States and the Soviet Union developed an accompanying ideology that directly affected Hollywood studios and film content. Anticommunist themes and the fear of outside aggression and internal subversion became increasingly linked to issues of atomic technology and its capabilities. These issues formed the basis of a common dominant ideology, a constructed belief system, which was openly perpetuated by many social institutions as a "universal order" or "universal truth" that organized, explained, and reaffirmed the world, "making us understand the existing social order as well as imposing it upon us."[12]

A major ideological clash was inevitable when the United States and the Soviet Union emerged as the world's two major power centers after 1945. Although conflict is not the necessary result of a two-power scenario, the superpowers' commitments to ideologically opposed systems, with each nation advocating and actively working to export its own system, made confrontation impossible to avoid. Both superpowers were determined to "rearrange the pattern of political relationships in the world in accordance with what each conceived to be the absolute truth."[13] This fundamental difference in point of view could not help but find expression in ideological conflict.

Both the United States and the Soviet Union concentrated on building "spheres of influence," usually via overt economic aid and often covert military aid.[14] On the part of the United States, such aid was designed to contain the spread of Marxism, whereas the Soviets used their aid for exactly the opposite purpose, to spread the ideology of Marxism. Although this overt expansionism was a manifestation of the power struggle between the two nations, expansionist policies could not be sustained on either side without a supporting ideology. As Edward Thompson points out in *Beyond the Cold War:* "The confrontation of the superpowers has, from its origin, always had the highest ideological content: ideology . . . has motored the increment of weaponry, indicated a collision course. . . . In both camps, ideology performs a triple function: that of motivating war preparations, of legitimating the privileged status of the armorers, and of policing internal dissent."[15]

The leading powers of each country were committed to an economic system that was the antithesis of the other. And in the name of ideology, each escalated the contest, justifying both expansionism and the arms race as the key to survival. The U.S. doctrine envisaged a world elaborately organized under law into a peaceful society of states, committed to free will, enterprise, and personal responsibility for one's actions. "Americanism" was conceptualized as idealistic, emotional, future-oriented, and optimistic; it glorified the dogma formulated by the Declaration of Independence and the Preamble to the Constitution. Convinced that the American way of life was superior to all others, it seemed the logical and even philanthropic to export these beliefs and values to an anxious world.[16]

On the other hand, communism's worldview was of a classless society where all lived and were treated as equals, with world order postulated as feasible and inevitable. The Soviet Union considered the ideal of communism as the basic motivation of all policy and was moved to action on behalf of its image of the truth. It was Marxist ideology, and the Soviet Union as its leading proponent, that posed a direct threat to the American way of life, which was based on private ownership and a free-enterprise system. Both of these national doctrines were universally applicable, leaving no room for the toleration of nonbelievers or for the compromise of their differences. The Cold War rapidly grew to become a way of life, an environmental factor to be factored into all conceptualizations of the contemporary world. The world was politically polarized, or at least was viewed by many as such.

Much Cold War rhetoric and rationale pivots on the competition for superiority in weaponry. Gregg Herken writes that the Truman administration viewed the atom bomb as a means to practice atomic diplomacy, as a bargaining chip or as the ultimate weapon should diplomacy fail. Since many scientists and military specialists predicted a twenty-year monopoly on the technological and practical development of the atomic bomb, this diplomatic mandate was based upon the fact of American exclusivity concerning the bomb.[17] Although this monopoly was destroyed in 1949 with the Soviet detonation of its own bomb, this "winning weapon" idea persisted into the postmonopoly period. The end of the monopoly caused no serious reappraisal of the central role of nuclear weapons in American foreign policy: The emphasis was merely shifted to a competition in the stockpiling of large quantities of more and more powerful weaponry. For example, for President Eisenhower, the "winning weapon" became the hydrogen bomb rather than the atom bomb. The hydrogen bomb was presented by the Eisenhower administration as a means to protect civilization, as a way to regain weapons superiority over the Soviet Union, and as a tool to further promote American initiatives in the Cold War.[18]

In selling the American public on the idea of atomic weapons testing, specifically of testing within the United States, the government promoted Cold War sentiments. The buildup of nuclear weapons was accompanied by constant assurances to the American people that such a program was in the interests of democracy. First, the strong anticommunist sentiments developing within the culture were played up—the critical need for testing was emphasized for a strong national defense against potential Soviet aggression. Second, nonmilitary benefits and peaceful uses of nuclear technology were stressed by politicians and bureau-crats, who based their claims upon the already existing utopian ideals regarding nuclear technology. Finally, citizens were being constantly assured that all testing and nuclear development was conducted with the utmost concern for health and safety, with absolutely no potential risk of radioactive fallout.[19]

Anticommunism played a major role in the justification of atomic testing and in convincing the public that nuclear development was necessary for security, even at the risk of fallout exposure. After the Soviets tested their bomb, named "Joe One," in the fall of 1949, the National Security Council (NSC) in Washington wanted a test site more militarily secure and closer to home than the Marshall Islands in the Pacific. When Nevada was chosen as a site, the AEC quickly stepped in to act as a public relations agency for atomic testing. In light of what was perceived as Soviet aggression in postwar international developments, many branches of government worked to foster a suspicious attitude toward the Soviets in their policies. Anticommunist activities by Congress included the actions of the HUAC and the investigations into individuals, programs, and agencies led by Senator Joseph McCarthy from 1950 to 1954. Known as "Tail Gunner Joe," McCarthy contributed to creating a climate propitious to the selling of the atomic bomb.[20]

Several laws were also enacted that reinforced Cold War paranoia and, conse-quently, atomic development and testing. In 1950, the McCarran International Security Act required members of the Communist Party to register with the Subversive Activities Control Board, by which they could be denied passports and employment in defense companies.[21] By 1954, Congress had passed the Communist Control Act, making membership in the Communist Party a felony.[22] Another factor that helped to foster a strong anticommunist sentiment was the government's preoccupation with issues of internal security. Such concern with security is exemplified by Executive Order 10450, issued by President Eisenhower in 1953, under which the mere suspicion of treachery brought termination of em-ployment. Eisenhower later boasted that 2,200 "security risks" had been elimi-nated from government service. In this climate, Julius and Ethel Rosenberg were convicted and executed for passing Manhattan Project secrets to the Soviets dur-ing the war.[23]

All major government organs utilized Cold War ideology in conveying the dan-ger of the communist threat to the public. The military aided in the creation of the Cold War environment, for example, during the war games and maneuvers conducted at the Nevada atomic test site—the aggressor enemy was always por-trayed as a communist force. Soldiers were indoctrinated from the beginning with the belief that should another major war appear, it would be fought against the communists.[24] The AEC reminded the American people in press releases issues throughout the 1950s of the danger of letting down their defenses. For example, a statement issued in 1955 before the Congressional Committee on Atomic Energy reads: "Soviet Russia possesses atomic weapons; there is no alternative but to maintain our scientific and technological progress and keep our strength at peak level. The consequences of any other course would imperil our liberty, even our existence."[25]

Widespread public animosity toward the Soviet Union developed after World War II, nourished by many politicians of both parties, by large segments of the mass media and the religious press, and by negative interpretations of Russian actions.[26] In May 1946, 58 percent of Gallup's sample responded that "Russia is trying to build herself up to be the ruling power of the world" whereas only 29 percent chose the more favorable view that Russia is "just building up protection against being attacked in another war." By October 1947, the percentage choosing "ruling power" had risen to 76 percent and the percentage choosing "protection" had dropped to 18 percent. A Gallup poll reported in late 1948 an "almost unanimous belief that Russia is an aggressive, expansion-minded nation."[27]

Because communism was presented as having world domination as its goal, proposals to improve relations with Russia were viewed with skepticism or hostility. The communists were seen as inherently untrustworthy: Conciliatory gestures on their part were camouflages to hide preparations for war. According to a 1949 Gallup poll, 60 percent of the sample believed that Russia did not want peace; by 1955, this had risen to 80 percent of the sample.[28]

In the United States, government agencies such as the United States Information Agency (USIA) attempted to popularize anticommunist themes in an effort to shape public opinion domestically and abroad. The power of the word was seen as a potent influential force, and terms such as "freedom," "democracy," and "the free world" became the arsenal in the "war to win men's minds and souls." This belief in the persuasive strength of words and ideas demonstrates the heavy ideological basis of the Cold War. In an address to the USIA in 1953, President Eisenhower said that the American system would eventually win the Cold War because of its "greater appeal to the human soul, the human heart, the human mind." The anticommunist propaganda campaign launched by the USIA in the early 1950s had three primary objectives: to promote the American ideal, to sketch out the adversary's characteristics, and to illustrate the strategies, dangers, and consequences of communism.[29]

Although the agency's operating assumptions concentrated on a worldwide effort to "sell the United States to the world, just as a sales manager sells a Buick or a Cadillac," the domestic media were not excluded from its mission. All entertainment not in the "national interest" was discouraged, with much criticism falling on Hollywood's film output as propagating dramatic stereotypes and unfavorable impressions of American life. The USIA stated in a summation of its objectives: "If Hollywood film output is harmful, the USIA should prevent harmful films from being produced." However, the agency could not directly modify the content of commercial films. Indeed, some of Hollywood's products were even seen as advancing the USIA's objectives, the agency being fully aware that audiences could learn values indirectly by watching films with no overt political content.[30]

Special emphasis was placed upon the consequences of losing the Cold War, and the ultimate loss was conceived as being subjected to a nuclear sneak attack.

At the same time, the impression judiciously permitted to gain currency was that the Cold War would some day culminate in a major crisis, perhaps an all-out war against communism, out of which either the United States would emerge victorious or the world would come to an end in mutual nuclear obliteration. In this manner, while the U.S. media indoctrinated the American public, it also engendered an atmosphere of paranoia borne out of the understanding that if the Cold War were lost and communism were not contained, civilization "as we know it" would all but cease to exist. Thus, the American public was browbeaten into accepting the position of the government and its ability to steer the country through the ideological perils that lay ahead.

Hollywood and the Cold War

The performance of the Hollywood film industry at this time can be viewed as that of a commercial enterprise responding to political and economic pressure in the pursuit of larger profits. The industry had enjoyed prosperity after the war as attendance increased and studios prospered. Fears in Hollywood that peace would be a commercial disaster were not fulfilled, and 1946 turned out to be, in box-office terms, the most successful year in the history of the film industry. The annual profits announced by eight major film companies totaled over $125 million, which, when compared to the average annual figure of $35 million in the 1930s, was a tremendous increase.[31]

However, in 1949 economic troubles began to develop, and the 1950s were devoted to attempts at economic recovery. Compounding the economic problems were the political purges initiated by the HUAC in 1947, resulting not only in studio blacklisting but also in the avoidance of controversial social topics. The blacklist reflected the nation's general insecurity, its image of the Soviet Union as an entity ready to devour the country and of communism as a constant and pernicious threat. Affected by the financial insecurity caused partly by the introduction of television, Hollywood's behavior can be seen as an attempt to pacify the government while the industry confronted its own economic problems.

The political climate of the 1950s was typified by the political purge initiated in 1947 by the HUAC; the stated purpose of the purge was to investigate communist propaganda in Hollywood films. Led by J. Parnell Thomas, the HUAC turned its attention completely to Hollywood in 1945 and 1946, citing the movie industry as one of the country's main centers of communist propaganda.[32] The hearings featured fourteen friendly witnesses, whose purpose was to provide evidence that communism was running rampant in Hollywood and in Hollywood's films. Showcased in Washington before live microphones, the witnesses charged that pro-Soviet and communist propaganda had been deliberately promoted in various films produced during and after World War II. From each witness, the HUAC sought support to outlaw the Communist Party and to blacklist party members.

Throughout the hearings, the committee attempted to get Hollywood leaders to approve of a blacklist, and in November 1947 the members of the Association of Motion Pictures issued a statement claiming that they would eliminate all subversives and communists from their industry.[33] Public opinion seemed to favor anticommunist measures, and Louis B. Mayer stated that the fear of film censorship and the belief that public opinion could be appeased led to the blacklisting of studio personnel suspected of communist sympathies.[34] The American Legion quickened the industry's decision to blacklist by threatening a national boycott of films and pickets in front of theaters.

Besides the Hollywood Ten, the ten screenwriters who were purged for refusing to cooperate with the committee, members of the Committee for the First Amendment as well as 208 actors of the Actors' Division of the Progressive Citizens of America, who had taken out an advertisement in *Daily Variety* to protest the hearings, were threatened. In 1951 and 1952, new names were continually added to the blacklist. Studios also compiled a "graylist," which contained the names of noncommunists who had radical leanings. These individuals weren't fired outright but were moved to innocuous positions and barred from promotion; many had great difficulties in finding new jobs.[35]

The HUAC's emphasis gradually shifted to claims that communists had been feeding on the reputations and the financial assets of various Hollywood individuals. In the past, funds had been raised by Hollywood employees to aid refugees from fascist countries or to buy ambulances for Spanish loyalists. This aid was perceived by members of the HUAC to have benefited the American Communist Party. The content of the movies became of far less importance to the HUAC than the naming of names. Many of the hearings were televised, which helped spread and popularize the suspicion that communists were indeed working within the Hollywood industry. These hearings continued sporadically until 1954, and by the time they were over 90 prominent industry figures had testified and 324 alleged communists had been blacklisted by the studios. During this time, the HUAC's hold on public opinion had been considerably strengthened by a series of national and international events: the fall of China to the communists, the first successful atomic explosion by the Soviet Union, the outbreak of the Korean War, and the conviction of Alger Hiss. The combined force of these events helped the committee achieve its goal of eradicating liberalism and radicalism in Hollywood.[36]

The studios were terrified that the charges of communism would wreck their industry. The American Legion and other right-wing groups promised to picket any movie if the name of any suspected communist appeared in the screen credits, and outside investment in any movies that could conceivable be a target for pickets would be nonexistent. Hollywood producers feared that millions of potential moviegoers would shun the films that the American Legion condemned. The legion, with three million members, rallied support in communities all over the country, conducting a letter-writing campaign and informing sponsors about the political affiliations of many entertainers. Demonstrations outside theaters showing Charlie Chaplin's *Monsieur Verdoux* resulted in the movie being withdrawn from circulation. Many theater owners and television stations were even dissuaded by the legion from showing Chaplin's silent films.[37] After the 1951 hearings, the heads of the five major studios promised not to hire anyone who had taken the Fifth Amendment and asked the legion for its own files of suspects so that the "loyalty" of employees could be checked against the legion's files.[38]

To a certain extent, Hollywood's motives in complying with the HUAC can be seen as an attempt to fend off political interference while the industry attacked a more significant problem—that of declining attendance. In 1949, a decline began as movie attendance fell to 70 million per week from 90 million per week the year before. The decline hit bottom in 1958 at 39.6 million moviegoers per week and stabilized at 40 million in the 1960s.[39]

The reasons for this decline are numerous. Television was a major factor. A 1951 survey concluded that theaters dropped 1 percent of their gross income for each 2 percent of homes within their market that had acquired a television.[40] Personal disposable income was also being diverted from movies to other items such as radios, televisions, and automobiles. During the period from 1929 to 1945, expenditures for motion picture admissions accounted for an average of 21.2 percent of the typical family's recreation budget, while home entertainment expenditures, covering the purchase and repair of records, musical instruments, and radios was 12.7 percent. Just after World War II, there were limits on goods available, and movies were an ever present alternative; for this reason, audiences were not terribly selective about the pictures they saw.[41] However, by 1949, home entertainment and motion picture admissions had reversed their relative standings; home entertainment expenditures now accounted for 24.3 percent of recreation expenses whereas motion picture admissions accounted for only 12.1 percent.[42]

Since the Hollywood industry was confronted with both political and economic pressure, it sought to pacify the political sector while trying to adjust to new economic realities. Perhaps the studios felt that they could not afford to irritate political authorities at a time when public opinion seemed to favor anticommunist measures. In any event, films with even moderately liberal trappings were no longer produced, since the HUAC investigations had implied that patriotic producers should avoid films with controversial social content. Even a conservative producer like John Ford were uneasy because, almost ten years earlier, he had directed *The Grapes of Wrath* (1940), which could be interpreted as a leftist film and which had been attacked when it was released. *Variety* sarcastically described the situation: "Hollywood's brass has been so busy trying to prove that the picture industry is a right-living, right-thinking and right-producing community that they have gone far out of their way to offend no one—whether it be Thomas, the Catholic Church, the Jews, the Negroes, the President, the American Dental Society, or the Institute of Journeymen Plumbers of America."[43]

Before the HUAC hearings, Hollywood had shown an interest in films that explored social problems such as anti-Semitism, racism, and demagoguery, and many such films, including *Gentlemen's Agreement* (1947), *Crossfire* (1947), *All the*

King's Men (1949), and *Home of the Brave* (1949) had been box-office hits. After the hearings, it has been speculated that producers lost their courage, and as a result the percentage of socially relevant films declined. Instead, "pure entertainment" films were emphasized, and a series of anticommunist pictures were quickly produced to repair the movie industry's tarnished image. According to John Cogley, the number of movies focusing on social issues decreased drastically between 1947 and 1954, although more than fifty anticommunist films were produced during those same years.[44]

These anticommunist films utilized themes such as atomic development and security; they include *The Red Menace* (1949), *I Was a Communist for the FBI* (1951), *The Whip Hand* (1951), and *My Son John* (1952). Such films capitalized on the stereotypes of communism developed in part by the USIA. American communists were portrayed as dark, unkempt, irrational fanatics aggressively intent upon destroying the United States. The public showed little interest in the Cold War fare, but as a public relations gimmick, the pictures helped restore Hollywood's image among the industry's right-wing guardians.[45]

3

Experimentation with Atomic Themes

A gathering of international scientists in *The Day the Earth Stood Still* (1951)

WHILE FILM STUDIOS WERE BUSY PUMPING OUT militaristic Cold War films in order to prove their patriotic zeal, they were simultaneously striving to discover commercially viable ways to exploit interest in atomic technology. Integrating atomic themes into a dramatic or docudrama production ran the risk of inviting government scrutiny, while direct military involvement with scripts and audience expectation that film content should support the dominant ideological stance also restricted the presentation of the atomic subject. Hollywood studios soon chose to experiment with genres that would allow more flexibility and attract less interference from outside interests, and hopefully make more money in the process.

Such experimentation capitalized upon popular interest in domestic atomic testing and concern with the effects of fallout; these films took the form of dark comedy (*The Atomic Kid*, 1954; *Living It Up*, 1954; *Ma and Pa Kettle Back on the Farm*, 1951), science fiction monster films (*The Beast from 20,000 Fathoms*, 1953; *Monster from the Ocean Floor*, 1954), and alien invasions (*This Island Earth*, 1954; *Killers from Space*, 1954). Narratives critical of the military development of atomic weaponry and the imagined disastrous effects of atomic war also managed to be produced by individual directors intent upon promoting their personal vision of the atomic future.

Atomic Comedy

The producer of *The Atomic Kid* (1954) anticipated that interest in the new domestic atomic testing and civil defense program would draw curious audiences to a film that made light of radiation's possible effects. Civil defense had become a dominant issue after the 1949 Soviet atomic bomb test. In order to ease public fears of the new vulnerability of the United States, President Truman created the Federal Civil Defense Administration (FCDA), which launched a massive public relations information campaign with the aim of forestalling mass panic in the event of atomic war with the Soviet Union.

In addition to establishing community bomb shelters, the FCDA scheduled regular air-raid drills and provided instruction on nuclear preparedness. Instructional films produced by the FCDA with the aid of the Strategic Air Command (SAC) were distributed to schools and organizations. For example, *Survival City* (1955) and *Atomic Survival* (1951) illustrated guidelines for atomic self-protection while offering dramatizations of Soviet atomic attacks and their imagined consequences. In 1951, the FCDA handed out 20 million copies of *Survival under Atomic Attack,* while a documentary film of the same name sold more prints than any film had ever sold before.[1]

By 1953, advertisements for civil defense and the FCDA were everywhere from newspapers to bus placards, while newspapers printed thousands of articles on the subject. School programs practiced "duck and cover" exercises, and some schools even handed out identification tags to children composed of "metal which could not be destroyed by blast or fire."[2] Operation Alert, a series of massive civil defense exercises simulating imagined Soviet nuclear attacks, involved literally thousands of citizens who sought shelter at the screeching sound of air-raid sirens. It was then the job of the media to report government speculation estimating how many millions of Americans would have succumbed in such an attack, providing detailed photographs of the deserted streets to press the point.

Followed by massive media coverage, the domestic testing program in Nevada was also well under way by 1953. Hundreds of reporters gathered to witness the atomic explosions from trenches. The televised tests included such novelties as a "doom town" complete with houses peopled by mannequins in living rooms and kitchens, posed in the midst of performing the daily activities of the average American. Such experimental props made the tests more attractive to the media, providing sensational photos while promoting military interests. After each detonation, the domestic destruction was publicized with graphic descriptions of the bomb's effects: "People played by dummies lay dead and dying in basements, living rooms, kitchens. . . . A mannequin mother died horribly in her one-story house of precast concrete slabs. . . . A simulated mother was blown to bits in the act of feeding her infant baby food."[3]

In focusing upon these contemporary images involving civil defense and doom towns, *The Atomic Kid* attempted to transform such issues into light comedy. Based on a story by Blake Edwards and produced and starring Mickey Rooney, the film portrays the absurd activities of two uranium prospectors in the Nevada desert who unknowingly spend the night in a doom town. Here again, the extensive use of stock footage in the film provides a basis of reality to exploit the unique nature of the doom town concept, not to mention economy of production. Mannequins are depicted sitting around the dinner table in front of their plastic meal, awaiting the predetermined bomb drop. One prospector (Rooney) remains with the mannequin family and discovers at the last minute that an atomic bomb will be detonated over his head. In a deliberately humorous scene, Rooney frantically tries to find a place to hide from the approaching explosion, only to close his eyes and stick his fingers in his ears as the bomb goes off.

Rooney survives the film explosion only to experience annoying physical reactions such as glowing eyes and "an internal chain reaction which doubles his basal metabolism." Despite such minor disturbances, his survival is touted by the press as "a victory of the human race over the atomic bomb, offering hope for the people of the world." When enemy spies try to capture Rooney for experimental purposes, the army saves him and cures him of his radioactive ailments, and he lives happily ever after.

The film attempted to ridicule the military, the scientists, and the media while incorporating the new concerns of atomic testing into this light comedy format. It was a box-office failure. Considering its historical context, it is hard to imagine an audience finding these issues humorous at a time when debate in society involved the dire topics of bomb shelters, the targeting of civilians, and radiation sickness.

The attempt to find humor in atomic technology was made again in 1954 with *Living It Up,* a Jerry Lewis–Dean Martin remake of the 1937 film *Nothing Sacred.* Here, Lewis portrays an alleged radiation victim brought to New York to capitalize on the publicity of his condition. As in the earlier film, in which Carol Lombard plays a victim of radium poisoning, the contamination element acts as a mere prop in the development of the story. Direct references to atomic testing and nuclear devastation as illustrated by mannequins being demolished in model suburban homes, and the portrayal of military personnel and scientists as incompetent buffoons, was not to be found again in film until the satirical doomsday humor of the very successful 1964 film, *Dr. Strangelove.*

Science Fiction Genre

Early speculation upon what life in the aftermath of a nuclear war might look like was, for the most part, confined to the science fiction genre. For example, *Rocketship XM* (1950) tells the story of an expedition to Mars that discovers a group of nuclear survivors, "crazed, despairing wretches" in a radioactive desert. This was the first widely distributed film to expound the fact that humanity now had the power to wipe out civilization entirely, and the first to show the possible effects of atomic devastation, albeit at a safe distance and on another civilization. In the film, a rocket is launched to the moon, but a swarm of meteors forces the ship out of its planned trajectory and it is forced to land on Mars. The planet is covered with artifacts and ruins much too radioactive to approach, and the crew members discover that there had once been a civilization on Mars that had destroyed itself with atomic warfare. Wild Martians, blind and disfigured from radiation, attack and kill three crew members; the remaining three return to Earth, only to die in a crash landing.

Film Daily commented that this film was "intelligently conceived . . . a far better treatment of the general subject than has ever been given in films." The original movie was scripted to portray a completely different Mars, one that had not suffered atomic war, but at the last minute Robert Lippert, the producer, and Kurt Neumann, the director, decided upon the bleaker story line. Emphasizing a nuclear theme allowed the film to exploit a topic popular in the public arena—that of the consequences of nuclear war.[4] *Rocketship XM* made over a million dollars and was successful enough to launch a line of films from the 1950s to the present day portraying postnuclear scenarios. However, this particular film is true to its time in that it reflects a pessimistic view of the postnuclear future—no "civilization" survives on Mars after the war, and the three who attempt to return to Earth with a warning about the perils of nuclear development fail. Later in the decade, depictions of postnuclear landscapes, even in films intentionally opposed to atomic technology, invariably show civilization reborn among the remaining survivors.

The most economically successful Hollywood exploitation of atomic themes can be found in the first picture debuting the radiation-produced monster, *The Beast from 20,000 Fathoms* (1953). The film kicks off a decade of appropriately grotesque monsters, all the result of atomic testing or research. The science fiction genre offered a forum basically free from direct government intervention and HUAC pressure. Debate concerning the residual themes of atomic development, which had been repressed in official public debate and in other genres, could be freely continued under the guise of the monster movie narrative.

A great deal has been made of the true significance of such apparitions, which denote, consciously or unconsciously, a variety of meanings, drawing upon older residual themes to develop new atomic imagery. For example, the rhedosaurus in *The Beast from 20,000 Fathoms* signifies atomic force, destruction, and extinction, since it was engendered by an atomic blast; the creature also signifies the fear of avenging nature that has been disturbed by man's technology. Many of these films suggest a subliminal anxiety about nuclear weapons. Rather than confronting the menace of nuclear war, some extrapolated the effects of unrestrained atmospheric testing. Lurking behind these monster films is the sense of immanent apocalypse and total destruction as giant creatures wreak havoc on New York, Los Angeles, and other locations.

What is clear about this particular genre is that it emerged and developed in direct relation with increasing public concern over the ability to contain the consequences of atomic atmospheric testing. Initially, official government channels had made light of radiation. When pictures from the first atomic test at Trinity were publicized, the radiological monitoring teams appeared standing at ground zero, taking no special precautions against radiation beyond wearing protective clothing. Less than two hours after the explosion, two scientists explored ground zero in a lead-lined tank, where they took soil samples from the bomb's crater.[5] This practice of allowing people to move about the test site a short time after a blast without elaborate special protection was repeated when military units were sent to "clean up" Japan after the war, later participating in mock nuclear conflict maneuvers during atomic tests in Nevada.

The concept of a radioactive cloud carrying fallout was acknowledged as a possible consequence of the Trinity test, and heavy fallout was identified after the test in an oval extending ten miles north of the test's crater, with readings in some places as high as 35 roentgens per hour. Most scientists involved were convinced that most of the fallout would remain in this fixed position.[6] Unknown to the scientists at the time, however, part of the cloud had strayed off course and passed over several cattle ranches. The cows lost hair on their backs and suffered from serious blistering of their exposed skin. According to government officials, the cattle had received only superficial damage, and no change was detected in their blood. However, the Atomic Energy Commission (AEC) still decided that all the cows should be observed for the duration of their natural lives so that evidence of their good or ill health would be available in case of future legal proceedings.[7]

The atomic tests in the Pacific drew further public attention to the effects of atomic testing. In the summer of 1946, less than a year after the Hiroshima bombing, Operation Crossroads was conducted at remote Bikini atoll in the Marshall Islands. These tests were arranged as a joint experiment involving all the services in order to discover exactly what atomic bombs would do to a target fleet of surplus battleships loaded with experimental equipment and animals. It also represented an important public relations venture in which the world press would view and report on nuclear explosions for the very first time. Two detonations were carried out, and more than a hundred journalists came to cover the much publicized "experiment."[8]

The two tests consisted of one air and one undersea detonation. The unimpressive performances of the bombs (instead of the fleet being instantly pulverized as expected, only a few ships were destroyed) helped to dispel the idea that atomic weapons were an uncontrollable destructive force. However, the navy took a precautionary measure against radioactivity by testing the military participants with Geiger counters. Because high levels of radioactivity were produced by the underwater test, the media focused on the dangers of radioactivity rather than on the immediate effects of the blasts themselves.

A Paramount newsreel released after the tests displayed animals with radiation burns. David Bradley, a Geiger technician at the Bikini test, went on to describe the terrible effects of atomic radiation to the public for the first time in his 1948 book *No Place to Hide*. Ships that entered the lagoon at Bikini had their saltwater lines contaminated by the radioactive seawater, and thousands of dead fish were found with radiation poisoning.[9] Popular magazines such as *Reader's Digest* began to publish articles on radiation; one article explained how an atomic bomb could shower a city with a "mist of death."[10] Such rampant speculation led to widespread paranoia concerning radiation contamination. Although fears of massive destruction from explosions subsided after the Bikini test, radiation became a much greater concern among the general population.

Based on a story by Ray Bradbury, *The Beast from 20,000 Fathoms,* which exploited public anxiety of the effects of atomic testing, is a prototype of a movie featuring a radiation-produced monster.[11] The film was produced by Mutual Pictures of California, a small independent company. Warner Brothers, smartly predicting the potential popularity of such a picture, purchased and released it in 1953. The film integrates a basic seek-and-destroy plot with a giant reptile disturbed by atomic testing, relying heavily upon stock military testing and imaginative pseudoscientific jargon. These elements became standard in films in this genre.

The film action opens as a voice-over narration explains a military exercise while the ever present stock footage shows military personnel preparing for action. In this case, the narrator explains that we are in the last few minutes of "Operation Experiment," an exercise in nuclear fission conducted in the atmosphere over the Arctic. As the clock ticks away the seconds, the military personnel and the government scientists prepare for the blast. The screen then displays familiar footage of a nuclear detonation. Minutes later, Dr. Nesbitt and his assistants are using various gizmos to record and measure radiation in the blast area. A blizzard is approaching as the group returns back to base. Suddenly, a huge roar dislodges the ice and covers Dr. Nesbitt—as he is dug out he cries that he saw "a monster!"

Gradually, as merchant ships begin to mysteriously disappear, scientists and the military combine in an effort to discover and destroy the monstrous creature. Not only has atomic testing brought new life to the previously extinct rhedosaurus but other giant sea creatures, disturbed by the atomic testing, have also begun to emerge from the deep. The rhedosaurus goes on to terrorize and destroy cities, and mass panic ensues. The military fights back, but conventional weaponry is to no avail. The blood of the beast carries a potent primordial virus that would unleash a plague of disastrous proportions if the beast were killed by conventional methods. An expert, not on prehistoric creatures but on atomic technology, is called upon to repel the monster. The atomic scientist is represented here as the one man who possesses the knowledge to destroy the threatening creature, by shooting a radioactive isotope into the beast's neck. The radioactivity, it is argued, will kill the creature and destroy the diseased tissues.

This basic scenario became the formula for numerous monster films of the 1950s. The narrative expressed paradoxical and contradictory attitudes toward atomic technology and science itself. Atomic technology created problems and solved them as well—the beast originated through atomic testing, and yet atomic technology was used to destroy it. Scientists, in their creation of the technology of the atomic bomb, consequently created the destructive monster, and yet only a scientist had the knowledge to repel the threat. However, the film is unique in that it displays one of the few instances in a Hollywood film where atomic power was used with positive results. Also unique was the role of the military. Although depicted as competent in their attempts to repel the monster, in the end they failed, ultimately deferring to the knowledge and actions of the scientist to save civilization. As the Cold War progressed, the military and military scientists were consistently spotlighted as the only heroes capable of saving humanity from the ravages of atomic monsters.

Personal Visions and Opposition

The first Hollywood products to overtly come out against the further development and use of atomic technology appeared in 1951. They represent an effort on the part of a few individuals to present a dissenting view on the implications of arms development. These few films don't support the dominant ideological line that such weapons are necessary for domestic protection from aggression. Such blatant questioning of the official policy on atomic weapons development became too controversial after 1951 for Hollywood to produce, particularly after the HUAC hearings. These oppositional films represent the last of their breed until the early 1960s.

Robert Wise's successful *The Day the Earth Stood Still* (1951) presents a cautionary tale concerning atomic annihilation and the loss of social control over technology while overtly promoting the world government agenda advocated by the Federation of Atomic Scientists. In the narrative, scientists and the "average American" are characterized as intellectually superior and beneficent when compared to the destructive and impulsive military. Although criticized for its "moralistic tone," the film enjoyed much success, which was attributed to its special effects and science fiction format. "[This film contains] sufficient science fiction lures and suspense [so] that only seldom does its moralistic wordiness get in the way," wrote a *New York Times* critic.[12]

The film tells the story of an emissary, Klaatu (Michael Rennie), from an organization of planets, who sets down his flying saucer in Washington, D.C., with the purpose of warning Earth's inhabitants: Anything resembling nuclear violence will be punished by the obliteration of the planet. He cautions that our international disputes and our development of nuclear weaponry endanger the entire universe. In seeking to present his message to the world, rather than to any one group or country, he must contend with three forces: the army, which wants to destroy him; the scientists, who are willing to listen to him; and a woman (Patricia Neal), who understands and helps him.

The military establishment is presented as ignorant and arrogant in their beliefs. They see all aliens as evil and immediately call out the troops to destroy the perceived invader. Klaatu is wounded by a trigger-happy soldier and is then locked up in a hospital. The visitor easily escapes and takes a room in a boarding house where he meets several ordinary people. He decides, despite the brutal military establishment, that there is inherent goodness on Earth; as a warning, however, he shuts down all electrical power worldwide for a brief period of time to demonstrate the abilities of the group he represents. The principal villain is a man who values personal fame and power more than integrity and love; he is willing to turn Klaatu over to the army, which shoots first and asks questions later. Klaatu is eventually killed, but with the help of his robot, he is brought back to life, delivers his message, and leaves. His message is that other planets have found an effective way to curb warlike tendencies by establishing a robot police force. "In matters of aggression we have given them absolute power over us; at the first signs of violence they act automatically against the aggressor. The penalty for provoking their action is too terrible to risk."

The film was based on a novella by Harry Bates, "Farewell to the Master," published in the October 1940 issue of *Astounding Science Fiction*. What the movie shared with the story was the idea that once humankind has passed a certain evolutionary level, technology becomes the master.[13] In the world of this movie, humankind was shown as having become the servant of nuclear technology—people were offered the option of mastering the atomic bomb or accepting destruction:

> For our policemen we created a race of robots. Their function is to patrol the planet in spaceships like this one and preserve peace. In matters of aggression we have given them absolute power over us. This power cannot be revoked. The result is we live in peace without arms or armies, free to pursue more profitable enterprises. . . . Your choice is simple: join us and live in peace or pursue your present course and face obliteration. We shall be waiting for your answer. The decision rests with you.

Stressing the violent nature of American society, the script chose not to present the standardized and expected image of the United States as entirely beneficent and foreign countries as inherently evil. For example, the American president's representative says, "I'm sure you recognize from our broadcasts the evil forces that have produced the tension in our world." Klaatu interrupts, "I am not concerned . . . with the internal affairs of your planet. I consider that your business, not mine." The alien, although not on "our" side, was one of the few Hollywood movie aliens who was depicted as beneficent.

Scientists are also characterized as positive social elements. Dr. Barnhardt, an Einstein-like character, is sought out when military and government leaders refuse to listen to the alien's message. Klaatu seeks out "the smartest man, the greatest scientist" to present with his revelation. Dr. Barnhardt physically resembles Einstein and is the movie's principal protagonist. Peter Biskind, in his review of films of the 1950s, commented that making Einstein the hero was a daring experiment for a film studio at this time. Einstein, together with many other scientists, had been severely criticized for his activist role in the Atomic Scientists' Movement and had been verbally attacked in the House of Representatives as a "foreign-born agitator" in 1945. Later, in 1953, Einstein had openly urged some witnesses not to testify before Congressional investigatory committees.[14]

The Einstein character calls a meeting of scientists from both East and West, which resembles the Cultural and Scientific Conference for World Peace held in New York in 1949 amid protest. They listen to the dire warning of the alien and propose to act accordingly. The army and the scientists are in conflict with each other, as the army sees the alien as a threatening invader to be repelled and destroyed whereas the scientists see the alien as a visitor with superior knowledge who can contribute beneficially to the human race. The film portrays the scientists as correct in their thinking and the army as an impulsive force that almost brings about the destruction of the world.

Another film that attempts to question the ethical aspects of atomic war is Arch Oboler's independent production *Five* (1951). Representing the first dramatic film to depict the survivors of a nuclear disaster on Earth, the film draws upon images of the heroic survivors' struggles in the post–nuclear holocaust environment.

Although this was the first film to deal with nuclear holocaust and its survivors, the fear of nuclear apocalypse was actually first expressed in the 1930s in science fiction stories, with a rapid rise in the number of such stories after 1946–1947.[15] Many of these films dealt with attempts either to defend the United States against attack or to survive after the attack took place. None anticipated that the war could be avoided, even by preemptive bombing, and most identified Russia as the enemy. Almost all end-of-the-world films had one thing in common: They assumed that it would be the human race that caused the final disaster and that the human race would survive.[16] The idea of nuclear devastation played upon the idea of survivalism, whose roots existed in American culture back in the frontier past. In most after-the-holocaust scenarios, the postnuclear world becomes a means of release from social constraints and the complexity of modern life. The polluted, overpopulated, and corrupt city is destroyed, and primitive and idealized survival-of-the-fittest adventures replace the mundane preholocaust life.[17]

For example, in *Five*, the nuclear war that wiped out most of the human race has already occurred as the film begins. The plot focuses upon the dramatic encounters of a handful of survivors struggling in postwar New York, three of whom eventually die. By the conclusion of the film, the two survivors seemed happy enough. "I hated New York, I'm glad it's dead," the young hero confides to his girl. Typical of popular end-of-the-world narratives, the film depicts survivors who scorn the now extinct civilization while happily using all its conveniences, free to drive any car or walk off with any product. Common to *Five* and other post–nuclear holocaust scenarios, likely realities are disregarded or altered in order to dramatize events. Human life is conveniently erased by the nuclear catastrophe whereas city buildings and modern conveniences remain intact. For example, in *Five*, the Earth's environment remains unchanged whereas all humans have mysteriously disintegrated into skeletons.

The romanticized idea that life would go on did not reveal the true potential of nuclear war for eliminating the human race. These films inevitably close with the image of the heroic survivors setting out amid sunlight and twittering birds to begin the world anew. *Five* even went so far as to quote from the Revelation of St. John: "I saw a new heaven and a new Earth" appears across the screen as the two remaining characters go on to repopulate the new world.

Although Oboler attempted to present an oppositional view concerning the benefits of atomic development, the overriding emphasis on American survival dampened the critical message. Future Hollywood products would inevitably adopt the heroic survivor theme when attempting to exploit audience interest in imagined postnuclear environments. In so doing, film studios helped promote the concept of the limited and survivable nuclear war, a concept increasingly emphasized in official government rhetoric and policy as the Cold War progressed.

This period of experimentation with genre and style gave way by the mid-1950s to science fiction as the only venue in which to package atomic issues. Economic and governmental pressures upon the Hollywood industry contributed to the creation of specific science fiction genres that worked to convey limited meanings to atomic technology, while also offering a venue for critical voices that were repressed in more official public channels.

4

Hollywood Science Fiction, 1954–1959

Few things reveal so sharply as science fiction the wishes, hopes, fears, inner stresses and tensions of an era, or define its limitations with such exactness

H. L. Gold, *Galaxy Science Fiction*

Into the mysterious mists with *The Incredible Shrinking Man* (1957)

AN ESTIMATED FIVE HUNDRED FILM FEATURES AND SHORTS produced between 1948 and 1962 can be indexed under the broad heading of science fiction. This rapid proliferation presents one of the most interesting developments in post–World War II film history, for never in the history of motion pictures has any other genre developed and multiplied so rapidly in so brief a period. "On a sheer statistical basis, the number of fantasy and horror films (including science fiction) of the 1950s . . . has not been equaled in any country before or since."[2]

Before 1950, few science fiction films came out of Hollywood. Immediately after World War II, early film serials like *King of the Rocketmen* (1947) appeared to be merely standard western narratives set in some future time and filled with imagined advanced technology. Then at the turn of the decade, images of blobs, enlarged insects, and mutated dinosaurs brought on by radiation began to figure prominently in Hollywood productions. Film themes began to explore the fear of science, the fear of alien invasion, the fear of the consequences of unleashed radiation, and particularly the fear that human beings were becoming impaired or diminished by their own technology. This last concern was depicted clearly and symbolically in *The Incredible Shrinking Man* (1957); the film opens with the image of a human outline dwindling as a mushroom cloud grows.

Generally, the growing importance of technology in society and the developing xenophobia of the Cold War contributed to the presentation of American society as vulnerable to malevolent elements, as gripped by emergencies that threatened not just national borders but the future of the human race itself. The potential for destruction from these imagined invaders and from radiation-produced creatures involved more than just the fear of the cataclysmic annihilation of civilization. These film narratives illustrated Cold War anxieties about the end of everyday, normal "American" life. Alien invaders from other planets or infiltrators from other countries on Earth subversively threatened to invade the United States or destroy it by stealing its atomic secrets.

Radiation, another major concern of the 1950s, manifested itself in films featuring an abundance of mutated animals, insects, and humans. Like the radioactivity from which they sprang or which caused them to emerge, the horrid creatures put the bombs' pollution of the earth into visible form. The radiation victims, usually either subjected to fallout or the unintended result of scientific experimentation, "provided a staple metaphor of runaway technology and nuclear paranoia for a generation."[3]

The genre played a crucial role in the evolving presentation of atomic themes in Hollywood film and the exploration of the negative aspects of atomic technology. By 1954, the majority of official dialogue concerning the future development of atomic technology was focused upon conveying its positive aspects. Direct pressure upon the Hollywood industry made any questioning of government nuclear policy on the part of Hollywood film productions almost impossible.

Because film in the docudrama and dramatic genres were subject to direct military scrutiny and script control, blatant questioning of the official dominant line was impossible. Yet public interest and concern over the effects of fallout and the transmutational properties of radiation was increasing daily, particularly in light of the continuing domestic testing program. At the same time, Hollywood was experiencing major economic troubles and vehemently sought to exploit any profit potential in contemporary issues.

Thus, Hollywood turned to the emerging film genre of science fiction to subtly capitalize upon the audience's concern with questions that were suppressed in official channels. Elements of this genre allowed flexibility in plot development and the depiction of controversial subjects not available in more restrictive narrative forms. The genre could offer its audience radical dislocations in time and space so as to create stages for action and to allow for experimentation with the social relationships supposedly required for a society's survival. Science fiction plots could transcend time and invent other worlds, unknown societies, universes, and races. An unsuspecting viewer is often unaware of the biases of a specific ideology that are presented under the guise of innocent science fiction stories. No other genre form, with the possible exception of children's cartoons, has such great literary freedom of invention and freedom from questioning and investigation.

The immediate popularity of science fiction in elaborating issues of atomic use contributed to the large-scale output of this type of film. Besides catering to public anxiety about science, atomic development, and what was perceived as the uncanny horror of radioactivity, the issues presented in these films worked to contribute new meaning and imagery to atomic technology and its use.

Radiation and Mutations

By the mid-1950s, science fiction films with atomic elements had developed into three basic forms. The most prevalent were stories about radiation-produced monsters, which combined ancient transmutation imagery with contemporary anxiety about hydrogen bombs and the effects of atomic testing and radioactive fallout. The emphasis upon the dangers and possible effects of radioactive fallout, particularly the mutation of common creatures, became a major element in films produced between the years 1952 and 1961.[4]

Scenarios involving the invasion of Earth by malevolent aliens, exploiting the contemporary Cold War concern about a subversive communist invasion, form the second most common theme of 1950s Hollywood science fiction films. Typically, these alien invaders are drawn to Earth to steal its atomic technology or its scientists or to invade and occupy the planet itself. Depictions of postnuclear civilizations either on Earth or on other planets make up the third category of film narratives incorporating atomic topics. Sometimes, these basic forms were combined; for example, an alien invasion could also include a postnuclear element as well as a mutated creature.

Although film has always sought to exploit the vicarious thrill of safely viewing the total destruction of established life, few films of this decade depict the actual destruction of civilization through the detonation of an atomic bomb, or even seriously address atomic war. Long before the nuclear scourge of the bomb could destroy the world, movie calamities could be found in Sodom and Gomorrah or in Gaza or Rome in Biblical spectaculars. However, with the real-life possibility of easy devastation through the detonation of a few bombs, the potential for complete world destruction became too possible and apparently offered little entertainment value. And although Hollywood productions could safely grapple with the implications of nuclear proliferation in the science fiction genre, they also wanted to provide gratifying entertainment, which meant avoiding any direct preaching or heavy-handed moralizing. Hence, as opposed to the period immediately after the Hiroshima detonation, Hollywood films of the 1950s exhibit a lack of content relating to the serious ethical implications of atomic use and development. Instead, American civilization was portrayed in film as threatened by gigantic radiation-produced monsters and evil aliens, images further removed from the realm of realistic possibility.[5]

The film narrative involving the radiation-produced monster can be conceptualized as a product of the 1950s. This type of film followed a formulaic story line and contained the mandatory elements including a mutated creature, scientists and soldiers as principal characters, innocent victims (usually children), and scenes of mass panic. The scientists themselves working within the military establishment were usually responsible for creating the monster, while the military either working alone or with cooperating scientists were required to destroy the monster and restore civil order. These film narratives presented a potentially critical element in the form of a cautionary tale, depicting what can happen when people are incautious or foolhardy, carelessly invading the realm of nature.

These atomic threats became increasingly combined with Cold War ideology as the decade unfolded. Particularly during this period, as Hollywood products were scrutinized by the HUAC as well as by studio chiefs and some segments of the American public for anti-American tendencies, the film's hero, helped along by the military, would inevitably defeat the threat to civilization. Scientists and the military together mastered and destroyed the radioactive monster or repelled the invaders, annihilating the creature with a radioactive isotope or blowing up the alien command post with an atom bomb. In these cases, the good atoms mastered the bad ones. The scientists joined government authorities in dispelling the threat; the irradiated monsters always succumbed to such authoritative intervention, leaving the world secure in its dependence upon the benefits of scientific technology. However, questions inevitably remained at the film's finale as to when the next threat might emerge. The human ability to predict or ultimately control the emergence of such threats always remained unresolved at the conclusion, for destroying the monster in a neat resolution could not cover up the deep anxieties that such threats could emerge anywhere.[6]

The recurrent theme of atomic technology disturbing sleeping monsters already hidden in the earth or creating new unpredicted terrors can be seen as a type of imagery springing in part from the guilt over creating and using the atomic bomb itself. Hollywood producers intentionally selected and perpetuated the residual images of the imagined consequences of violating nature's secrets through atomic research, extending fears about the transmutational properties of radiation to extreme limits. The popularity of this type of film points to a resistance to more overt and realistic presentations of atomic development and use.

Since the early 1950s, social observers had noted that many Americans were refusing to face the issue of nuclear war, as if a denial mechanism had set in.[7] To test this idea directly, psychologist W. A. Scott showed a test group a set of drawings related to nuclear war and asked them to make up stories about the drawings. The more explicit the drawings were, the less people would allow the idea of war to creep into their stories.[8] Psychologist Joel Kovel equates this phenomenon to a "state of nuclear terror," the inability to channel positive emotions such as outrage and anger into constructive action. The response, rather, demonstrated a mood of resignation and a perceived uselessness of action, which in turn promoted a refusal even to consider the issues or to recognize one's state of compromise or despair. The terror was instead deeply sublimated and incorporated into the narratives of Hollywood science fiction film.[9]

Susan Sontag, in her essay on post–World War II science fiction cinema, suggests that audiences, not daring to think about atomic war, projected their fear onto a monster in order to defeat it vicariously.[10] Displacement, a hostility that shrinks away from what is too threatening and directs itself onto some other target instead, might have been at work in the creation of these radiation monsters. A combination of fear and hostility toward the bomb, and consequently toward the potential destruction of civilization, was a threat that many found too great to face:

> A mass trauma exists over the use of nuclear weapons and the possibility of future wars. Most of the science fiction films bear witness to this trauma, and, in a way, attempt to exorcise it. The accidental awakening of the super-destructive monster, who has slept in the earth since prehistory, is, often, an obvious metaphor for the Bomb. But there may be explicit references as well. . . . Radiation casualties—ultimately, the conception of the whole world as a casualty of nuclear testing and nuclear warfare—is the most ominous of all the notions with which these science fiction films deal.[11]

Science fiction has traditionally been a literature that questioned individuals' abilities to effectively utilize the power they might be capable of creating. Very often this power is symbolized by some terrible weapon of destruction, so naturally atomic development was immediately linked to science fiction scenarios. In 1914, H. G. Wells first named the destructive force of radioactivity an "atomic bomb."[12] Until recently, any fiction that discussed nuclear weapons and the results of their development was considered science fiction.

Thus, the uneasiness about atomic technology and scientific development itself was manifested in the development of a specific science fiction film genre.

Particular genres tend to be popular at certain points in time because they embody and work through those social contradictions that the culture needs to come to grips with, that people may not be able to squarely acknowledge except in the realm of fantasy. As such, popular genres often function similarly to the way myth functions—working through social contradictions in the form of narrative so that very real problems can be transposed to the realm of fantasy and apparently solved there.[13] The attraction an audience finds toward one type of genre points to issues within their contemporary social and cultural moment. Although dismissed as "cheap and simple plotting" by some, the popularity of radiation-produced science fiction monsters points to concerns within the culture exploited by Hollywood filmmakers.[14]

However, the film images that developed at this time were not merely simplistic constructions formed from some generic social anxiety. Many film scholars view 1950 science fiction as a transparent reflection of society's anxiety about increasing technological prowess and its responsibility for the gigantic forces of destruction now available. The genre is assumed to reveal the "wishes, hopes, fears, inner stresses and tensions of an era, or define its limitations with exactness."[15] Francis Arnold is typical in characterizing the upsurge of science fiction films in the 1950s and 1960s as a reflection of the public's concern with the existence of the atomic bomb and the Soviet Sputnik satellite.[16] It has also become a convention of critical analysis to accept the paranoia of 1950s science fiction film as a symptom of sublimated nuclear anxiety.[17]

Conceptualizing Hollywood-produced genres in this way ignores a major area of influence in the production of these images. The ability to freely mirror society's concerns is impeded by the economic and structural constraints of the commercial nature of Hollywood, dictates that work to determine the content of any genre film. These economic priorities greatly determine the selection of particular ideas and images that the producers hope will appeal to the audience. In this process of selection, a myriad of potential issues and events are bypassed. The proliferation of certain notions linked with atomic technology is due to specific economic changes within the Hollywood industry as much as to the result of the social queasiness surrounding atomic development.

Economic Troubles in Hollywood

The Hollywood industry underwent many changes during this period, which had a marked effect upon film content. Three factors particularly affected the industry: the increasing popularity of television, the shift in film audience demand, and the implementation of the government antitrust decrees. These economic and structural evolutions had a profound influence upon film production and contributed in their own way to the selection of specific depictions of atomic use that would be promoted by Hollywood products.

The economic structure of the Hollywood industry was being quickly transformed with the implementation of the government antitrust action. Traditionally, the movie industry held a vertical monopoly, with the major companies controlling production, distribution, and exhibition. The advantages enjoyed by the major studios over independent producers included the setting of rental rates, discriminatory privileges over first runs, and the ability to influence distributors' sales policies. This arrangement also enabled the major studios to mass-produce films and market them as a package. Economic integration had become more or less complete by the end of the silent period, and by the 1940s the film industry was controlled by five fully integrated organizations (Paramount, MGM, Twentieth Century Fox, Warner Brothers, and RKO); two partially integrated producer-distributors: (Columbia and Universal); and one distributor: United Artists. Between them, these eight companies controlled most of the important theaters and produced the majority of American films.

The change in the industry's structure began when the Justice Department filed a legal blockbuster known as the Paramount Consent Decree, or the "Paramount case," which attacked these monopolistic procedures as unfair trade practices. The Supreme Court handed down its decision in 1948, which forced the big studios to divest themselves of any affiliation with exhibition. This decision was the culmination of the government's efforts to attack vertical integration; it required the divestiture of production and distribution from exhibition and prohibited several other practices including block booking, stipulating admission prices, establishing any fixed system of clearance, and granting to circuits any contract except on a theater-by-theater and picture-by-picture basis.[18] Previously, the five major studios had held contracts with extensive theater chains and gave preferential treatment to one another's pictures. Using block booking and blind buying, the majors had preempted the playing time of key theaters nationwide.

The Paramount Consent Decree removed the base for vertical integration and left in doubt whether the major studios would continue to dominate or whether the industry could even continue to be profitable. The provisions contained in the decree included the prohibition of unfair distribution practices, so that each picture would be rented on a separate basis, theater by theater, without regard for other pictures or exhibitor affiliation; the splitting of existing companies into separate theater and producer-distributor companies with no interlocking directors or officers; the divestiture of all theaters operated in pools with other companies and of all theaters in closed towns, that is, where those theaters had no competitors; and the establishment of voting trusts to prevent shareholders in the former companies from exercising common control of both successor companies.

The process of divorce between production and exhibition was undertaken gradually. Between 1948 and 1953, theaters previously owned by producer-distributors were sold to independent corporations that could follow their own best interests instead of being subordinated to the overall control of a corporation that also operated production facilities.[19] The transformation of the industry due to these decrees increased competition between the five major studios, since the studios and the affiliates were forced to deal with each other at arm's length, creating

more competition at the exhibition level. They could not give one another preferential treatment without the threat of possible contempt of court charges. Since independent exhibitors were no longer forced to buy a full line of pictures in order
to get the one movie they wanted, they gained more control over the business.[20]

Open market competition was forced upon the major studios at a time when
the whole market was shrinking, for the most part, because of television.
Television had begun its real commercial expansion in 1948. By 1949, 1 million
American homes had TV sets, and in 1954, the number had risen to 32 million.
By the end of the 1950s, nearly 90 percent of homes in the United States had TV
sets. Television had grown to replace movies as the dominant leisure activity of
the American people. Along with this shifting trend, annual box-office receipts
declined from $1.692 billion in 1946 to $1.298 billion in 1956, or about 26 percent. More than four thousand theaters closed during this period.[21]

In an attempt to reduce overhead, actors, writers, producers, and directors were
taken off long-term contracts. Without captive venues, marginal films of limited
appeal were more difficult to book than high-powered blockbusters whose grand
scale and big stars could be counted on to generate business. Also, by 1953 the
overseas market accounted for 60 percent of total receipts, surpassing domestic
business for the first time.[22] A new production strategy for the big studios involved action-packed, simply plotted blockbusters with wide audience appeal.
This strategy forced a continuing reduction in the number of films produced each
year. Because big studios no longer cared to spend money on cheap formulaic
films that only appealed to smaller selective audiences, they subsequently farmed
out their low-budget drama and science fiction productions to subsidiaries.

The big studios' blockbuster strategy enabled the smaller studios, such as
Universal and Columbia, to capture a larger share of the market by producing
lower-budget products. Simultaneously, independent producers found a market for
their products among the growing teenage audiences and a venue for exhibition
among theaters eager for products. From 1946 to 1956, the number of independent
producers more than doubled to around 150.[23] The changing relationship between
exhibition and independent producers was described in *Variety* in 1956:

In recent months exhibitors have clamored for film fare that would appeal to
teenage customers whom they regard as their best audience. . . . The product
shortage has brought about a new theory of assembling a show, a practice that has
been adopted by several independent producers and distributors. . . . The distribs,
according to the booker, launch these pictures with a hefty advertising campaign.
"They line up a big group of theaters," he explained, "and grab their money and
run. It's not legitimate film fare as such. It attracts an audience many of us in the
industry consider undesirable."[24]

Because of product shortage and the absence of secondary films, low-budget independent productions were aggressively packaged and sold to eager theater owners.

At the beginning of the decade, when movies were America's most popular
form of entertainment, the majority of films were produced primarily with adult

appeal. Big-budget films, including those in the science fiction genre such as *The Thing* (1951) and *The Day the Earth Stood Still* (1951), were directed almost entirely at adults.[25] By the mid-1950s, when television had overtaken film as the most popular form of entertainment, the studios found it necessary to increase the appeal of going to the movies. Some studios chose to narrow their focus and attract one group with the requisite income, leisure, and garrulousness to frequent the theater. Since older Americans tended to stay at home, many studios began to target a younger market, which still sought entertainment outside the home. Experiments with the moviegoing experience, such as the introduction of 3-D, the emphasis on science fiction and horror genres that provided vicarious thrills, and the development of drive-in theaters all were undertaken in the effort to cater to young audiences.[26]

The Hollywood film industry experimented with technological enhancements in the effort to attract a younger audience. The process known as 3-D was introduced in 1952 with the production of Arch Oboler's *Bwana Devil* (1952). To experience the three-dimensional effect, the viewer was required to wear specially designed Polaroid glasses while the film was run simultaneously through two projectors. This stereoscopic method was marketed as "a true third dimensional experience," and *Bwana Devil* was hailed by the trade papers "as historic in its box office hype as was Jolson's Jazz Singer."[27]

In the wake of 3-D's success, other studios imitated the technique, using it to enliven science fiction monsters and aliens. In Universal's *It Came from Outer Space* (1953) flying saucers and alien monsters lunge out of the screen into the audience with a contrived but potentially terrifying effect. The success of the 3-D gimmick was short-lived; complaints of headaches from the glasses and of repetitive plots sounded the death knell for this technology. Drive-in theaters couldn't offer the 3-D experience, and major studios refused to experiment with creative plots and explore the potentials of the innovation. By 1954, audiences had lost interest, and 3-D pictures were no longer produced.[28] But the interest in science fiction fare 3-D promoted and capitalized upon remained to be exploited.

Science fiction fare provided an advantage to Hollywood studios that the medium of television didn't enjoy. Theaters had their own unique properties, which made them ideal for offering frightening experiences to willing audiences. Television couldn't offer the wide screen and the darkened theater ambience that film could: "The screen is too small, the set too much within control, the commercials too frequent to build the mood, the reality of who you are, where you are, are too insistent."[29]

Studios found that science fiction and monster movies were not easily adaptable to the television format with its small screen, its difficulty in creating and portraying special effects, and its sponsor censorship. Television truly catered to the lowest common denominator; sponsors insisted upon inoffensive family fare and science fiction monsters were potentially too disturbing and controversial to be acceptable. Television had little to contribute to science fiction programming until the series *The Twilight Zone* appeared in 1959, with *The Outer Limits,* capitalizing upon the success of the former, appearing soon after.

Most science fiction television had been confined to young children's programs with such classics as *Captain Video* (1949–1956), *Captain Z-ero* (1955), and *The Invisible Man* (1958); these programs were entirely inappropriate for offering any frightening or thoughtful representations of atomic development. Generally, they consisted of oversimplified versions of Cold War struggles. For example, although the heroes of *Captain Video, Rocket Rangers, Space Ranger,* and other science fiction shows were affiliated with future intergalactic organizations, it was quickly evident that these good, simple heroes were just ordinary Americans operating in some distant future time, protecting our solar system against evil foreign influences. These space series introduced their young audiences to the distinguishing characteristics of tyrannical regimes and to the moral legitimacy of battling against such tyranny, all in stylized Cold War fantasies in which the champions of democracy triumphed over totalitarianism.[30]

Science fiction had always appealed to teenage audiences, and since it was not, for the most part, offered on television, studios found that this genre had great marketability. Gradually, the smaller studios and particularly the independent producers increased their output of this type of film. Low-budget science fiction films with unknown actors and directors were produced in bulk by independents and small studios alike, which sometimes invested the majority of the budget into high-powered sensational advertisements. In some instances, the film's title and advertising campaign sold the film to distributors before the story for the script was even conceived.

This shift in marketing strategy and production has been called the "juvenilization" of Hollywood film, and cheap science fiction fare produced during this time fell under the label of "exploitation film."[31] "Exploitation" had been traditionally used in Hollywood to describe a film's content; for example, in 1946 *Variety* portrayed the "exploitation film" as containing "some timely or currently controversial subject which can be exploited, and capitalized on, in publicity and advertising."[32] However, by the mid-1950s, the term had assumed a negative connotation referring to a low-budget concoction, hastily conceived and produced, which drew upon the public curiosity and free publicity surrounding a current event. As a production strategy for small studios and independent producers in the 1950s, the exploitation formula had three elements: controversial, bizarre, or timely subject matter; a substandard budget; and a teenage audience. As "exploitation," these films were "triply exploitative, simultaneously exploiting sensational happenings for their story value, their notoriety for publicity value, and their teenage audience for box office value."[33] Labeled "weirdies" by the trade papers, these films were constrained only by budget and available technology.

Producers of these exploitation films preyed upon topical news events and contemporary social concerns for their film narratives. For example, forty-three science fiction film projects were announced in the trade papers the day after

Sputnik was launched; these were advertised in trade publications as "an opportunity to cash in on today's headlines . . . to cash in on history's biggest news!"[34]
Hydrogen bomb tests in the Pacific and underground testing in Nevada in 1956
and 1957 prompted a slew of film monsters, all in some way related to these real
events. Just as scientists and politicians depended upon images already in the culture to convey the meaning of these new occurrences, so the producers of exploitation films, with little time and even less money, quickly constructed their
products around easily accessible cultural meanings. Hence, atomic technology
and its perceived misuse by humanity creates mutated monsters and evil technology, which attempts to destroy the civilization that created it. The genre of the
mutated radiation-produced monster and the evil alien invader had begun.

The appeal of these exploitation films, according to some studio executives,
rested on plots or gimmicks with proven success. For example, when Warner
Brothers' 1954 production *Them!* a science fiction movie featuring giant atomically
mutated ants, was a box-office success, there was a flood of imitations parading a
multitude of giant radiation-produced creatures. Low budgets and short production schedules contributed to the style and plot of this type of film becoming rou-
tine. Stylistically, most used the semidocumentary narrative and the flat, gray, "realistic" cinematography made popular in crime and spy films of the late 1940s,
originally adopted because it was inexpensive to produce and required no expensive
atmospheric lighting or special effects. The extensive use of newsreel and military
stock footage with voice-over narration also typifies this type of science fiction film;
these elements were easily incorporated for the sake of economy. Basically, all a producer needed was a high-concept title. The energetic exploitation of the teenage audience was, dollar for dollar, a better investment than big-budget science fiction
crossovers that aimed to appeal to both teenage and adult audiences.

All too soon, these science fiction monster films became repetitious, only differentiated by the endless variety of radiation-produced creatures: giant insects,
sea creatures, dinosaurs, even humans loomed on the screen seeking human prey.
Predictably, they are all destroyed by military intervention, and just as predictably
the films all close with speculation upon the nature of atomic development and
the unforeseen hazards that lurk in its shadow. The same conventions were used
repeatedly: recognizable characters, well-worn plots, similar film styles. Because
of the redundancy of these images and the unique qualities of the science fiction
genre itself, these films seemed to capitalize upon the fears and concerns of
American society and were able to point out flaws within the dominant culture.

Science Fiction and Independent Production

Independent filmmakers sought to capitalize upon science fiction's success with a
variety of films in this genre. These producers, just gaining a foothold in
Hollywood after the breakup of the studio monopolies, sought to attract audiences with films produced on limited budgets. Instead of contributing new and

varied film subjects and styles, the independents found themselves in competition for financing and exhibition deals, and thus they produced formulaic repetitions of previously successful films.

The major obstacle faced by independent producers was in finding financing for their pictures, and the dependency upon obtaining bank loans was yet another aspect determining film content. Production loans from banks were restrictive; they required information concerning script content such as whether the script "was of a controversial nature from religious or ideological points of view, or whether the subject had limited appeal."[35] Most independent producers found that it was easier to gain financial backing if their product resembled previous successful films, and consequently most films remained within relatively narrow subject boundaries.

A genre film differs fundamentally from other films by virtue of its reliance on preordained forms, familiar plots, and recognizable characters. A set of common codes and assumptions underlie production parameters and viewer expectations. Consciously or unconsciously, the audience and the genre filmmaker are aware of the prior films and the way in which each of these concrete examples is an attempt to embody once again the essence of a well-known story. Popular genres are important for the Hollywood film industry because they allow film producers to resort to tried-and-true formulas that have proved profitable in the past. Elements in a commercially successful genre film are imitated until that genre is no longer profitable.

Film genre is perpetuated by the fundamental intertextuality of Hollywood film. One film draws upon another and may draw upon other media as well, such as science fiction literature and even commercial advertisements. Every Hollywood film is to some degree an intertextual network, relying on patterns of meaning already existing in other films and other cultural forms. Most science fiction films incorporate an "intertext," or elements from other films. Such incorporation could include everything from an entire genre of films or a single reference to a specific film. For example, each film featuring a radiation-produced monster contains elements from previous films of that genre. *War of the Colossal Beast* (1958) was made as a sequel to the previous *The Amazing Colossal Man* (1957). The character Robbie the Robot used in *The Invisible Boy* (1957) was recycled from the earlier science fiction film *The Forbidden Planet* (1956). The fabricated atomic explosions created for *The Beginning or The End?* were used in *Above and Beyond* as well.

Particular images are continuously selected and become dominant because of their role in a successful formula, whereas other less successful images that portray the same ideas are ignored in order to avoid low box-office returns. During the Hollywood studio era and in most television production today, this type of production also holds down costs, since sets, costumes, and props can be used over and over again in shows of the same genre. In-house writers need only copy previous plots, and expenditures on high-priced original properties are averted.

Insight into the production priorities that determined the selection and repli-cation of certain specific images of nuclear use over others can be found in the work of Roger Corman. Corman was perhaps the most successful of the indepen-dent filmmakers working in the low-budget science fiction genre during the mid-to late 1950s. His production methods and the economic priorities that deter-mined the content of his films are typical of independents of this time. Individually, he has the distinction of having produced and directed more films dealing with nuclear issues than any other filmmaker, with such titles as *The Day the World Ended* (1956) and *Attack of the Crab Monsters* (1956).[36]

Independents like Corman produced low-budget exploitation films intended for release as parts of double bills. Most major studio productions in black and white cost between $1 million and $2 million, whereas the typical Corman feature ran under $100,000. Corman, working through his distribution company American International Pictures (AIP), began producing films specifically for release as dou-ble bills for increased profits. Typically, a second feature got only a flat price from exhibitors, whereas a first feature earned a percentage of the ticket sales. By com-bining two features together, a producer earned a percentage of the ticket sales by selling the combination as a percentage package. Exhibitors agreed to pay the same rental figure for two independently produced low-budget films that they paid for one major studio film. Considering that more than eight thousand theaters de-pended on features, small independents had ready customers, with exhibitors using these cheap exploitation pictures to bridge the gap between blockbusters.[37]

AIP soon found that it could outgross the major studios with ads promising "giant all science fiction double bills" that catered to the teenage market.[38] The practice of combining two science fiction films on the same double bill went against the traditional practice of mixing genres; such mixing aimed at crossover appeal in an attempt to attract a larger audience. Since these films were produced specifically to lure teenagers and young adults into indoor and drive-in theaters, the double-bill strategy had both biology and culture on its side. One exhibitor explained: "A young couple go out to get away from home. They come to the the-ater. They don't want to be back two hours later. They may not absolutely want to see two pictures, but it makes them feel good to know they're getting two for the price of one, and it occupies the whole evening for them."[39]

Film content was conceived to appeal to this specific audience, and genre audi-ences were drawn to these movies for their science fiction elements or their shock value.[40] As Corman relates, "Mastering low-budget filmmaking techniques for the 'exploitation' market of the 1950s consisted of telling an interesting, visually en-tertaining story that would draw young people to the drive-ins, and not take yourself too seriously along the way."[41]

Independent producers added to their double-bill exploitation-film strategy by producing movies in set pairs. For example, AIP at one point promoted a package in which the second feature would be a sequel to the first. Billed as "events lead-ing up to the global finale," *The Day the World Ended* was followed by *Last Woman on Earth,* in which the actress from the preceding feature survives the nuclear obliteration with seven men.[42]

Corman's films were produced with this double-bill strategy in mind and, as are most films in Hollywood, to make as much profit as possible. But, unlike major studios who might have created a more thoughtful presentation of nuclear issues for prestige as well as profit, or big-budget independent directors like Stanley Kramer or Stanley Kubrick who felt they had a personal message to promote, Corman focused upon realizing the maximum profit with the minimum investment. Typical of independent producers, Corman worked on all aspects of his films, from preproduction and production through postproduction, frequently writing the script himself and conceiving of the promotional campaign as well. Some independent producers even went so far as to star in their films. For example, producer Robert Clarke directed and starred in *Hideous Sun Demon* (1959). Most independent films like Corman's were shot within ten days and for under $100,000. Most ideas for the scripts derived from what could be produced on a budget, incorporating the most inexpensive special effects. Like most independent productions, Corman's films were very low-budget and were sold to distributors before the actual shooting began, or even before a script was written. AIP's creative process was described in this manner: "In most cases we have no more than a title to start with. We think up the title then kind of pre-test it by springing it on one of our exhibitors. If he likes it—and if it's gory enough, of course— we give it to a writer and tell him to write a script for it, and then we get on to more important things, like the promotion campaign and the publicity."[43]

Advertising campaigns involved posters "obviously overdrawn for the deliberate and calculating purpose of bringing people into theaters"; the film monsters themselves, brought to life with cheap special effects and surrounded with by now familiar formulaic scenarios, could never live up to their advance billing in the posters. Still, teenage audiences attended in large numbers with the hopes of being entertained, shocked, and amused.[44]

With such efforts devoted to providing images that would offer vicarious thrills, AIP wisely managed to avoid the wrath of the Production Code Administration (PCA), which directly influenced the content of Hollywood film. This self-regulating mechanism was established in 1934 by the major studios in an attempt to quell growing criticism of film content by various pressure groups such as the American Legion. Members of the Motion Picture Producers and Distributors of America (MPPDA) had to submit their pictures to the PCA, which determined if content adhered to the Production Code. The code outlined specific issues and representations of society that were deemed morally and politically unacceptable by the PCA. Pictures that failed to gain approval could not be exhibited in theaters owned by the MPPDA, which constituted about 90 percent of all theaters.[45] A major factor in the administration's approval of science fiction gore was that it was quite busy, along with various citizens' groups, with more seriously compromising fare such as *Peyton Place* (1957) and *God's Little Acre*

(1958). The major studios were desperately attempting to attract audiences by trying to push the extent to which the censors would allow more explicit sex and violence in film. In 1958, AIP noted that its sixteen recent films had received the PCA seal, citing the "comic touch" and "tongue in cheek humor" that tended to disarm potential critics. One studio chief at AIP noted: "Our stories are pure fantasy with no attempt at realism. Because of this it is difficult to see how anyone could take our pictures so seriously that psychological damage could occur. . . . In our concept of each of our monsters, we strive for unbelievability."[46]

Since the demand for science fiction was high thanks to the double-bill strategy, films had to be produced quickly and have specific audience appeal. Little experimentation with style, plot, or characters took place because of these requirements. These films imitated the formulas of earlier successful films, which generally were released by larger studios. Hence, the radiation-produced giant monsters in *Them!* were replicated in cheap films until audiences gradually lost interest. Corman's selection of nuclear images was determined by a combination of perceived audience taste, the imitation of previously successful science fiction formulas, the incorporation of current events in scripts for exploitation value, the ability to cheaply produce a specific atmosphere or special effect, and the easy accessibility of location for settings. These factors together worked to determine what specific images of nuclear use would be constructed.

According to Corman, he monitored his teenage audience's tastes by interacting and discussing ideas with small groups. Here, he describes a small test session:

> We geared ourselves up for the teen genre movies where the title was the most important drawing card. . . . We really designed our movies for kids. Every Friday and Saturday my kids would bring 30 or 40 of their friends to the house and I'd run movies to see what they liked and what they didn't like. I'd run our movies. I'd run other people's movies. . . . That's where our ideas came from. We learned what not to make as well as what to make.[17]

After discovering what imaginative scenarios interested teenagers and what films they enjoyed, Corman went on to conceive of a film title and concept. His ample use of nuclear images stemmed from his own interest in science fiction and from the wide public curiosity in the issue: "I had always read science fiction as a kid, and most of the low budget films of the day were Westerns and mysteries. It was the dawn of the nuclear age, so I thought doing science fiction and using the nuclear idea would add some excitement and novelty."[48]

Most of Corman's films utilizing nuclear themes were imitative, with slight variances in monster appearance and gimmick. This is aptly illustrated in Corman's first film as an independent, *Monster from the Ocean Floor* (1954), which involves a man-eating mutant created by atomic testing that begins devouring fishermen—a clear imitation of *The Beast from 20,000 Fathoms* (1953). The "monster," another superimposition of a squid, differentiated its film action from that of its predecessor by incorporating a miniature submarine. Corman concocted this contrivance after reading a *Los Angeles Times* article about an electric-powered one-man submarine. Corman didn't write the story until he was sure he could use the submarine, which was donated for the movie by a local company, Aerojet General.[49]

Despite the submarine episode, Corman's film stands as one in a long line of intertextual imitations. Mutated sea creatures were offered to film audiences every year from 1953 to 1957, each film drawing upon the previous in plot and visual style. *It Came from Beneath the Sea* (1955) showcased yet another giant squid, this one specifically created by hydrogen bomb explosions off the Marshall Islands. Next, a gigantic mutated sea creature who guards an underwater deposit of uranium is shown in *The Phantom from 10,000 Leagues* (1956). Next, giant mollusks begin hatching from the effects of radiation in *The Monster that Challenged the World* (1957).

Corman stated that his film ideas came from a reflection of "what you see around you," and his adoption of current events and general items of public interest into his film scenarios is clearly evident. For example, Corman claims that he got the idea for the radiation-mutated crabs used in *Attack of the Crab Monsters* (1956) from watching Jacques Cousteau's first undersea adventure film. Linking a perceived interest in marine life with the contemporary concerns of fallout and the Eugelap hydrogen bomb tests, Corman produced a film concerning sea crabs mutated by atomic radiation on a South Pacific island. A group of people are stranded on an island near the test site, and fallout has destroyed all animal life except land crabs and (conveniently) seagulls. Not only has the effect of fallout caused the crabs to become gigantic but it has given them superior intelligence as well. Inexpensively filmed during a Hawaiian sojourn, the film was made for $70,000 and grossed over $1 million in rentals.[50]

In similar fashion, *War of the Satellites* (1958) attempted to exploit the national dialogue and speculation surrounding the launch of Sputnik and public interest in the impending launch of the U.S. Explorer satellite. Imitating another science fiction invasion film, *Kronos* (1957), alien forces attempt to halt a U.S. atomic rocket mission and indeed all space exploration from Earth.

Not only did independents imitate formula plots and monsters, so too did these films replicate one another in style. Primarily, they were filmed in black and white, with few camera setups, for the sake of economy. There is no special lighting or rapid editing involving numerous camera angles and wide pans. Creatures, when not superimposed giants, were rubber masks or wire-and-paste puppets. Since many of these creatures were not visually frightening, their appearances were usually brief and were shrouded in fog, wind, sand, or darkness. The tense buildup to the monster's first appearance involved most of the action, with emphasis upon hostility or upon the mysterious quality of the environmental setting from which the monster emerges.

Ultimately, all filmmakers are restricted by the available technology for the images they can capture. As mentioned earlier, superimposition techniques made

producing giant mutations cheap and easy, hence the proliferation of these images. Likewise, major studios and big budgets could provide an imaginative postnuclear landscape, but low-budget films were restricted to readily available settings. This factor didn't prevent independents from exploiting the audience
interest in such imagined scenarios of *Total Destruction Day* or *The End of the
World*. Since no nuclear devastation could be constructed for Corman's post–nuclear war film, *The Day the World Ended* (1956), he simply envisioned the
postholocaust world as no more hostile or strange than his own backyard. He
shot the film in a forest behind a restaurant off Ventura Boulevard. To fit this setting, he manipulated the story line to involve a group of people who had survived
nuclear war because they had been in a valley where the surrounding mountains
and winds had shielded them from radiation.[51] *Last Woman on Earth* (1960), also
by Corman, introduces three survivors of a nuclear holocaust who happened to
be skin diving during the bombing and surface to find the lush tropical setting
unchanged except for the fact that the entire human population is dead.

This use of familiar settings was necessary because of practicality and budget
constraints, but this also promoted the impression, albeit unintentionally, that the
consequences of nuclear war were not so completely devastating. These movies
forecast no nuclear winter, no blackened earth. Trees, vegetation, even birds and
animals survive; humans are left to repopulate the Earth again. Later, as films of
the 1960s tackled the consequences of nuclear war and its environmental destruction more seriously, logistics and budgetary considerations still play a part in
watering down the effects of war. *On the Beach* and *The World, the Flesh and the
Devil* show only deserted cities; the citizenry has been destroyed but the planet remains quietly intact.

Thus, the rise of independent filmmakers, a consequence of the breakup of big-
studio monopolies, contributed to the development and dissemination of a set of
images relating to atomic technology. Hoping to exploit teenage interests, they drew
upon deep residual cultural concerns such as anxiety over tampering with nature,
the transmutational effects of radiation, and the creation of monsters. The radiation-produced monsters appeared the way they did because of budgetary constraints and the availability of cheap special effects. And due to the intertextual nature of Hollywood film production, particularly the tendency of films to copy
previously successful plot formulas, the replication of these same imagined effects of
radiation and atomic development continued throughout these science fiction films.

The following chapters offer an overview and analysis of three major science
fiction genres that popularly incorporated atomic themes: the radiation-produced monster film, the alien invader film and the corresponding atomic espionage films that featured communist invaders, and films with postnuclear scenarios. An investigation into these genres will illustrate how the various factors of
Cold War ideology, contemporary context, and the institutional and economic
priorities of the Hollywood industry helped to determine the selection of specific
images associated with atomic issues.

5

Radiation-Produced Monsters

Them! (1954)

*When man entered the atomic age, he opened a door into a new world . . .
what he will eventually find in that new world, nobody can predict.*

Them!

Mutated insects in *Them!* (1954)

DESPITE HOLLYWOOD'S COLD WAR EMPHASIS upon the military establishment in the 1950s, the incorporation by filmmakers of residual cultural elements into the science fiction genre to give meaning to atomic issues points to an uneasy public grappling with the topic. The specter of the uncontrollable transmutational property of radiation as a result of the atomic testing program, the image of nature's indomitable power over humanity, the linkage of fictional horrors to real world events all reverberated concerns of the time, and these themes are ultimately critical of the dominant government ideology of widening nuclear proliferation. The intertextual nature of Hollywood production ensured that these images were repeatedly disseminated in film scenarios. One film replicated the previous, creating a genre that capitalized upon contradictory and unsettling premises.

The connections and ensuing contradictions involving radiation-produced monsters, residual cultural elements, and Cold War ideology are graphically presented in the prototypical movie of this genre, *Them!* (1954), in which mutated ants emerge near the Trinity test site. The desert setting, the flat and colorless visual and narrative style, and the positive characterizations of the military juxtaposed to more critical portrayals of scientists became formulaic elements of the radiation-produced monster films produced in Hollywood between 1954 and 1959. Warner Brothers' production of *Them!* imitated some of the same plot devices of the successful *The Beast from 20,000 Fathoms* (1953), including the depiction of a giant creature transformed as a possible result of radiation, and followed a basic "seek and destroy" story line in quasi-documentary style. It also copied from other science fiction films, borrowing, for example, the unique sound effects from *War of the Worlds* (1953).

The premise of *Them!* speculates upon the possibility that common insects might mutate, generation by generation, to so large a size that they could conveniently add humans to their diet. The idea that ordinary creatures could be mutated as a result of radiation was merely an extension of the seminal beliefs associated with atomic energy, elaborated by Frederick Soddy in 1908. *Them!* and the ensuing barrage of cinematic mutated creatures served to strengthen this association.

Genre Narrative and Style

Most movies in the radiation-produced monster genre were not made by large studios but were cheaply and hastily made for distribution by independent producers. The easily imitated special effects, the high audience interest, and the low cost of production made these kinds of films perfect material for the newly emerging independents. Low-budget films typically were more likely to present unpleasant and unsettling events than major productions, relying upon the exploitation of current events and catering to audiences seeking vicarious thrills. Thus, most films dealing with radioactivity and its effects or with postholocaust worlds are of this variety, and merely replicate the genre elements of previous films.

The transmutational effect of radiation was used as a gimmick because it was technically possible to do so. Special effects had developed to the point where the superimposition of moving images, one over another, was easily accomplished. Using a combination of film footage of garden ants superimposed onto human characters and large articulated puppets of huge ant limbs, an effective image of giant insects was created. Earlier, models of giant dinosaurs and painstaking frame-by-frame filming had produced the jerking, unnatural movements of film monsters. The development and availability of this newer technology made the selection and subsequent repetition of one specific imagined effect of radiation prevalent.

These genre films followed a basic plotline exemplified by the script of *Them!* The narrative of *Them!* begins as local police from a small desert town discover a small girl, suffering from shock and unable to speak, wandering alone in the desert. Soon they discover a trail of demolished buildings, strange tracks in the desert, and various dead bodies randomly strewn about. A plaster cast of a mysterious footprint found near the destruction is sent to Washington, and two entomologists, an old eccentric man and his daughter, arrive on the scene. Thanks to the help of the FBI and a variety of military personnel, the cause of the destruction is discovered. Giant ants, "a fantastic mutation, probably caused by lingering radiation from the first atomic bomb," have become numerous enough to begin emerging from their desert habitat. After much discussion between the scientists and army officials, the army firebombs the nest. But, unfortunately, the menace is not so easily contained. The scientist discovers that two queen ants have escaped and predicts that the menace will quickly spread across the United States, infiltrating cities, consuming their human populations, and eventually ruling the planet.

A military command post is quickly and efficiently established to monitor all national news reports, and army personnel search for evidence of mysterious deaths and strange occurrences. The concern for the unseen infiltration is kept from the unsuspecting population as the army tries secretly to eradicate the hidden threat. Gradually, one queen and her male followers infest a cargo ship and consume its unfortunate crew. Soon after a navy destroyer quickly dispatches the ship and its insect marauders, a larger nest of giant ants is discovered in a storm drain in Los Angeles. Martial law is declared over the city, and an army of troops mobilizes against the hoards. The people of Los Angeles leave their fate to the military establishment. The audience is not presented with scenes of mass panic or of giant ants terrorizing the population. The ants' presence is covert; they lie multiplying under the city, unseen by average citizens. Only the military understand and can destroy this concealed enemy. Left in capable military hands, the army blasts the ants into oblivion in the movie's conclusion.

Besides showcasing mutated creatures and the military's ability to destroy them, this seminal film displays other conventions of the genre. There is constant emphasis upon the relationship between real contemporary news events and the fictional plot, lending credence to the cinematic action. Most film narratives in the radiation-produced monster genre explicitly link the plot to real-life atomic tests while devoting large amounts of film time to military stock footage, frequently presenting footage of actual atomic tests. Earlier nuclear films portrayed an imaginary, nameless test or vaguely mentioned lingering radiation as the cause for the emergence of the beasts. For example, a generic and unspecified polar test, referred to as "Operation Experiment," is blamed for disturbing the sleeping monster in *The Beast from 20,000 Fathoms.*

In contrast, the scientists in *Them!* are shown pointing to the words "Trinity test site" on a map depicting the geographic location of the creatures. Later, the emergence of the ants is specifically linked to "lingering radiation from the first atomic bomb test." Subsequent radiation-produced monster films furthered this extrapolation of the film story to the real world, either through the use of newsreel footage or through voice-over narration, in order to link the fictional story with actual events or to the state of science and technology in the familiar world. For example, a scientist lectures upon the intricacies of astronomy as we zoom through the universe in *Invaders from Mars* (1953).

Using U.S. government stock footage of atomic tests for specific film sequences further emphasized the importance of military personnel and technology as necessary for national defense, and it also served to link the responsibility for the resulting calamities onto specific events or social institutions. Such images of tanks, jeeps, cannons, jets, missile launchers, and bombs became repetitive and recognizable, functioning in the same way the use of newsreel footage did, as a reference to the real world. Blame for the emergence of radiation monsters lay with the government's atomic testing program, with specific tests at pinpointed sites, and with the scientists and military personnel who had developed the technology without fully understanding the consequences of their actions.

Evidence of further critical emphasis can be found in the choice of setting for films of this genre. Typically, the radiation-produced threat emerges from a largely unknown and unexplored geographical area, most often the desert, the sea, the arctic, or outer space. For Hollywood studios, the near proximity of the desert and the long California coastline offered a convenient, and more importantly economical, stage for movie production. Specifically choosing the American desert also served to directly relate the depicted events to the Nevada test sites and the lingering radiation at those sites. Some scenarios involved Los Alamos itself, which in the early 1950s was alive with activities connected with the production of thermonuclear weapons.

The desert setting became an important element in linking fact with fiction. The landscape itself conjured images of a postnuclear terrain, not the familiar smoking rubble of Hiroshima but the barren and unlivable environment that massive nuclear bombing could leave behind. But the vast sandy expanse tended to take on deeper significance as a landscape, becoming an additional character in the action of the movie itself. The setting played a large role in these films as an angry and hostile force, as if nature itself had begun to destroy or at least threaten civilization. Nature, violated by man's tampering with its secrets through the manipulation of the atom, had angrily turned against civilization. The revenge of nature has been a predominant theme throughout human mythology, and it is hardly surprising to find film scenarists "depicting Mother Earth fighting back against the obscenity of the atomic forces unleashed by mankind's folly."[1]

For example, throughout *Them!*, sandstorms and howling winds obscure sound and vision as the characters fight the elements to discover an even greater menace. In one scene, a policeman searches a deserted house as the wind howls, repeatedly bangs the front door, and causes the lights to flicker. He peers out into the dark isolation of the desert, and violently blowing sand slaps into his face. We see him next as a corpse on the desert floor, mere bones, his gun belt carelessly tossed by the mandibles of a giant ant. The isolation and hostility of the desert environment is constantly alluded to in dialogue: "The wind is pretty freakish in these parts"; "Who can tell what's out there in this wasteland."

The inaccessible and largely unexplored environment of the desert sets the menace in relative isolation from the civilization it threatens, shrouding it in mystery. The monster is born out of and emerges from this realm. It strikes out from the unknown, the unexplored, and then submerges itself in the desert's expanses. Only experts, the scientists, through the investigation of a trail of destruction, can uncover the nature of the threat. After this discovery, the military works to destroy the threat as it inevitably encroaches upon populated areas.

Another common element in this genre is found in the depiction of the primary victims. It is usually young children, animals, the elderly, or the simpleminded upon whom the beasts initially prey. The monster soon moves on to larger populations in its aim to terrorize and destroy cities and civilization for its own purposes. One could compare this motif with the contemporary Cold War concern of communist infiltration and invasion—fear of "the other." Widely promoted at the time was the idea that the poor, the uneducated, the young, and the simpleminded were especially vulnerable to communist ideology.[2] Once such subversives gained a stronghold over these more vulnerable members of society, it was only a matter of time before the communist hoards would advance, taking over whole countries and eventually the entire free world. Hence, the invading "other," be it a monster or an alien, at first consumes unknowing and vulnerable victims before expanding its activities to destroy entire cities.

But the choice of children and animals as the innocent initial victims of atomic proliferation point to another factor. Despite the massive Atomic Energy Commission (AEC) public relations campaign, which attempted to reassure the public that atomic testing posed no danger, concern over the effects of radiation on livestock and contaminated milk on children was always at the forefront of public concern.[3] Of particular worry was the threat to the "future generations" that the tests potentially imperiled, and the possible widespread poisoning of large sectors of the population through their unknowing consumption of beef and dairy products exposed to radioactive fallout. Hollywood's choice of victim of the radiation-produced monster certainly capitalized on this concern.

The conscious evocation of biblical prophecy to convey the grave import of events is another common element of the genre. For example, in dialogue, in voice-over narration, and in closing sequences, these films invariably draw upon some prophecy concerning the fate of mankind or the Earth. *Them!* was typical in this respect as well. For example, when the scientist Medford first discovers the mutated ants, he solemnly declares: "We may be witnesses to a biblical prophecy come true . . . and there shall be destruction and darkness come over creation, and the beasts shall reign over the earth."

Although atomic technology had always invoked religious exhortation, it had usually been in reaction to some discovery or event, as in Robert Oppenheimer's quote from the Bhagavad Gita, or in reference to atomic power as "the power of God." As the imagined consequences of nuclear development began to take cinematic form in Hollywood, filmmakers relied upon Christian prophecy and allegory for dramatic impact and to portray nuclear phenomenon in familiar terms, using rhetoric that the public already associated with atomic technology. Bringing up the Revelation of St. John, for example, endowed nuclear phenomena with deeper and graver import. Such examples include the opening scene from *When Worlds Collide* (1951) in which a heavenly choir accompanies the images of an opening Bible. The deep-voiced narration propounds: "And God looked upon the Earth, and behold, it was corrupt, for all flesh had corrupted his way upon the Earth. And behold, I will destroy them with the Earth."

A similar godlike commentary opens a film that features giant mutated crabs. *Attack of the Crab Monsters* (1956) begins with a string of stock-footage atomic explosions, and the booming voice warns: "And the Lord said I will destroy man whom I have created from the face of the earth."

Allusions to biblical prophecy also worked to lend an inevitability to nuclear development and its consequences, however terrifying they might be. Whatever happens was "as it should be," or an "act of God." Such rhetoric furthered the naturalization of atomic technology, linking it to familiar and largely accepted religious beliefs, while its inherent fatalism made any protest against atomic development appear irrational.

The Cold War: Glorification of the Military

The heightened Cold War ideology of society in the 1950s pervades the images and narrative of the radiation-produced monster genre. Unique to films incorporating nuclear themes during the mid- to late 1950s is the emphasis upon the absolute necessity of military authority. The cinema portrayed the military and its might succeeding against invading monsters and aliens, with the population in full support. Brian Murphy, in his study of monster movies of the 1950s, labels this glorification of the military and its technology a "celebration of militarism."[4]

This attitude differs from the common narrative in atomic films produced immediately after the dropping of the atomic bomb. Instead of portraying scientific knowledge and expertise as essential for the destruction of the threat, science fiction films of the 1950s emphasize military force and technology. For example, the scientist in *The Beast from 20,000 Fathoms* is a crucial player in controlling the knowledge upon which the world's salvation rests. He alone quells the monster with his nimble handling of a radioactive isotope. Military personnel play a lesser part in the action and never directly assist in the actual destruction of the monster. Yet, by 1954, civilian scientists in these movies had become secondary to military characters. Depicted as always in control and ready for action, the military hero in these movies was often a scientist as well, but unlike the civilian scientist, this hero always placed humanity and the preservation of American society over scientific gain.

Typical to the genre, the main focus of the action and dialogue in *Them!* revolves around an FBI agent. Perpetually in control and ready to vanquish the adversary, the FBI hero is only hindered by the bumbling scientist in his personal quest for scientific knowledge. "Why don't you just let me go in with bombers and wipe out that nest?" the agent impatiently complains. The FBI agent never "looses his cool" in anger or fear, and he alone has the ability to communicate with the scientists, the army, and government officials alike. In fact, the agent explains the nature of the menace to government committees, translating in "simple terms" the unintelligible scientific jargon of the etymologists.

He performs all this while never losing sight of the human dimension, of the familiar way of life being threatened by the insect invaders. This character's concern for humanity and empathy with the victims stands in direct opposition to the purely research-oriented agenda followed by the scientist. Their opposing positions are illustrated in the following exchange. A government official wishes to destroy the ants' nest in Los Angeles, even though two young boys might be trapped inside:

> GOVERNMENT OFFICIAL: Are we supposed to jeopardize the lives of the
>   people of this city for the sake of two children who in all probability are
>   already dead?
> FBI MAN: Why don't you ask their mother, mister.
> SCIENTIST: I've told you before, we can't destroy the nest until we're sure
>   no new queens have hatched out.

The FBI agent epitomizes the ideal American military hero and, as such, works to glorify the military establishment. He is strong, virile, and fearless, and takes a strong moral stand while spouting lines laden with xenophobia and Cold War rhetoric. In one exchange with the scientist, he complains, "Why don't we all speak English, then we'd have some basis for understanding." Additionally, agent character is involved in the mandatory romantic flirtation with a woman scientist, when he is not displaying the capabilities of a high-powered bazooka or leading the ant firebombing brigade.

Hand in hand with the increased role of the military came the Cold War focus upon secrecy and containment. Specifically, this involves hiding the existence of a threat from the unsuspecting public, particularly by censoring the mass media. In *Them!* as in most movies of this genre, the emphasis upon secrecy is abundantly displayed. In an early scene, as the policeman investigates the eerily deserted house, a barely perceptible radio program discusses a mysterious "closely guarded secret." Later, after the mutants are discovered, the scientist warns a military committee that "something incredible has happened in the desert" and that "it must be kept a secret to avoid a nationwide panic." He goes on to emphasize that "absolute secrecy is essential, there isn't a police force in the world who could handle the panic." Throughout the film, the military refers to the ant crisis as "top, top secret," setting up their headquarters with high-tech radio transmitters and hoards of personnel. Various scenes depict journalists hovering outside the mysterious headquarters, speculating upon the purpose of the military presence and questioning a government official about the activity:

JOURNALIST: How about telling us what's going on in there, Senator?
SENATOR: Sorry boys, no comment, can't tell you a thing, sorry.

The military is depicted as in control of the flow of information, including the activities and movements of the scientists. As in real life with the Manhattan Project, the media and the public in *Them!* were kept ignorant for the sake of "national security." It is suggested that even the army personnel searching across the nation for "strange occurrences" were also uninformed regarding the specific reason for their work.

The American public must have been accustomed to this type of censorship in relation to atomic development. *Them!* was released in 1954, the same year as the Bravo hydrogen bomb test. AEC Chairman Lewis Strauss and President Eisenhower held a news conference after the test that made evident the classified nature of national defense activities. When the press asked for a general description of what had happened when the bomb went off, Eisenhower replied that "the information was classified." Eisenhower insisted that the words "thermonuclear," "fusion," and "hydrogen" be left out of press releases and speeches. Because the administration sought to restrict the discussion of the hydrogen bomb, press reportage of nuclear issues was subsequently heavily censored.[5]

In direct correspondence to this real-life situation, the military establishment in radiation-produced monster films is depicted as going to great lengths to censor, for security reasons, the extent of each monstrous invasion. Film dialogue explains this priority as motivated by concern for "the public's own good," in order to avoid mass panic. When the public does learn of the approaching menace in these films, it usually reacts with relative calm as the military marches through streets, positions troops on every corner, imposes curfews, and assumes complete authority. There are absolutely no signs of dissent or discontent, and the scenes of mass panic depicted in earlier monster movies are replaced with orderly public behavior as the military efficiently rallies to repel the beasts. The country appears unified it its battle against invasion, whether the invaders be extraterrestrial or the product of its own defense program.

Typical of this genre, the radioactive monster's encroachment is treated as an incoming invasion, with troops mobilizing, officers issuing commands, and scientists hovering about, just as in an actual war.[6] When the giant ants in *Them!* are discovered nesting in the drainage pipes under Los Angeles, the military acts just as it would against a known threat such as an invasion by a foreign country. They take over the city, contain and control the population by declaring martial law, and censor all mass-media broadcasts. The radio broadcasts from military intelligence inform the public: "This is the most serious crisis this city had ever faced. . . . It is not known . . . [but] other American cities, even now, might be infested." In Universal's *The Deadly Mantis* (1957), the threat from the invading creature and the idea of a communist first strike against the United States are virtually interchangeable.[7] Instructions are issued via television to members of the "Civilian Ground Observer Corps" from "Continental Air Command" to vigilantly prepare for the invading mutated insect:

> We have every reason to believe that the mantis is flying south along the gulf stream and we believe it will be one of you devoted men and women of the Civilian Ground Observer Corps who will spot it next time it appears. . . . You spotters should listen for a loud droning sound much like that of a squadron of heavy bombers flying in formation. . . . If the mantis is sighted, the procedure will be the same as though an enemy aircraft has been sighted.

In allowing the military complete social control, the public is rewarded by the destruction of the threat. Military power and a complacent public are portrayed as necessary not only for the continued existence of the "American way of life" but for the survival of the human race itself.

The Nature of the Threat

The specter of a subversive attack upon American society encapsulates the period's concern with containing communist aggression. The aliens, or the hoards of creatures, were always an emotionless, sometimes irrational threat, lacking any moral or ethical nature. Representing threats as insects and ravaging beasts served to establish their "otherness."[8] While J. Edgar Hoover was being commended for "catching Communist agents like killing poisonous snakes or tigers" and for equating communism with "barbarians beating at our gates from without and moral termites from within," movies depicted the communist threat as subversive creatures, an evil menace that could appear unpredictably and unexpectedly anywhere and at any time and that could never be completely contained.

This emphasis upon an alien threat stems from Cold War ideology and the resulting xenophobia represented in fear of "the other." The quest for security through an arsenal of nuclear weapons has been described as a quest for security based on the dualism of "our side" and "the other side," becoming a battle of absolute good against absolute evil.[9] The nuclear shield becomes a wall of total separation, justified because its development means "total power for America, because Russia is total evil."[10]

This dualism may have developed before the advent of nuclear weapons. World War I was marked by a sense of total confrontation between two polarized forces. It has been suggested that trench warfare, with its "collective isolation," established a psychological and political polarization in which the distinction between combatants and noncombatants was virtually erased.[11] The enemy as a real person disappears, only to be replaced by an abstraction—"the enemy" or "the other." The only possible attitude toward such an unredeemable evil is to hate it and to use every means possible to destroy it. Hence, in this situation: "Whole populations can be regarded as legitimate targets. . . . We quickly reach, by benefit of propaganda, that terribly simplified morality with a single absolute: Any act that helps my side win the war is right and good, and any act which hinders it is wrong and bad. This drive toward moral absolutism of a totalitarian sort affects all other aspects of warfare in our age."[12]

In a Cold War, all citizens are potentially on "the front line," and such attitudes tend to be widely shared. This attitude is both fostered by, and reflected in, ideological slogans that serve to legitimate it. These slogans became symbols in themselves, anticommunist slogans and atomic bomb security rhetoric joined together to weave a tightly knit fabric of interlocking symbols. The key factors in this ideological framework were the assumptions that the United States represented "freedom and dignity" whereas "the other" stood for oppression and totalitarianism. "The other" may represent a threat to "our side" on a number of levels. It may threaten our economic base, our power over other peoples, or even our social system and cultural values. In the Cold War, each side fears what "the other" might do in concrete terms, but ultimately the biggest insecurity comes from what "the other" might do to "our" world order, its stability and its meaningfulness.[13] Both world wars were fought by the western alliance to defend "our civilization," "our way of life," against an enemy depicted as uncivilized, barbaric, and even animal.

During the Cold War, the ideological goal of the United States was promoted as one of freedom, whereas communism's goal was seen as the absolute cessation of that freedom. The U.S. government rhetoric during the Cold War portrayed the communist doctrine as puritanical, humorless, and atheistic, devoted to the destruction of existing institutions and patterns and their replacement by an entirely new order—the total communization of the world.[14] The publicized image of communist countries was that of ideological empires that, like the medieval church, acknowledged no limit to their aims. "They are obsessed by messianic zeal to convert the heathen, with world domination as their goal."[15]

The ants in *Them!*, with their communistic social organization, represented "what Americans in the 1950s were most programmed to fear," and their organized military and emotionless manner neatly functioned as an analogy to the communist threat.[16] The Cold War emphasis is found in the nature of the threat as well. It was the character of ants themselves, as well as their size, that made them so menacing. "Ants are the only creatures on earth, besides man, who make war," Medford states; the scientist then goes on to explain "the nature of the creatures we're up against": "Ants are savage, ruthless, and courageous fighters. Ants campaign, they are chronic aggressors, they make slaves of those they can't kill. . . . They have a talent for industry, social organization, and savagery which makes man feeble by comparison."

The predominant, stereotypical image of communists at this time was of massive collectivities, willing to sacrifice individual lives in their quest for world domination. Communist governments ruled by fear and terror, always attempting to "enslave human souls."[17] Drawing on a creature as common and familiar as the garden ant and transforming it into a threat also worked to emphasize the ever present potential for subversion. Anyone who has ever watched ants assault a picnic lunch is familiar with their organizational capability, and ants are well known for their self-sacrifice for the good of the nest. So too were communist aggressors known for their warlike nature, aggressive intentions, and militarized uniformity.

Residual Elements

The depiction of such alien threats pointed to the need for a strong and vigilant military, to the necessity for the public to leave such affairs to these "experts" for the sake of national interests. But it also questioned the competence and wisdom of the government's policy of nuclear development and testing, as indicated by residual themes resurrected by Hollywood filmmakers to exploit audience anxiety about fallout and its effects. Although on one level the ants in Them! act as a metaphor for invading communist hoards, they are also the unexpected result of the domestic atomic testing program. The idea that such experimentation violated nature and engendered unpredictable threats offers an alternative view to the Cold War agenda that emerges, like the monsters, from the depths of these film scenarios.

This critical posture in radiation-produced monster films is manifested in their lack of a satisfying and comforting closure before the final credits roll. These films end on a note that reminds the audience of the continuing threat, for which the military must always be ready. After the army eliminates the menace in *Them!*, the FBI agent speculates upon the possibility, and even the inevitability, of future invasions. "If such horrors followed the first bomb test, what would come of all the bombs exploded since?" Although this lack of closure allows the opportunity to develop sequels, it also implies a skeptical questioning of the military's capability of controlling forthcoming threats. In denying the traditional closure found in, for example, the gothic horror genre, the film leaves the audience with the foreboding sense of a perpetual continuing threat.

Radiation-produced monster movies stand as a warning against the development and use of atomic energy. Ultimately, such creatures can be seen as nature seeking revenge for the exploitation of the secrets of the atom and the use of these secrets for destructive purposes. They warn that humanity must learn to use atomic energy safely and responsibly and must rectify its errors or, as is stated in *Them!* "we will vanish from the Earth and the beasts will reign."

The genre was Hollywood producers' way of safely exploiting contemporary interest in nuclear fallout as this subject appeared more and more on the public agenda. As media reports increasingly positioned the debate on fallout and its effects at the forefront, the number of Hollywood-produced films in this genre increased. After the box-office success of *Them!*, the largest-grossing film from Warner Brothers that year, it was easy to predict that Hollywood studios would continue to take advantage of the theme. Soon, giant monsters, all the result of radiation, invaded billboards with promises of even more bizarre and unimaginable movie entertainment. Direct imitations of *Them!* incorporating giant insect images with all the previously illustrated genre elements include *The Black Scorpion* (1959), the giant spider in *Tarantula* (1955), mutated wasps in *The Monster from Green Hell* (1957), giant grasshoppers in *The Beginning of the End* (1957), and a giant praying mantis in *The Deadly Mantis* (1957).

The plausibility of atomic testing creating such aberrations seemed to be undoubtedly accepted by the public. Hence, radiation and giant mutated creatures became forever linked in cinematic terms. The media praised *Them!* for its realistic portrayal of a possible consequence of radiation. *Newsweek* stated that the film "had a fine atmosphere of fact," whereas *Saturday Review*'s Arthur Knight found the movie "as persuasively realistic a horror story as one could possibly imagine . . . maintains a high level of plausibility."[18]

The concept of radiation that could transform living flesh, heal ills, or create monsters began as a connection between radiation and life, a connection found throughout history from ancient transmutation myths to modern science. Spencer Weart, in his overview of the history of images associated with nuclear fear, cites the concept of the association of a life force with magical rays that carry hopes and fears as an archetypal theme deeply embedded in human culture and embodied in radiation imagery. Ancient transmutation imagery had borrowed the concepts of heat, primeval light, and the creation of the world, and radiation imagery incorporated these archaic symbols of vitality and rebirth, these seminal understandings of the goodness of the rays of the sun, these religious myths and cosmic energies. Consequently, when doctors reported that atomic rays could heal, they seemed to confirm the link between radiation and life force. For example, in their first paper on atomic energy, Frederick Soddy and Ernest Rutherford described the "evolution" of atoms and went on to describe transmuted atoms, the "daughters" of radioactive "parent" atoms, further emphasizing the concept of the relationship between the power of creation and atomic technology.[19]

The public concern over the effects of radioactive dust, or fallout, was merely a continuation of the fears of radiation first expressed after the 1946 Bikini detonation. When the AEC started the Nevada tests in 1950, it uniformly denied that the detonations posed any danger, stating that people would be safe as long as they remained a few miles away from the bomb explosion. The AEC had committed itself to a massive public relations campaign in an effort to reassure the public concerning the safety of such tests, in the hopes that future tests would not be impeded by any controversy. The press also repeated these reassurances, scarcely bringing up the issues of fallout and other consequences of radiation. This was not only because the reporters believed the experts who said that there was little danger but also because the press didn't want to impede the tests, which were presented as necessary for national security.[20]

Irrepressible rumors about the hazardous effects of fallout began to spread in 1953. Testing was thought by many to destroy health, cause birth defects, contaminate fish, vary the Earth's orbit, melt the polar ice caps, and threaten a chain reaction that would engulf the world in flames. Still, most of the American public had faith in the safety of the testing program. Just after the 1954 Bravo test, 71 percent of Americans surveyed responded that the United States should proceed with the rest of the planned hydrogen bomb tests in the Pacific, despite the news coverage of radiation damage.[21]

In April 1955, the Congressional Joint Committee on Atomic Energy had its first public hearings devoted to global fallout. The committee joined the AEC in denying there were problems, and the press repeated the official AEC reassurances. Despite these pronouncements, public anxiety began to grow when it was discovered that the Bravo fusion test at Bikini on March 1, 1954, had produced fallout that went far beyond what had been predicted by the AEC. This fifteen-megaton hydrogen bomb explosion produced lethal levels of fallout over a 7,000-square-mile area of the Pacific, heavily contaminating a group of American personnel and Marshall Islanders. About a hundred miles downwind, natives on Rongelap atoll had to be evacuated and sailors on a Japanese fishing boat were exposed to fallout, one dying from what was believed to be radiation sickness.

Meanwhile, the explosion had propelled fine radioactive dust into the stratosphere, and independent scientists, not associated with the AEC, began to warn of the possibility that explosions in one locale could have wide and dangerously unpredictable results in distant areas. Unusual birth defects began occurring in communities hundreds of miles away from the explosion site. Contaminated fish were discovered in Japanese waters, which set off a radiation scare in Japan. Despite growing evidence to the contrary, the AEC denied responsibility for the fallout, or even that the bomb test had been responsible for the contaminated fish and radiation sickness. A 1955 AEC report attempted to promote the Bravo test in the best possible light: "If we had not conducted the full scale thermonuclear tests mentioned, we would be in ignorance of the extent of the effects of nuclear fallout and therefore we would have been much more vulnerable to the dangers from fallout."[22]

The AEC's public relations campaign consistently denied that any damage could result from low-dosage levels of radiation. Hundreds of press releases argued the position that exposure below a certain "threshold level" would not cause permanent damage, citing the fact that the environment was constantly bombarded by natural radiation.[23] Soon, a public relations campaign called Project Plowshares was instituted, which included the distribution of booklets to Nevada residents and an effort to eliminate unfavorable press comments on atomic testing by directly pressuring editors. In 1957, the AEC distributed thousands of copies of *The Green Book* to people living around the test site; the publication promoted the idea "that it is extremely unlikely that there will be fallout on any occupied community greater than past low levels."[24] The AEC also started promoting "atom bomb watching" as a tourist attraction for vacationers in Nevada, releasing a partial schedule of the tests so that tourists could plan to view them. The Las Vegas Chamber of Commerce launched promotional measures around "bomb watching," and news stories, such as "Desert Capital of the A-bomb," started appearing in the *New York Times* travel section. These stories gave information on the best viewing locations and local accommodations, assuring travelers that there was "no danger from radioactive fallout."[25] Typical statements used to reassure readers included the following:

> The American people can be assured that the rigorous safeguards which govern the tests are designed to prevent injury to the people of any community or city. . . . Precautions are taken to hold fallout from Nevada test shots to an absolute minimum. Suitable weather conditions are selected. . . . Most of the Nevada explosions occur well above the surface of the earth, with the result that only small amounts of earth are drawn up into the cloud.[26]

Journalists were invited by the government to cover the tests, and they sat on bleachers atop a small hill ten miles from ground zero, a spot that came to be known as "News Nob." Their accounts focused on the visual effects of the explosion and the aftermath, while they consistently praised the government for its success in nuclear testing. All the while, the media repeated the AEC stand on the absence of radiation hazards.[27] A typical description was: "The dust cloud which swept across the trenches was choking and blinding. . . . It was a horrible feeling to see that monster cloud, loaded with radiation, rising in an expanding ring virtually over our heads. But the scientists' calculations were correct, the cloud drifted directly away from us. We were safe from radiation fallout."[28]

Gradually, the AEC's reputation began to suffer amid a growing international outcry against atmospheric testing. Even AEC staff members were admitting that bomb tests might cause occasional death, yet few suggested that the tests should stop. Prominent opponents of testing such as Linus Pauling and Albert Schweitzer found that they could draw attention to the problem by talking about the potential far-reaching consequences of fallout contamination upon milk. By 1959, the U.S. Public Health Service, which had begun to monitor fallout in foods, noticed a sharp increase in the amounts of the isotope strontium 90 in milk. Within a few years, the concentration of this isotope had doubled in American children. Worries about contaminated milk prompted thousands of letters to Congress; the issue became so serious that dairies were concerned about potentially declining sales.[29]

Much of the growing public anxiety over atomic testing and its effects was due to publicity generated by newly formed antinuclear groups that focused upon the dangers of fallout. By 1956, several independent scientists, including Schweitzer, Pauling, Nobel Prize winner Hermann Muller, and others were openly criticizing the AEC and the bomb tests that were threatening the environment with deadly radioactive dust. Adlai Stevenson's presidential campaign brought the bomb test issue into the limelight, as he warned against the hazards of global fallout. National groups such as Leo Szilard's Council for a Livable World, Physicians for Social Responsibility, and the National Committee for a Sane Nuclear Policy (SANE) organized against bomb development and testing. Hundreds of citizens, not only members of pacifist and religious groups but also businesspeople, administrators, and labor union members, wrote to President Eisenhower in opposition to the bomb tests.

SANE and the Campaign for Nuclear Disarmament in Great Britain were formed of countless smaller antinuclear groups, and survived on donations and volunteers. The groups aimed to promote a constructive fear of nuclear weapons by reminding people of Hiroshima; they relied on general moral appeal and hoped for action through disarmament. A typical SANE advertisement linked the threat of bombs with fallout from atmospheric testing; a typical slogan was "Nuclear bombs can destroy all life in war . . . nuclear tests are endangering our health right now."

Although atomic testing was perceived as necessary for defense purposes by the majority of Americans, the idea that atomic scientists had somehow violated the order of nature and would cause the world to suffer for their indiscretion surfaced more and more in public opinion after the Bravo test.[30] There is much evidence that Americans were becoming concerned about the existence and effects of fallout, their anxiety being further enhanced by the fact that radiation from fallout could cause genetic defects and cancer. In May 1957, 52 percent of Americans felt that fallout from testing was dangerous, and a year later 46 percent felt that continued testing could result in a "threat to the health of future generations."[31] For example, early in 1957, the World Federation for Mental Health called for a study of the mental health implications of the peaceful use of atomic energy. The federation believed that the public needed protection from "undue anxieties and fears" and thought that nuclear power might arouse "many irrational fears, or irrational degrees of fear . . . because of the very special types of threats inherent in our popular concepts of atomic energy."[32]

Fear of Transmutation

The concept that exposure to radiation could cause transmutation is central to all radiation-produced monster films. Transmutation, the process of being changed into another substance or nature, gained popularity in the Middle Ages with the conjectured possibility of converting base metals into gold and silver by an al-chemistic process. The alchemist, with his ability to transmute matter in such a way, was believed to have powerful and secret knowledge of the universe at his command; he could use this power to transform society for the better, or to de-stroy it. As the first individuals to have knowledge about atomic energy, the scien-tists were nearly always the first to connect it with ancient myths, and they used the concepts of transmutation and a utopian future as a way to make their find-ings understandable to the general public.

The linkage of the transmutation of elements to atomic technology was empha-sized in 1901, when Soddy and Rutherford found radioactivity to be indicative of fundamental changes in matter. With the pulse of radiation, the atom was trans-formed into a different element while maintaining its original chemical properties. The media and the scientists themselves couched this discovery in rhetoric appro-priated from discourse used in alchemy, emphasizing the scientists' enthusiasm about the new discoveries by using traditional images to describe the new techno-logical developments.[33] The media also conveyed such a relationship: "The trans-mutation of the elements is regarded as the nearest approach yet to be made to the finding of a modern version of the 'Philosopher's Stone' of the alchemists."[34]

Just as the atomic bomb had been described as a socially positive creation, doc-tors and scientists were initially convinced of the beneficial quality and potential marketability of radium, drawing upon the residual theme of harnessing the "healing rays" of nature to promote their discovery. Low doses of radium were ad-vertised as therapeutic and stimulating to the life processes. The healthful proper-ties of radium were touted by such peddlers as Dr. W. J. Morton. Morton distrib-uted a product called "liquid sunshine," which he touted as a cure for diseased organs; the product would "bathe a patient's entire interior in ultraviolet light. . . . We know of the value of sunshine on the outside . . . and we believe it will have a similar effect on the inside."[35] Radioactive patent medicines appeared in the form of tablets, toothpaste, injections, and suppositories, which promised re-lief from aliments ranging from baldness to old age.

The capability of radiation to create genetic mutations that could be passed down through generations was publicized in 1927. Hermann Muller applied radi-ation to biological forms in an effort to investigate its potential to reshape living things, suggesting that such a process might help scientists control the evolution of plants, animals, and humans. Scientists had subjected the eggs of primitive life forms to X rays and radiation and found that if the embryo wasn't destroyed, it would grow into a mutation. Muller, however, was the first to alter genes deliber-ately with radiation; he dosed flies with X rays and found mutations appearing in later generations. Not only did Muller's experiments promote the concept of transmutation and its connection to radiation (he called his discovery the "artifi-cial transmutation of the gene"), but he furthered the image of the scientist's own power, as one who could create strange beings or further the process of evolution at will.[36]

The Image of the Scientist

From the very beginning, the discovery of radium was linked to images of the scientist as an alchemist who not only held the secrets of the transmutation of matter but also had the knowledge to create a utopian world through this capability, and to destroy that world. Frederick Soddy himself wrote that in order for society to benefit from the advances in modern technology, the public must "acknowledge its real master," namely science, and choose as rulers "those who are concerned with the creation of its wealth," namely scientists.[37] Such reliance upon the development of technology left great power over the future in the hands of scientists. The vision of the utopian city made way for the idea that some fool in a laboratory had the power to doom the earth. By 1903, Sunday newspaper supplements were describing radioactive devices that could destroy the earth at the touch of a button and explosive waves of radiation that could transmute the whole mass of the globe into helium or some other gas.[38]

That notion that radioactivity was somehow "contagious" from one atom to another and the possibility that atomic experimentation could create a global chain reaction became themes that were discussed by the general public. The idea that such destruction could be caused by one scientist underscored the specter of the evil and power-hungry scientist, an image that was to cling tenaciously to stories about nuclear energy. Although an individual destroying the Earth appeared in fiction as early as 1901 in *The Purple Cloud*, the concept of a planetary chain reaction provided the first rational description of how one person might be able to accomplish such a feat. Newspapers repeated such thoughts, claiming that the whole universe might accidentally be "fired like a train of gunpowder"[39] and expounded the risks of the atomic experiment.[40]

The stereotypical scientist-as-sorcerer, who wielded great contaminating power, stemmed from fictional characters such as Dr. Faustus and the traditional magus; these images were combined in popular culture to create a new "scientist" who endangered society with his mixture of demonic and scientific powers.[41] Throughout the nineteenth and early twentieth centuries, scientists were most commonly stereotyped as well meaning, if unworldly and absentminded. With Mary Shelley's *Frankenstein* (1818), in which the scientist is capable of producing a "race of devils" that would lead to annihilation, the vision of the dangerous scientist inventor, or the satanic scientist, emerged. This stereotype involved certain aspects that remained constant throughout the development of atomic themes—the scientist was remote from everyday life, he avoided women's love, he was obsessively devoted to the search for dangerous secrets, he seized powers over life and death, and he usually died a violent death.[42]

Because of their very nature, scientists could not always be trusted to make wise decisions for the benefit of civilization; they might rather wish to reshape society to their own liking. Intending to put the world in order, scientists would plot to master and control people by using their own privileged knowledge and devious inventions. This idea of scientists misguided by their own megalomania, defending and setting right the ills of the world, had been featured in popular fiction as early as 1896. H. G. Wells's *Island of Dr. Moreau* introduced a mad doctor turning animals into half humans in order to create a dictatorship based on his own technological dominance.[43] Usually "mad," such individuals have their own rationale for destroying the world; some see life as only suffering and therefore believe that "it would be better to destroy the world forthwith";[44] others plot to destroy the world "in the name of freedom."[45]

American movie serials of the 1930s depicted favorite heroes such as Gene Autry and Crash Corrigan battling villains who planned to enslave the world using "the atom—the most destructive force known to science."[46] In the 1936 film *Things to Come*, H. G. Wells rendered the well-meaning if not overzealous scientist attempting to force humanity to follow his own particular morality or be destroyed.[47] The 1940 movie *Dr. Cyclops* showcased an evil scientist who chose to seek "the cosmic force of creation" to gain total control over life through the transmutation of flesh. Here we have a scientist who put his knowledge to evil use by miniaturizing humans to gain control over them; he was named Cyclops "for his moral as well as his physical myopia."[48] In the 1936 Universal picture *The Invisible Ray*, the mad scientist builds a radium ray projector with the ability to smash cities and cure illnesses.

Stories about evil scientists became associated with atomic energy because of the invisible and unforeseen properties of radiation. The uneasiness that people felt with technology was encapsulated by the idea that humanity was too unsophisticated to cope with the powers of technology, or that delving into the mysteries of nature was a crime against God. For example, in these mad scientist tales, the scientists inevitably die lonely, horrible deaths as a punishment for their inquisitiveness, for prying into "secrets we are not meant to probe."[49]

Robert Oppenheimer himself was stereotyped as Dr. Faustus, as the overweening genius with dangerous access to the secrets of the universe. In reference to the development of the atomic bomb, in 1956 he declared: "We did the Devil's work." In traditional cultures, such figures are dangerous and are usually purged in one way or another from society. The fate that Oppenheimer met, being ritualistically cast out of the loop in the witch-hunts led by Senator Joseph McCarthy, matches the destiny of Dr. Faustus. Both the atomic scientist and the fictional character were ambitious, individualistic, and immersed in science.

Most pre-Hiroshima films portrayed mad scientists as misguided villains; these characters employed radium-based energy to drill into the Earth (*The Tunnel*, 1943), created a deadly bomb (*The Greatest Power*, 1917), invented a powerful tank (*The Great Radium Mystery*, 1919), transmuted lead into gold (*Gold*, 1934), and mutated minuscule humans (*Dr. Cyclops*, 1940). Radium's destructive potential was also illustrated as radiation that could destroy by touch (*The Invisible Ray*, 1936), as destructive radium emoting death rays (*Queen of the Jungle*, 1935), and as a radium tube ray gun that destroys mail planes (*Ghost Patrol*, 1936).

Gradually, scientists portrayed in Hollywood film of the mid–1950s had evolved into two types—the heroic military scientist and the bumbling and fairly incompetent atomic inventor. The evil-minded scientists are replaced in these films by well-meaning but incompetent figures, unable to fully understand or control the unintentional results of their experimentation, the atomically created threats that are ultimately unpredictable and uncontrollable. It is the inhuman threat, either the alien invader or the mutated creature, rather than the scientist, who embodies malicious evil.

The public image of the atomic scientist had suffered to a certain extent by the late 1950s. To some, the applied scientist seemed a rootless, emotionally inadequate person, prone to corruption at the urging of evil companions and willing, for a pittance, to sell secrets to the Russians. The pure scientist seemed an impractical, incomprehensible bungler whose activities were of no benefit to anyone.[50] The civilian scientist was portrayed more and more in Hollywood as a sort of Einstein caricature, bumbling, self-centered, thinking of an impending catastrophe as "a great scientific find," with little regard for the threat to human life posed by such catastrophes. This version of the scientist character can be found in the majority of films of this period. For example, *The Phantom from 10,000 Leagues* (1956) features an emotionless oceanographer more interested in examining the beast than in saving San Francisco from destruction. A slew of bungling scientists are ineffective in containing the rage of *The Amazing Colossal Man* (1957). Although their experimentation with atomic technology may have charitable motivations, it invariably leads to disaster. In *Tarantula* (1955), the scientist's quest to discover a cure for a specific disease leads to the development of a giant spider. In *The Beginning of the End* (1957), scientists, hoping to end world hunger by developing irradiated food, are foiled by grasshoppers who mutate after feeding upon experimental vegetables being grown in a Department of Agriculture facility. In the end, it is always conventional military might rather than scientific discovery that eventually halts the impending disaster.

For example, in *Them!* the primary scientist character, Medford, is portrayed as old and feeble, in contrast to the virile and capable FBI hero and the military characters. The scientist stereotypically speaks with a foreign accent and is absentminded; he wears glasses, which he is always losing. Bumbling and stumbling, he is portrayed as incompetent in everyday life, requiring assistance in walking, even in using a communication radio. Few understand his scholarly gibberish. And, as opposed to the FBI and military characters, the scientist stoically regards the mutated giants as "a scientist's dream come true." He hinders the military's efforts to destroy them until he can gather "more information," ultimately endangering the American population and the world in his personal quest for knowledge. The fate of human society is secondary to his interests, as he nonchalantly comments that "man, as the dominant species of life on earth, will probably be extinct within a year." The inherent callousness of the scientist is demonstrated in opening scenes of *Them!* in his method of jolting the little girl out of her trance-like stupor. In order to interrogate her, the scientist forces the girl to inhale formic acid. This produces a hysterical scream, and the girl runs to a policeman's arms for comfort.

Narratives in this genre always contain contradictory notions of the value of scientific knowledge. Although it is this unsentimental quest for technological knowledge in the drive to develop the atomic bomb that creates the menace, it is the scientist who wields the knowledge and intellectual expertise to understand the nature of the threat. And even though the military obliterates the beasts, scientific knowledge is still portrayed as necessary, although better controlled by the more responsible and responsive members of the military.

Radiation-Produced Human Monsters

By 1956, the radiation-produced monster genre had incorporated the imagined effects of radiation upon humans into its typical narrative. Human mutations received the same basic treatment in movie action as their animal and insect counterparts had. Exposure to potent radioactive materials created bizarre consequences, and the innocent human victim was soon relegated to the role of destructive menace. Scientists could attempt to hinder or reverse the mutation process, but their efforts were always to no avail. The human victim inevitably lost its "humanness" as the mutation resulted in insanity or megalomania, and inevitably homicidal tendencies. Despite the fact that many human victims were themselves members of the military, the military efficiently and uncompassionately dispatches the threat to civilization by the conclusion of the film.

An early example of the evolution of this genre is illustrated in *First Man into Space* (1959), in which a radiation-exposed navy pilot undergoes a metamorphosis into an inhuman monster with a thirst for blood. During an altitude test in an experimental jet, his plane breaks through the Earth's atmosphere and crashes to the ground. The wreckage is found to be covered with a strange substance, and the body of the pilot missing. Soon, back at the navy's experimental headquarters deep in the desert, a scientist works with the military to analyze the transmutated metal of the fuselage. He finds: "It has undergone a complete transformation . . . possibly by cosmic rays we do not know or understand. We know very little, only by some mysterious means the cells controlling growth and reproduction are changed by exposure to some cosmic rays, beyond that, we can only guess."

The blood-seeking pilot, now grotesquely mutated, slaughters cattle and young women and eventually finds himself in the scientist's lab. A navy commander manages to maneuver the monster into a high-altitude chamber and restrain him there. In a futile attempt to reverse the mutation process, the scientist only succeeds in bringing an early demise to the unfortunate pilot. The closing dialogue between scientist and military characters seeks to justify this sacrifice of human life in the quest for scientific knowledge: "We're conquering a new world, the danger has to be faced, someone has to be first. . . . The conquest of new worlds always makes demands upon human life, and there will always be men who accept the risks."

Typical to this genre, the film ennobles the military and its technology by presenting lengthy stock footage of jet planes and military hardware and by focusing upon military heroes in the story. In contrast, the scientist is pictured as a mysterious foreigner. He never demonstrates compassion or concern for this pilot-turned-monster, and he only wishes to study him to gain scientific knowledge. However, the scientist's attempts to contain the menacing pilot, or to help him, fail. Ultimately, the scientist is impotent against the unknown forces he is trying to understand, and military heroism instead eventually saves the day.

Independent producers immediately jumped upon the novelty and popularity of this simple extension of the radiation-produced monster genre. The year 1957 saw over five features based upon the disastrous effects of radiation upon humans. All portrayed ineffective scientists who were unable to aid the mutated victims and efficient military personnel who could. The human mutation itself is presented as any stock monster, without regard for the "humanness" the victim once possessed. *The Amazing Colossal Man* (1957) depicts a navy colonel accidentally exposed to the nuclear explosion of a "plutonium bomb." He survives the blast, only to become a bald fifteen-foot giant. Although his external wounds from the blast are insignificant, the exposure has an unseen effect upon his cells, causing him to grow at a rate of "eight to ten feet a day." His heart, mysteriously enlarging at a slower pace, will eventually burst if his growth cannot be checked. Scientists rush to halt the mutation, while keeping him a secret at a remote desert army base. Soon the diminishing supply of blood to his brain contributes to a megalomania and causes him to run rampant through the desert, killing all he meets. Military intervention eventually drives him to his end, as he falls off Hoover Dam.

The Cyclops (1957) also dealt with a gigantic, deformed human, this one twenty-five feet tall with a swollen left eye. The giant and several animals suffer from elevated levels of ground radiation. Indeed, it seems that radiation in film could transform almost anything, following no scientific logic. Some films feature monsters as radioactively resurrected zombies. In *From Hell It Came* (1957), an enlarged radiated stump emerges from the grave of a South Pacific islander who had died of radiation burns resulting from an atomic test. The stump walks around and terrorizes villagers before it falls into a bog and presumably drowns.

The Incredible Shrinking Man (1957) involves an unfortunate character named Scott Carey who, while relaxing on his small pleasure boat at sea is enveloped in a mysterious cloud. Later, he begins to notice that he is losing weight and visits a military specialist. Soon it is revealed that Scott's condition is the result of a chemical reaction—he had walked through a shower of insecticide and, while on his boat, had passed through a radioactive cloud. This causes his body to shrink, and, despite the efforts of the scientists to discover a remedy, he continues to wither into nothingness. This effect of radiation is even glamorized in the closing sequence, as Scott becomes a bit of dust, as minute as an atom itself. New worlds and possibilities through radiation were pondered in the closing narration: "Still a human being . . . or was I a man of the future? If there were other bursts of radiation, other clouds drifting across seas and continents, would other beings follow me into this vast new world?"

Manifestly, these human mutation films stress not only the ability of the military to control and discharge any threats to the United States but also the need for unselfish sacrifice in the interest of technological progress. Just as the American population was asked at this time condone and accept the AEC's unpopular domestic atomic testing program, these films were emphasizing the need for just this kind of sacrifice. Unfortunate causalities may occur, as evidenced by the fate of the mutated monsters, but they are a necessary investment in the continuing technological development needed to maintain American global dominance. Atomic development is clearly something to be feared in these movies, but they propose neither its abandonment nor its curtailment. Science is simply too important to be suppressed.

The basic motif of the transformation of innocent people into monsters stems from the fear of the violation of nature and nature's punishment for such violations, just as in the mutated beasts scenarios. But radiation's effects on humans transforms them truly into "the other," changing their entire nature, not merely their size, as in *Them!* Mild-mannered citizens and compassionate military personnel alike become raving, murderous aberrations; radiation strips them of their humanity. The development of atomic technology brings with it the loss of a genuinely human life and emotion. These mutated humans do more than merely symbolize a retribution for man's technological tampering with nature, "the same message propounded by the 'mad scientist' films of the 1920s, 1930s and 1940s."[51] Unlike these mad scientist films, in which the scientist himself usually falls victim to his own unnatural experiments, most nuclear victims of the 1950s are innocent and unaware of their vulnerability to the threat. These newer films depict unlucky humans who are scientifically victimized through exposure to radioactivity and are transformed into inhuman creatures hated by all. These victims become devoid of feelings and emotions; they are impersonal, transformed into "no living animal at all, but a sort of blind substance made of radioactive isotopes."[52] In one sense, the corrupting potential of the bomb indeed turned people into monsters lacking emotion and compassion, echoing the Cold War stereotype of the effects of communism.

Of course, not all film monsters produced in the 1950s were the result of radiation; some emerged from biological and chemical experimentation. However, atomic rays and radiation were the most common plot devices, and radioactivity was sometimes involved in these films even when other explanations were offered for the creation of the monster. When the movie scientist remarked "It's radioactive," audiences learned to expect something terrible and inhuman to emerge. These stories not only took advantage of the public's concern over atomic development but also reinforced the specific association between radioactivity and monsters.[53]

6

Alien Invaders and Atomic Espionage

The atomic destruction of the utopian cities of Metaluna in *This Island Earth* (1954)

INVASION FILMS, WHILE NOT ENTIRELY TIED TO ISSUES OF ATOMIC USE, became the second most popular form of science fiction film during the 1950s. Andrew Tudor, in his genre analysis of Hollywood horror films, notes that 18 percent of all horror films produced between 1956 and 1960 were based upon alien invasion from space.[1] The apprehension over the survival of individual humans as well as the human species, the fears of atomic technology and its effects, and the projection of a terrestrial threat onto extraterrestrial settings underlay virtually all of the period's science fiction movies. Many film narratives manifestly mixed fears of subversive and overt alien invasion with concern over atomic development and its consequences.

Typically, the alien invasion scenario depicts a technologically superior civilization that comes to Earth (more specifically, to the United States) to invade the planet or use its resources, transforming humans into emotionless clones or taking control of unsuspecting minds. The invaders are usually portrayed as an uncompassionate, ruthless force that requires the planet Earth or its inhabitants for its own use; the invaders need human bodies (*Invasion of the Body Snatchers,* 1956), brains (*It Conquered the World,* 1956), blood (*The Thing,* 1951), or scientific knowledge (*This Island Earth,* 1954; *Killers from Space,* 1954), or simply wish to assume social and political control (*Earth vs. Flying Saucers,* 1956). The invaders work unseen as they begin to infiltrate everyday life; friends and relatives suddenly begin acting strangely, and police officers and doctors are transformed into the pawns of the devious alien enemies. If the aliens are allowed to carry out their plans, they would cause the destruction of American life, of all humankind, and sometimes of the planet itself. However, their intentions are inevitably foiled by the swift intervention of American military might and scientific know-how.

Radiation-produced monster and alien invasion films all link concerns about alien infiltration to anxieties over transmutation and atomic development. The nature of the threat poses a crucial difference between these invasion films and their predecessors. In the 1930s, threatening monsters were predominantly anthropomorphic, but by the 1950s, it is the American "way of life" that is threatened by invaders, by aliens with whom we share little.[2] Both alien invader and radiation-produced monster films emphasize the fear of transmutation: Either radiation turns the normal into the abnormal or communist infiltration and its accompanying corrupting ideology transforms ordinary Americans into something alien and foreign. Both hazards operate covertly in their attacks against American society; radiation is unseen, its presence undetectable and only discovered through its resulting horrific mutations. Communism is also the all-pervasive threat that can arise anywhere, without warning. Both elements are ultimately uncontrollable, destroying life "as we know it," preying upon social as well as personal fears.[3]

The Cold War and the Military Scientist

Because of their emphasis upon threatening invasions of Earth by hostile forces eager to enslave or obliterate the citizens of the United States, the alien invader films are heavily laden with the imagery and the language of the Cold War. As in the radiation-produced monster genre, the typical scenario emphasizes the need for a strong and organized military establishment that exercises complete authority over the population. Also stressed is the importance for the wider population to remain constantly vigilant against invasion by foreign powers; the value of scientific knowledge when controlled not by the civilian scientist but by competent military personnel; and, most crucially, the alien nature of the ideology, the "otherness," of the forces that threaten American life. Alien invasion scenarios provide content that reinforce the conviction that the United States must defend itself against invaders—"an obsession that may have been all the more acute because we had never experienced a war on our own turf."[4] Confronted by "the other" in these films, Americans have only one possible response—using every means available to destroy the invader.[5]

The United States during the Cold War has been described as paranoid in its fear of the "Red Menace." That fear, and the "better dead than red" slogan it spawned, guided many actions at home and abroad and also prompted the continuing development of atomic weapons. The Red Menace became real to the United States almost as soon as the Soviet Union was born. As the first Marxist state, the Soviet Union provided to western Marxists a living organism from which they could draw inspiration for their own revolutionary plans. The evidence of a Marxist state in the Soviet Union, along with the emotional appeal of Marxism, was to the West clear evidence of the dangerously infectious nature of the Marxist virus:

> What American statesmen now saw themselves faced with, in the person of the new Russian Communist regime, was . . . a government faction, installed in the seats of power in another great country, which had not even dreamed of declaring war formally on the United States but which was nevertheless committed, by its deepest beliefs and by its very view of its place in history, to a program aimed at the overthrow of the entire political and social system traditional to American society . . . a damage more monstrous in the eyes of most Americans than any they might expect to suffer from even the worst of purely military defeats at the hands of the traditional sort of adversary.[6]

This anticommunism is echoed in the alien invasion genre films. Transformation by foreign ideologies, forced subservience to alien powers, and the loss of free will were depicted as a fate worse than death. The prospect of the "robotization" of family members and the transformation of society as a whole into a population of unemotional, cold, obedient humanoids was a fear that directly related to dominant notions about communism. Scenarios in which a friend or relative began to act in an unusual manner corresponded to the images of brainwashing and thought control linked to communism at this time. Film aliens transformed human victims into unfeeling zombies; happy and unsuspecting individuals were changed into stoic and obedient slaves. Sometimes the victims were reassured that they would be born into an "untroubled world," free of the cares of personal ambition. The transformed zombies outwardly appeared physically unchanged, but they "had lost their souls." As the entire population transformed into these unemotional robots, everyone would become alike, a subservient hoard controlled by their alien masters.

An example of this scenario is found in *Invasion of the Body Snatchers* (1956), which pictures seed pods from outer space that take possession of human bodies, forcing them to become "hosts to an alien form of life." These doubles perform the same everyday duties as their human counterparts, but lack any emotion, just as the inability of people living under communist "siege" to impulsively display emotions was attributed to the effects of communism. The film also draws upon the contemporary government rhetoric comparing communism to a fatal disease. Adlai Stevenson's campaign speech in 1952 stated that communism was "a disease which may have killed more people in this world than cancer, tuberculosis, and heart disease combined," and that the goal of America's enemies was "total conquest, not merely of the earth, but of the human mind."[7]

So too is the need for vigilance against subversive attack stressed. Each American citizen must be wary or suffer an unhappy fate. The main character in *Invasion of the Body Snatchers* cries to unsuspecting passersby, "You fools, you're in danger . . . ! They're after us! You're next!" *The Thing* concluded with another plea for vigilance against unseen invaders: "Tell the world . . . Watch the skies—everywhere—watch the skies!" Similarly, in *The Blob* (1958), an indestructible, inhuman invader capable of consuming entire towns illustrates the unseen horrors of an evil ideology that might return to corrupt an unsuspecting country at any time. Consisting of a mass of jellylike material whose growth in size and power corresponds to its increasing number of victims, the blob's tenacity knows no physical bounds as it oozes under doorsills and down chimneys. No area of human activity is safe from this invader, and only military intervention can impede its ever expanding consumption. Such invasions could only be impeded, never permanently prevented; whereas one attempted invasion might be aborted, another is surely being planned by the alien force. The message was unmistakable: The population must always be wary and on the alert.

The heroes of these struggles were inevitably military men or government agents who, with the extensive use of advanced technology and with superior intelligence, protected a population that had no means to protect itself. Again, through the use of stock footage and scenes of fully equipped troops massing to repel the invaders, the value and necessity of the military establishment was emphasized. The films presuppose a faith in the legitimacy of established authority. In this xenophobic universe, "we can do nothing but rely upon the state, in the form of the military, scientific and governmental elites. Only they have the technical knowledge necessary for our defense."[8]

As in most science fiction, the scientist in these invasion films plays an important role. The hero increasingly is a military scientist, a figure who becomes prevalent in science fiction films from 1954 onward. The military scientist is usually the first character to realize the extent of the invaders' ill will and the only one who has the knowledge and technology at his command to defeat them. Typical in its exaltation of the military scientist is the hero of *This Island Earth* (1954). Amid a multitude of scientific hardware, the scientist Cal works alone in his lab single-handedly making scientific discoveries. He is able to fly a jet plane, assemble a alien gizmo consisting of "9,000 parts and components," throw a left hook that can floor an eight-foot mutant, evade capture by the aliens, and romance the female love interest. The civilian scientists he meets are incompetent, albeit brainwashed; their purpose in the movie is only to provide moral outrage at their early and violent demise.

The uneasiness and suspicion that many Americans felt about scientific advance and intellectuals in general was evident in the various portrayals of civilian scientists. Sometimes serving only to offer explanations for the strange occurrences, scientist fall victim to the alien invaders as easily as any civilian members of the population. At other times, scientists are a malevolent force working on the side of the aliens for their own evil gain; they are presented as wild-haired figures willing to hand over the country to invaders in order to learn more about the secrets of the universe, or to receive special favors. Either they are destroyed by the invaders they have tried to protect or they switch allegiance before the film's conclusion when they realize that the invaders do not share humans' traditional values and social structures.

Examples of the varying images of the civilian scientist can be found in a selection of films. *It Conquered the World* (1956) showcases a cucumberlike creature who, aided by an evil and intensely power-hungry scientist, attempts to take over the world by turning the population into subservient zombies. The alien invader in *Kronos* (1957) possesses a benevolent scientist and uses him for evil purposes. *The Thing from Another World* (1951) features a vegetablelike creature from another planet who crashes on the North Pole and begins devouring dogs and humans in its quest for blood. In this movie, the scientist's personal quest for scientific knowledge jeopardizes the safety of everyone involved because he wants to preserve the creature for scientific study. "All I want is a chance to communicate with it," claims the scientist, before he is devoured in his attempt.

Good and Bad Atoms: *This Island Earth* (1954)

The alien invasion narrative that addresses atomic issues and elaborates Cold War ideology is exemplified in *This Island Earth*, which combines the glorification of the military scientist and the utopian potential for nuclear use, while warning about nuclear energy's destructive potential when misused by a corrupt civilization. Here, the invading aliens are the unfortunate victims of their own abuse of atomic power, their crumbling civilization evidence of the destructive potential of atomic development and serving as an example for the United States if it fails maintain a strong nuclear arsenal as deterrence. The narrative adopts the residual themes of scientific discovery's potential for progress or destruction, but here it is linked to blatant Cold War representations—technology's impact is dependent upon the political system that employs it.

By the mid-1950s, the dominant atomic imagery circulating in the public sphere had been relegated into two polarities, that of "good" atoms that could be used for peaceful purposes and of "bad atoms" that was epitomized by the destructive potential of the bomb and the hazards of radioactive fallout.[9] The government-sponsored Atoms for Peace campaign sought to support the proposed International Atomic Energy Agency's attempt to institute nuclear technology for peaceful uses, in an effort to develop a legitimate nuclear industry and divert concern away from the buildup of nuclear weaponry toward notions of technological progress and international cooperation.[10] The campaign also sought to keep the United States ahead of other competing countries in the development of this technology for domestic purposes. In keeping with the new policy, Congress passed the Atomic Energy Act of 1954, designed to encourage the commercial development of atomic energy.

Emphasizing these issues, President Eisenhower delivered an "Atoms for Peace" speech to the United Nations on December 8, 1953, which included the announcement that the United States wished to share the anticipated benefits of nuclear technology with the rest of the world. The speech turned the phrase "atoms for peace" into a widely used slogan and, with the use of rhetoric ("This greatest of destructive forces can be developed into a great boon for the benefit of all mankind"), linked the campaign with the idea that the power of the atom could unleash unlimited material abundance and new hope for a nuclear utopia.[11]

The "Atoms for Peace" speech launched a media and public relations blitz at home and abroad, which proclaimed that the world was on the threshold of a utopian "Era of Atomic Power." However, public anxiety about nuclear weapons was so strong by this time that Atoms for Peace campaign could only hope to counteract the negative connotations by offering marvelous and awe-inspiring visions of a nuclear future. Animated films such as *A is for Atom,* Disney's *Our Friend the Atom,* and *The Atom and Eve* were shown on television and in schools. These films typically showed an evil bomb monster, representing the power of the atom, that could be harnessed and controlled by scientists to work wonders in energy production, agricultural growth, nuclear propulsion, and medical advances. The main image used to describe the promise of nuclear energy was that of a genie in a bottle, like the genie and the fisherman in the *Arabian Nights*. Scientists had released the genie as a terrible atomic bomb, and now they needed to use their scientific knowhow to turn the genie to peaceful and productive tasks.[12] The films also included demonstrations of how nuclear energy would make life easier for housewives by powering toasters, hair dryers, and dishwashers. By 1960, 2.5 million people had seen these films.[13] The Atoms for Peace campaign also distributed atomic energy information kits to elementary, high school, and college students and sponsored elaborate traveling exhibits, including five walk-through exhibit vans.

A large government-sponsored public relations campaign continued into the 1960s in an effort to convince the public that a little fallout in the atmosphere was tolerable and to associate bomb tests with positive feelings. Testing was presented as necessary to ensure national security; to discover a method to perfect a fallout-free device, or "clean bomb"; and to develop a useful explosive with the potential of developing agriculture on the earth. The scientists involved in Project Plowshares praised the Atomic Energy Commission's testing program, which, in addition to protecting American national security, brought the dream of using nuclear technology to better the world closer to reality.[14]

Project Plowshares optimistically speculated that nuclear explosives could be used to dig subway tunnels, deepen harbors and canals, flatten mountaintops, heat underground chambers to generate steam for power, blast loose mineral deposits, and generally "change the Earth's surface to suit us" by "planetary engineering."[15] These ideas were presented at the Second International Conference on the Peaceful Uses of Atomic Energy in 1958, along with plans to close the Strait of Gibraltar, which would supposedly cause the Mediterranean to rise to the point where it could be used to irrigate the Sahara.[16]

Although the government put much effort into the distribution of positive propaganda about the atom, particularly in the Atoms for Peace campaign, most Hollywood entertainment programming at this time consistently depicted atomic energy, and the consequences of its use, in a pessimistic light. *Crack in the World* (1965), for instance, portrays the Project Plowshares rhetoric in a negative manner, as an overzealous scientist fires an atomic bomb down a mine shaft hoping to obtain energy from the Earth's magma. The disastrous results include earthquakes and devastation, and the planet breaks apart into two pieces, which then whirl off into space.[17]

However, in *This Island Earth*, the nuclear scientist, Cal, explains his view of atomic energy using Project Plowshares rhetoric. He is shown holding a press conference about his work with the "Committee on Atomic Energy." Standing before his military jet, he expounds upon the benefits of the industrial use of atomic energy: "We need to link atomic energy with electronics, then we will have the horse and the cart. . . . We will soon enter the push-button age. . . . An entire factory will be run with a generator the size of a matchbox. . . . Laying a four-lane highway at a mile a minute would be simple."

Much of the film footage is devoted to scenes of Cal speeding around in his military jet. Back at the lab, he assembles a gizmo with strange parts received from an unknown mail-order company. The contraption turns out to be a communication device, and with it he meets the character Exeter. Exeter's odd appearance, complete with exaggerated forehead and unnatural white hair, doesn't seem to give Cal a clue as to his alien nature. Unsuspicious, Cal agrees to be flown to an unknown destination, where he finds an international group of scientists, including two other Americans, working on a mysterious project. Exeter explains that he represents a group of investors who "seek to put an end to war through new discoveries . . . particularly the discovery of limitless amounts of free nuclear energy." Exactly how nuclear energy would end wars on Earth is not explained at this time. Later in the film it becomes clear that "peace through strength" and a strong nuclear defense capability is being promoted in the narrative.

As Cal begins working with these scientists, he gradually learns that Exeter, as an officer in an invading army from the planet Metaluna, is brainwashing human scientists. As Cal and an American woman scientist, Pat, attempt to flee the laboratory, they are sucked up into a giant flying saucer and taken to Metaluna, while the remaining scientists are callously destroyed. Soon we discover than Metaluna is at war with a neighboring planet and needs Earth's atomic expertise to reinforce its protective shield. The consequences of a weak defense system are vividly illustrated as the space travelers view enemy warheads exploding on the planet's surface. Exeter laments: "What you are witnessing may be the end of our world. As our power diminishes, our protection fails." But by the time Exeter returns, it is already too late for the planet; meteoric bombardment by the enemy has caused the shield to fail.

Fear of Totalitarianism

The repressive social and political system depicted on the alien planet in *This Island Earth* was fatally flawed, which contributed to its ultimate destruction. Although the aliens are technologically and intellectually more advanced than humans, their "otherness," their "unhumanness" and regimented social system, is offered as an explanation for their society's demise. Exeter takes the captured Earth scientists on a brief tour of the planet on their way to consult the planet's leader, "the controller." The ruins of Metaluna reflect a utopian world, a city of futuristic spiraling towers and pastel dome-shaped structures, encompassing a society "superior to Earth's." However, their "educational complexes and recreation centers are now rubble." The planet was ruled by a militaristic dictator who "brainwashed" his citizens at will. The society breeds mutant slaves to do manual labor, has little regard for free will and human life, and is godless.

For example, Exeter nonchalantly blows up the remaining scientists, simply saying "it was necessary" and "we aren't all masters of our own souls." As the invading force, Exeter and his fellow aliens are emotionless and militaristic; complete obedience is expected by "the controller," who explains that they "do not permit any dissenting opinions." Dissenters are simply lobotomized by a machine that "destroys the power of the will." Crucially, they have no religion. The following dialogue occurs between "the controller" and Cal:

THE CONTROLLER: Typical of you Earth people to refuse to believe in the superiority of anyone but your own. You are like children looking into a magnifying glass, imaging the image you see is your true size.
CAL: Our true size is the size of our God.

The presumption that individual lives and emotions are "natural" and will flourish "come what may" provided a recurrent message in these movies, making the point that repressive systems are fundamentally flawed. President Eisenhower spoke of the "grave weaknesses and internal contradictions of Soviet Communism" in its reduction of its population to "slave labor."[18] The communist system became "the most insolent hoax in history," and "fooling all of the people all of the time" became "the essential function of the state apparatus."[19] The "Red conspiracy" was explained away as fallacious and irrational dogma that was contrary to human nature. According to the American point of view, the individuality of the human spirit could not be successfully adapted to the brutal conformity of a social collective under strict government supervision, which supposedly was the fate of the communist worker. Since the totalitarian state was seen as violating the individual's rights, it was not only different from American beliefs and values but was an inherently irrational system as well.

Once Russia was designated as the "enemy" by American leaders, Americans transferred their hatred of Hitler's Germany to Stalin's Russia with considerable ease. President Truman himself had remarked in 1947 that "there isn't any difference in totalitarian states. I don't care what you call them, Nazi, Communist, or Fascist."[20] Similarities between these "totalitarian states" helped formulate specific anticommunist themes. Communism as a personal way of life was portrayed as being "different" from the American system in standards of personal and political freedom, social values, and lifestyles. The communist political-economic system, usually represented by a communist government, was presented as demanding and achieving conformity of word and deed from its citizenry, planning their every thought and move in ways that would be unthinkable in the western concept of social relations. The predominant stereotypical image of ordinary people in communist countries was usually as a part of a massive collectivity, marching in military or athletic displays; as a totally submissive mass, "completely militarized from youngest childhood."[21]

Echoing this logic, "the controller" in *This Island Earth* explains to the human scientists that the remaining population of Metaluna intends to relocate on Earth, where their "knowledge of weapons will make [them] superior" to humans and eventually will make slaves of Earth's population, just as their own mutant slaves had filled that role on Metaluna. He then instructs Exeter to brainwash the captive scientists. However, as the brainwashing is about to begin, a meteor kills the controller and the mutant slaves revolt, indulging in a killing rampage. Their relocation plan fails as the control center is smashed by a bomb. The flawed social system of Metaluna's population, their inhuman nature, and their weak defense system contributed to their failure, as the planet burns up and becomes a lifeless radioactive sun.

Before the final destruction, Exeter decides to return the Earth people to their own planet. Safe in Exeter's flying saucer, the humans watch as Metaluna becomes an incandescent globe of destruction. Exeter expresses the hope that the planet's dying light will warm the surface of some other dying world. After dropping the two scientists safely off, Exeter's blazing ship crashes into the sea. As Cal and Pat return to Earth, Pat remarks: "Thank God it's still here." After having witnessed the possible consequences of nuclear abuse, they return to the realm of the utopian use of atomic power, convinced in the wisdom of a mighty nuclear defense capability and in the ultimate superiority of the American political system.

Typical of this genre, no one on Earth except the scientists had even known of the infiltration of these aliens, much less of their evil intentions to divert Earth's population and resources for their own prosperity. Often, these films depicted the invaders fleeing their own planet, which had been destroyed by the abuse of nuclear power, only to attempt to establish their alien and ultimately flawed social system on Earth. For example, *Night of the Blood Beast* (1958) features outer-space creatures whose world has been destroyed by atomic war seeking to bring their civilization to Earth by implanting their embryos in human bloodstreams. In the end, the creatures are destroyed, but it is made clear that others are likely to follow.

Fear of Scientific Development

The majority of films of the 1950s address the risk inherent in science itself. Exploring nature's mysteries, in particular experimenting with atomic energy, inevitably attracts the unwelcome attention of alien forces, consequently placing the planet in jeopardy. Because of scientists' knowledge and potential for discovery, they become valuable commodities, often leading to disastrous results. This point is better illustrated in another invasion scenario typical of the time, exemplified in the movie *Killers from Space* (1954). The film opens with an atomic mushroom cloud exploding over a desert test site. A military jet piloted by a scientist circles ground zero. Spotting something unusual in the cloud, the pilot dives to investigate and crashes. Mysteriously, the body of the scientist is never recovered. Later, he is found on the air force base suffering from memory loss and a large scar on his chest just above his heart. Soon, his wife reports that he is behaving strangely and is probably engaging in espionage. The FBI arrive and monitor the scientist, concerned about risks to classified information and security. After he is given truth serum, the scientist describes an operating table in a cave and remembers that his heart was suspended in the air above him.

Soon, it is revealed that aliens are responsible for bringing the scientist back to life after he was killed in the plane crash. They are hiding deep in the Earth in a cave and need the scientist's knowledge of atomic power to fulfill their plan to invade the Earth using giant mutated animals and insects. The aliens explain: "We are accumulating the energy released in each of your atomic explosions. . . . We have stored several billion electron volts as a result of your atomic tests. . . . After your next atomic test, these animals will multiply at a rate beyond imagination, at the proper time we will unleash them. . . . They will spread to every continent and devour every living thing on earth."

The aliens offer to save the scientist's life if he cooperates with them, but he nobly declines. Therefore, they brainwash him to "listen to orders and obey." Yet he overcomes the indoctrination through his own strength of will and shuts down an electrical plant from which the aliens have been siphoning power. This shutdown causes the alien's cave to explode in an gigantic atomic cloud. The scientist saves the planet although, through his own knowledge and atomic experimentation, he was the one who had initially endangered it.

Not all invading forces had evil intentions. Some, as in the seminal *The Day the Earth Stood Still* (1951), stressed the destructive force of atomic weapons and the gloomy fate of the Earth if their warnings were ignored. *The Space Children* (1958) features aliens using children to thwart the launching of a hydrogen rocket, believing that "the Earth is not yet ready for such a weapon." In *War of the Satellites* (1958), an alien power warns the United Nations to cease its rocket experiments or witness the destruction of the Earth. For the most part, however, all aliens, whether extraterrestrial or from a closer proximity to the United States, had ominous and threatening intentions. Attempted invasions of alien ideologies were portrayed as equally pernicious and covert, as illustrated by films depicting communist spies pursuing elusive atomic secrets.

Atomic Espionage

Fears of invasion, whether by earthbound or extraterrestrial elements, were linked to issues of atomic development throughout films of the 1950s. Film noir, a style of filmmaking popular in the late 1940s, was also adopted by Hollywood producers to portray themes of subversive communist activity and communist attempts to infiltrate American cities and steal atomic secrets. Although not of the science fiction genre, the atomic espionage spy film proliferated "as the paranoia of the Cold War commenced with the suspicions over atomic secrets."[22]

These films featured undercover communist agents seeking mysterious atomic secrets or substances in America. The subversives were intricately involved in various plots concerning foreign invasion and hostile acts against the United States; the plots invariably rested upon acquiring American atomic weaponry or technology. Unlike the films made directly after World War II, which featured the atomic scientist as the main character, these later atomic espionage stories showcased the role of government agents, usually from the FBI, working in conjunction with local police departments. Not only did these stories praise the military and the police, they celebrated the functioning of such real-world agencies as the FBI and the CIA.

The need for centralized and omnipotent security agencies to guard against the technologically competing and ideologically threatening Soviet Union and "fellow travelers" had become a national issue. The "Red scare" was a consolidation of dangers such as the vulnerability of atomic weapons technology, the potential infiltration of American society by communist subversives, and the susceptibility of the American public to the unethical and aggressive methods of the communists.

Films that focused on these concerns reinforced the image of the evil inhuman communist subversive while graphically illustrating the crucial need for government surveillance and security measures. In reference to Hollywood's products of this time, Michael Rogin stated: "The cold war consensus produced political power in the 1950s. It helped build a national security apparatus that survived the breakdown of the consensus and dominated the 1960s. By the time the cultural consensus stopped producing power, the powerful institutions were in place. We can see their genesis in our films."[23]

The public consensus seemed to accept the principle that communism was so deeply shrouded in mystery and so distorted an ideology that the only explanations as to why an adult, American or otherwise, would join the Communist Party were force, trickery, or naïveté. Deluded followers throughout the world could be manipulated "quite ruthlessly" to "serve the purposes of the Soviet State." Supporters of communism were depicted as psychotic, complex conspirators driven by fanaticism or motives of personal gain. A Gallup poll in 1961 found that the words "warlike" and "treacherous" were most commonly used to describe the Russian people. In the same poll, these terms did not even appear in descriptions of Germans and Japanese.[24] The stereotypical communist leader was sinister, gaunt, with a "lean and hungry look," subjugating and manipulating his nation's population with terror and oppression.[25]

Equating communism with a religion that forced unquestioning obedience can be found at all levels of the culture. Describing communism as a "secular religion which preaches a secular messianic message," this concept was further promoted with the common usage of such words as "doctrine," "creed," and "party faithful" to emphasize the religious aspect of the communist belief.[26] Reinhold Niebuhr, an American theologian, went so far as to state in 1960 that "Communism is a secularized religious apocalyptic creed" that created a tyrannical oligarchy devoid of either internal or external checks upon its power.[27] Communism was condemned as a militant faith determined to generate world revolution, to liquidate all nonbelievers, and to "kill millions of Americans" as well.[28]

Strong popular sentiment looked upon the communist political-economic system not only as an irrational adversary of U.S. interests and values but also as an inherently false and evil regime. Communist governments were committed to imposing their systems "upon an unwilling world, by any means, fair or foul," as demonstrated by their acts of violence, blackmail, brainwashing, and coercion by terror.[29] Russian military might and aggressive foreign policy was seen as evidence of their desire for world domination and as a threat to U.S. beliefs and values. Indeed, communism was so far removed from American values that scholars urged diplomats not to think along the lines of old-fashioned diplomacy and Christian ethics when dealing with communists, because "none of these concepts appear in the communist dictionary."[30]

Internal subversion was the communists' main tactic for achieving their goal of world domination. The rapid disintegration of capitalist countries was to be hastened by "native subversion," with communism feeding and growing upon chaos and breakdown. Political upheaval and confusion left a nation vulnerable, "letting communism in much the same way unsanitary conditions breed vermin and disease."[31] The communists were always searching for trouble spots in the free world, "to seize more countries, to enslave more millions of human souls."[32] This fear of internal subversion is embraced in the famous slogan of the McCarthy era, "Reds under the bed," which almost inevitably accompanied any report involving communist "infiltration." This popular slogan served to expound the need to alert the average American to the insidious and all-pervasive Red threat, by reaching people where they felt the most secure, off guard, and relaxed.

Hollywood film incorporated these concepts into characterizations in atomic spy films. Scientists, when they appear at all, are relegated to two groups. They are depicted either as renegades who want to sell their secrets to the communists for their own personal gain (*Tangier Incident*, 1954; *The Thief*, 1952) or as mere vessels of information vulnerable to kidnapping and extortion. Scientists figure marginally in *The Atomic City* (1952), which has been hailed as the prototype of this genre.[33] Here, the son of a Los Alamos physicist is kidnapped by communist spies and held for ransom for hydrogen bomb secrets. *World for Ransom* (1954) has the scientist himself kidnapped for the purpose of extracting atomic secrets. In no case is the scientist heroic; he must invariably be rescued by the more capable government agents.

Usually, these films follow the classic film noir style. They depict a world of contending, sometimes ambiguous, moral forces in which deception, treachery, and murder are commonplace. The dialogue is abrasive and the style is characterized by nighttime shooting, dark shadows, sharp lighting, skewed camera angles, and convoluted narratives.[34] The emphasis upon law enforcement and government agencies centers the film action upon security and surveillance operating in an underworld society of suspicious characters in shadowy settings. It is the government agents who keep the "American way of life" safe, by confronting not only subversive activity but also elements in society that are vulnerable, because of their disregard for the law and accepted social norms, to exploitation by communists. The police, although hindered by the self-serving interests of a few disreputable characters, manage to triumph over the communist aggressors because, in the end, even crooks turn noble and patriotic in the face of the true social evil—communism.

The depiction of atomic materials in these films reflects the ambivalent and contradictory attitude toward atomic issues prevalent in society at this time. Typically in these films, the sought-after scientific treasure and the reason for its value is rarely explained. The object of everyone's attention usually consists of equations reproduced on film or written in notebooks, or a mysterious substance in a sealed container. These atomic secrets are of value only because they are "classified," "necessary for national defense," and "potentially disastrous in the wrong hands." Superficially, American nuclear technology is portrayed as neutral; it is only the intentions of the possessors of that technology that render it a threat. All atomic spy films are based on the assumption that only the American bureaucracy can deal ethically and responsibly with such a potentially destructive force and that the world would suffer atrocities on a grand scale if atomic secrets were to fall into the hands of the conscienceless communists. Hence, the endless depictions of communist agents randomly slaughtering innocent people, beating and shooting old women, and leaving behind a trail of senseless murder as they strive to attain atomic superiority offer a glimpse of what could become commonplace if they were to attain their goal. So inhuman a foe turns even hopelessly hardened and cynical street criminals into sympathetic characters; even America's worst criminal offender is ethically superior to a communist agent.

Common to this genre is the use of documentary and newsreel footage to blur the distinction between real events and movie drama, just as in the early radiation monster movies. Subtle visual clues also reinforce the darkened atmosphere and the sense of paranoia. For example, as the police trail a communist agent in a subway station, a civil defense poster behind them displays a shadowy figure looking out over a city skylight. "Ever vigilant for defense—the blood of life," it reads. In another film, an FBI agent, while searching an apartment for communist spies, is shown looking under the bed—an obvious allusion to the "Reds under the bed" slogan popular at this time.

The communist conspirators are depicted as ultimately threatening and barely human. Constantly skulking in the shadows, their voices lilting with foreign accents, they haunt dark rooms and smoke incessantly as they unemotionally plan out their next moves. Usually their faces are never shown; their shoes and pant cuffs are all the audience sees of them. It was popularly believed that communists could pass as ordinary citizens, but, like extraterrestrial invaders, the communists in these films are sinister and eccentric; they are far from ordinary. Through various intrigues, they manage to convince susceptible American citizens to do their bidding, controlling them behind the scenes. Communist agents operate as scouts, the first line of infiltration of a secret international conspiracy that threatens the American system and way of life. As they operate undetected, taking their orders from "headquarters" in Moscow, they torture and kill innocent victims in their quest for atomic secrets. Nevertheless, American technology and brain power are always superior to anything these aliens, Soviet or otherwise, can ever hope to produce.

The typical elements of the atomic spy film are found in *Pickup on South Street* (1954). In it, a pickpocket unwittingly lifts film containing classified atomic information from a courier's purse. The courier herself is unaware that she is working for communists, believing that she has merely been doing a friend a favor. The police and the FBI attempt to persuade the pickpocket to give them the film, appealing to his sense of patriotism: "If you refuse to cooperate, you'll be as guilty as the traitors who gave Stalin the A-bomb. Do you know what treason means?"

Unconcerned by this talk, the pickpocket keeps the film out of personal interest, hoping to make a deal with the communist agents. Claiming that "a red's money is as good as anyone else's," he almost sells out. A friendly colleague tells him in disgust: "What's the matter with you, playing footsies with the commies? I thought you were a regular crook. Even in our kind of business, you have to draw the line somewhere."

Soon, shocked by the communist agent's killing of innocent people, the pickpocket single-handedly captures and turns in the communist gang. Even a good-for-nothing turns to the side of the law when confronted with the evil and callousness of communists.

But it is *Kiss Me Deadly* (1955) that epitomizes the personal and social paranoia of the nuclear age, submerged in the popular rhetoric of the times. It also characterizes atomic technology as a body of knowledge so corrupting and destructive that it can only be comprehended and managed by government authorities. This adaptation of a Mickey Spillane novel includes federal agents, communist spies, and atomic secrets commingled with a deeper theme promoting a collective social ethic. It has been suggested that the death of individualism, which operates outside the clearly defined strictures of the postwar national security consensus, is the film's central theme.[35] According to Peter Biskind: "By 1950, the stakes had become too high for the down-and-out shamuses doing their own thing. *Kiss Me Deadly* is a Cold War cautionary tale, and the message is clear. There is no room for neutrals playing both sides of the street."[36]

This idea is conveyed by the consequences of the individualistic lifestyle of the protagonist, Mike Hammer. Almost all the characters he comes in contact with eventually die, as he does himself. His world is insecure and dangerous; no one is honest, except the police and the FBI, and no one can be trusted. Hammer is repeatedly warned of the dangerous secret substance the communists are seeking— but his own self-interest hinders him from cooperating, with disastrous consequences. The sought-after prize is so secret that the authorities cannot allow him knowledge of its true nature. The communists also keep the contents secret and their importance ambiguous, answering Hammer's queries with: "What is it we are seeking? Diamonds, rubies, narcotics? How civilized this Earth used to be. But as the world becomes more primitive, the more fabulous become its treasures."

Later, in attempting to break Hammer's self-interested attitude, the FBI investigator nervously whispers these words: "Now listen, listen carefully, I'm going to pronounce a few words, they're harmless words, just a bunch of letters scrambled together, but they're meaning is very important. Try to understand what they mean: 'Manhattan Project, Los Alamos, Trinity.'"

These words alone are enough to change Hammer's mind; he gives the authorities the key to the hidden substance. However, throughout the film, the secret remains a Pandora's box sealed from view in a lead container. Classical allusions abound as, at the end, a communist conspirator warns of the consequences of curiosity: "The box contains the head of Medusa, and whoever looks on it is not turned into stone, but into brimstone and ashes."

The destructive potential of the atomic substance is revealed at the film's end as Hammer, the communist agent, and their immediate surroundings are obliterated in a mushroom cloud. But the secret itself, the reason that the element is so precious, is never revealed. The contradictory positive and negative images that always seem to be evoked in relation to issues of atomic development are displayed here as well. To the Americans, nuclear power is a necessity for national defense (hence the allusions to Los Alamos and Trinity); to the Soviet agents, an unattainable treasure. And yet it has the potential for inconceivable destruction and corrupting influence. Just as radiation monsters awoke from the depths of the earth, the forbidden atomic secrets depicted in these spy movies are usually hidden, whether they are underground, deep in the sea, or in a secret locker. It exists as an unspeakable secret, the knowledge of which causes all associated with it, except those in authority, to die.

By the late 1950s, the atomic espionage theme had diminished to where it only operated as a subplot in the science fiction monster genre. *The Phantom from 10,000 Leagues* (1956) and *The Atomic Man* (1956) depict communist spies only in small portion of their narratives. Although the glorification and justification of law enforcement agencies' roles in national defense may have appeased the House Un-American Activities Committee, the fact that nearly every such film lost money had the studios gradually decreasing the production of this type of film.

By this time, the Soviet Union had successfully developed and tested its own hydrogen bomb. Its ability to match U.S. offensive technology proved the assumption of the superiority of American technology obsolete. Public attention increasingly focused upon the weapons delivery systems, namely ballistic missiles with intermediate range. By 1955, these missiles were in place in England, Turkey, and Italy, while the Polaris nuclear submarine was launched in 1960. Gradually, Hollywood began to release films depicting more catastrophic effects of nuclear destruction and the consequences of fallout.

7

Postnuclear Scenarios

Devastation of American cities in *The Day the World Ended* (1956)

TOWARD THE END OF THE 1950S, the cinematic spectacles of giant mutated insects and space invaders threatening the planet were less and less common. Teenage audiences were showing their preference for more gory offerings such as *Horror of Dracula* (1958) and *The Screaming Skull* (1958) over atomically mutated creatures, and independent producers began to abandon science fiction in favor of the horror genre.[1] Although fallout shelters and civil defense measures were presented by government officials and media broadcasts as adequate protection against any Soviet attack, speculation on the consequences of atomic use began to provide profitable, if sobering, film fare. Attempts at a less sensational and more realistic confrontation with atomic concerns began to emerge from the larger studios. However, Hollywood covered their postholocaust fabrications with a cosmetic sheen, for films dealing with post–atomic war scenarios rarely portrayed decaying corpses or radiation sickness. Rather, the aftermath of such conflicts was illustrated in fictional and unscientific terms that would be palatable to larger movie audiences. In trying to exploit the dismal idea of the potential destruction of civilization and the planet itself, Hollywood films portrayed the postnuclear environment as survivable and perhaps even advantageous.

As the atom was promoted by the Atomic Energy Commission (AEC) as a beneficial element, the Soviet Union was simultaneously promoted by most official organs as the enemy, with the threat of a Soviet attack a constant condition. The AEC gained public support by assuring people that "fallout was much less dangerous than falling behind the Russians in the arms race."[2] Before 1957, the Soviet Union had no physical capability to launch a nuclear strike on the mainland United States. Yet the years 1955 through 1957 were devoted to conjuring up the idea of a "bomber gap," portraying the United States as "lying almost defenseless under the menace of a vast Soviet bomber armada."[3] Promoted by industrialists, politicians, and generals, this concept helped to continue the vast investment in the Strategic Air Command.

Since 1953, a contingency plan for using atomic weapons in limited wars had existed, and with it a policy called the "New Look," which involved the overseas deployment of tactical nuclear weapons intended for battlefield use in Europe. Military exercises in Europe relied upon the assumption that atomic weapons would be used in any future war. To prepare for such warfare, American soldiers conducted maneuvers close to atomic detonation sites so that they could be tested and trained for real-life combat. By 1954, the official U.S. response to Soviet aggression entailed "massive retaliation." The United States also began to fly U-2 reconnaissance planes over the USSR in 1956.[4]

The general impression of American technological superiority over the Soviet Union was quickly altered with the November 1957 launch of the first earth satellite, Sputnik. The launching of Sputnik generated panic among many Americans, who feared that the Soviet Union had begun to excel in technology, an area long dominated by the United States.[5] Americans began to worry about whether the United States was falling behind in high technology, or if it could consistently compete and remain superior to the ever expanding Soviet expertise. Edward Teller declared on national television after the Sputnik launch that the United States had lost "a battle more important and greater than Pearl Harbor."[6]

What was lost in the publicity surrounding the Soviet satellite was the fact its launch was part of the USSR's contribution to International Geophysical Year (IGY), a cooperative multinational effort to research and better understand the planet. In association with the National Science Academy and with the support of UNESCO, the IGY involved 60,000 scientists from sixty-six nations. The year 1957 coincided with a sunspot cycle and was chosen by the cooperating scientists as a period in which they would cooperatively participate in such joint projects as observing and measuring wind patterns, investigating the Earth's magnetic field, and documenting the impact of cosmic rays upon the Earth's atmosphere. Such research results would be shared internationally—scientists had begun to cooperate despite Cold War hindrances.

This fact was largely bypassed by the media in favor of speculation upon the consequences of losing the Cold War, losing the battle against communism. As a result, the ultimate destruction was conceived as a nuclear sneak attack. At the same time, the impression was judiciously permitted to gain currency that the Cold War would some day culminate in a major crisis, perhaps an all-out war against communism, out of which the United States would either emerge victorious or the world would come to an end in mutual nuclear obliteration.

The rhetoric of the Cold War involved images of mass destruction, with the United States surviving relatively intact to begin anew. Narratives of nuclear survival found in the popular media of the time act as an extension of the American belief of its own invulnerable omnipotence.[7] Throughout most postnuclear films of this period, the United States system remains invulnerable and survives all attempts at annihilation. Typically, films of this genre operated upon the premise that one need only hide in a shelter for a short time while fallout dissolved away and Communism was eradicated by nuclear destruction. Then a newly cleansed, renewed United States would emerge, with its familiar concerns and social relations intact. An example of this ideology can be found in a 1945 issue of *Life,* which offered a summary of global nuclear war. The article is illustrated with drawings showing New York City as a crumbling ruin, yet with the Public Library's lions still standing. The final line reads: "The United States wins the war."[8]

Hollywood drew on the concept of survival not only from the popular rhetoric of the time but also from a long history of science fiction literature. The most pervasive nuclear war theme in all of science fiction is the "myth of the heroic survivors" who, after an appropriately brief glance at the destruction of their civilization, begin to build a new and improved society from the ruins of the old.[9] The postdisaster landscape served as a convenient testing ground for the old virtues of self-reliance and simple living, proving that American institutions and values were eternal and natural to humankind. Although the use of nuclear power had not exactly provided the predicted "atomic utopia," at least it had worked to clear the slate so that a new and improved America could begin afresh.

The epitome of the survivalist idea is found in *Five* (1951), a movie that went on to become a formula for countless imitators such as *The Day the World Ended* (1956), *The World, the Flesh and the Devil* (1959), *Last Woman on Earth* (1960), *The Omega Man* (1971), and *The Silent Earth* (1989). The formula introduces survivors in a postatomic world who are saved through some accident and then set out to make it in the new world. The survivors are confronted in some way with the old prejudices or social mores of the preholocaust civilization, which they then address and usually resolve before the final scene. There is never any attempt to confront the horror of the overall situation; the reality of the nuclear destruction is not allowed to interfere with the mostly illogical contrivances. For example, the dead populations have conveniently disappeared and are only fleetingly referred to. The lingering effects of radiation are not realistically depicted; in these movies, the effects of the blast and the fallout last only a few days, and then normality returns to the Earth's ecosystem. Environmentally, the planet suffers only a minor inconvenience; nuclear war is like a cloth that wipes away the accumulated ravages of history and allows a clean, fresh world to be reborn.

Most post–nuclear war films rely upon the image of a deserted metropolis, in which the survivors collectively begin to rebuild society again in more or less its original form. Survivors typically battle imaginatively conceived mutants and each other before beginning their new life, with predictable biblical allusions. Philip Strick postulates that these landscapes, in response to disaster, "carry a powerful symbolic charge, representing not only the summation of former mistakes but also the prospects for rebuilding. . . . Above all, Armageddon simplifies: questions of morality and responsibility may legitimately be set aside in favour of basic matters like survival and the perpetuation of the species."[10]

Two typical examples of the "after the bomb" film is *The Day the World Ended* (1956) and *The World, the Flesh and the Devil* (1959). Both open following an atomic war, and they conclude in similar fashion. *The Day the World Ended* portrays several people who find their way to an isolated valley after the "almost total destruction of the world." The valley contains a shelter owned by a man named Madison and his daughter, who had been prepared for atomic war and its aftermath. The group of people, presumably the only ones left on Earth, arrive in search of shelter, some already suffering the effects of radiation. Soon, a wild mutant starts threatening the group, and the survivors, involved in a sexual conflict, begin fighting among themselves.

Eventually everyone dies except, predictably, one male and one female character. All other survivors are mutants living in the radioactive fog, battling each other for supremacy. Mutants in these "after the bomb" movies all look similar, but in no way reflect any scientifically plausible form. For example, mutants in this particular film had gigantic, balloonlike heads with three eyes, four arms, and horns. How this instant mutation of living human beings is possible is never explained. Nor is any explanation offered when a sudden rainfall kills the mutants just as they are attacking the last two humans in the movie's climax. The closing title, as the Adam and Eve characters embrace, informs us that this is "the beginning."

The World, the Flesh and the Devil also presents the survival myth while trying to encapsulate the problems of surviving nuclear war in the midst of racial and sexual conflicts. The main character, an Afro-American man named Ralph, is trapped in a mine for five days, unknowingly protected from the destruction of world civilization by atomic war. After digging himself out of the mine, he finds a vacant city. The answer to the mystery is revealed as a newspaper headline tells of retaliation for an atomic attack, a special radioactive salt having disintegrated all human, but not animal, life. Ralph begins to enjoy the bounty of the destroyed civilization—he moves into a Park Avenue penthouse, connects a portable generator, and gathers canned food, which apparently the radioactive salt has not penetrated. Soon, Sarah, another survivor who found shelter in a decompression chamber for five days, joins Ralph. Since she is Caucasian, a racial element emerges, which is further complicated by the arrival of yet another Caucasian survivor, Ben. Soon, the friendships degenerate into a shooting contest between the two men over the woman, which is resolved when the rivals find that they cannot kill one another. The three walk off hand in hand as the closing title reads "The Beginning."

Most reviewers found this film unsatisfactory and silly in its presentation of the issues.[11] One critic found the ending so theatrical that "you wouldn't be surprised to see the windows of buildings suddenly crowded with reintegrated people, cheering happily and flinging ticker tape. The drama of humanity's survival collapses into an irrelevant wrangle about racial discrimination.[12]

Films on time travel were also used as a way to ponder the consequences of nuclear war and the possibilities of survival. For example, in *World Without End* (1956), four astronauts, on their return to Earth from Mars in 1957, experience technical difficulties in flight and find themselves near an unidentified planet on which they are forced to land. Upon landing, they are attacked by giant spiderlike creatures and deformed cave people. Soon, they discover an underground civilization and learn that they are on Earth after an atomic war in the future, in 2508. The astronauts find out that after the war, a civilization was founded underground in order to avoid the mutated "surface beasts" living in the open. Since the men can no longer return to the Earth of their own time, they help the weakened underground dwellers blast the surface beasts with bazookas, and the great outdoors is restored to the "normal people," who then can begin civilization anew.

A more pessimistic view of the future is found in *Terror from the Year 5,000* (1958), in which a scientist's secret experiments with a "time vault" materialize a mutated woman from Earth's radioactive future. The woman explains that fresh pre-atomic genes are needed to start an uncontaminated race, and she tries unsuccessfully to take the scientist into the future with her. Despite their individual plot variations, these films never suggest that the human race would not survive a full-scale nuclear confrontation. Humans, albeit in mutated form, continue to thrive.

Although, in these films, the United States ultimately wins any confrontation through the survival of its system, the strategic details of the nuclear conflict are rarely made clear. Which country was responsible for the aggression and who launched the first strike are insignificant details when considered against the consequences of the quarrel. It is humanity's ultimate tampering with nature itself that led them down the road to destruction, or at least to a point where society must begin again. Although Hollywood was hesitant to offer realistic portrayals of atomic destruction or the effects of radiation, instead relying upon survival myths to make the nuclear future more palatable, the real future was becoming increasingly questionable as ballistic missiles were aimed at the United States. Order is inevitably restored in the post–nuclear war films of the 1950s, but they foreshadowed a cultural transformation in which the future was portrayed as overwhelmingly pessimistic.[13]

8

The Nuclear Future, 1960–1964

What we fear from the next war is famine and disease and bestiality, tyranny and the loss of whatever human dignity we have inherited from past genera-tions. To suppose that the atom will bring quick death for the millions and a bright, clean world for a bright, clean boy and girl to repopulate is to tell a fairy story to the soft-minded.[1]

Civilization after the atomic holocaust in *The Time Machine* (1960)

FAMILIAR THEMES IN SCIENCE FICTION FILMS, such as radioactive mutations and alien invasions, lingered into the first few years of the 1960s, but the increasingly redundant depiction of such scenarios was quickly losing its box-office appeal. The gimmick of the radiation-induced mutation had become all-important in the genre; the particular configuration of the mutated creature became the only aspect that differentiated one film plot from another. Soon, these products seemed to lose the interest of even an undiscriminating audience. In extreme attempts to squeeze any remaining profit from the fading genre, conglomerations such as *The Beast of Yucca Flats* (1960) blended communist agents, secret atomic information, invading extraterrestrial aliens, and giant radiation-created mutants into one convoluted and confusing plot. But low box-office returns killed off these mutants and invaders faster than any military intervention could ever hope to do.

However, alternative scenarios and new applications of the nuclear theme had begun to evolve in Hollywood productions. With the contemporary issues of global fallout, doomsday machines, and mutually assured destruction on the military agenda, many films began questioning the exalted portrayal of military leadership and the feasibility of a survivable nuclear future. Since the atomic bomb and the military industrial complex that created it had enjoyed, for the most part, a positive image throughout the 1950s, an examination of their unattractive and contradictory aspects offered new material for Hollywood producers. The fear of communist subversives and alien invaders gradually gave way to fear of fallout and more pessimistic assessments of the nuclear future. Cinematic military scientists began to appear as power-hungry madmen, while the survivors of the imagined postnuclear world found that their continuing existence was unattractive and even impossible. Critics lauded Hollywood's attempt at portraying nuclear issues without "grotesque eighty-foot monsters looming across the horizon in the wake of nuclear explosions, no papier-mâché skyscrapers toppling into Times Square, and no concentration on the B-film brand of sex and violence to contend with . . . without the super-science and melodramatics that seem to be standard procedure for films of this genre."[2]

Despite the Department of Defense's insistence that a nuclear war was survivable, cinematic depictions of a survivable post–nuclear war environment had begun to thin out, making way for more cynical predictions of the future. By the early 1960s, the contradictory images of nuclear technology, one as savior to the nation and the other as destroyer of worlds, had begun to undermine each other in the public sphere. Government bureaucracies pushed for further weapons development, arguing that the U.S. nuclear arsenal was the only deterrent that stood between the United States and communism aggression. The utopian promises of Project Plowshares had yet to be realized, and the public was becoming increasingly skeptical of its supposed benefits to American society and the world. Clearly, the Atomic Energy Commission was losing the battle in trying to present the nuclear buildup as an ultimately beneficent and peaceful activity. While the specter of radioactive fallout had by this time been forever linked to images of mutation and contamination, greater segments of the public were also becoming suspicious of the far-reaching control that government authorities held over nuclear energy.

However, exploitations of the by now standard "heroic survivor" scenario of future human existence, which downplayed the fatal effects of fallout while insisting that American civilization would inevitably survive, were still being produced in Hollywood. For example, *Last Woman on Earth* (1960) presents once again the familiar love triangle among the last three survivors after the world's population is destroyed by atomic radiation. The predictable ending leaves the last man and woman alone to attempt to repopulate the new postholocaust world.

Other examples in this vein include *Panic in the Year Zero* (1962), which replicated the scenario introduced a decade earlier in *Five* depicting the adventures of a typical middle-class family fighting to survive after an atomic attack on southern California. The greatest danger of nuclear war, it would seem, was not radioactivity but common looters who must be fended off with shotguns. The characters fight with frontier gusto, excitedly exclaiming, "We are on our own, Ma. No rules, regulations or laws!" After the family members are exposed to acts of barbarism, they become killers themselves, and then it's back to civilization again with the military fully in control. The film ends with the survivors thanking God for the United States Army as two soldiers welcome them into a restored Los Angeles, where they can begin life anew. The fade-out concludes with the words, "There must be no end, only a new beginning."

But gradually films began to emerge that questioned the assumption that the nuclear future would be hospitable and the premise that American society, much less the military establishment, would endure at all. Independent filmmakers, particularly individuals who had made a name for themselves and had established a loyal following, were able to capture their personal visions on film and exploit the expanding market for their products. Soon, the once "heroic survivors" of nuclear war were confronted with situations that made their continuance impossible and Earth's ultimate future undeniably grim. And the effects of radiation upon Earth's inhabitants were also shown in a more authentic and believable light, offering the film audience more serious and sobering representations of the consequences of nuclear war.

Personal Visions: *On the Beach* (1959)

The first example of this wave of movies imagining a pessimistic future appeared in 1959. Suggesting that the atomic bomb might completely destroy the world and all life upon it, Stanley Kramer's *On the Beach* (1959) was praised as a deterrent to further nuclear armament and was credited with initiating a public dialogue that questioned the efficacy of using nuclear arms to prevent World War III.[3] Such socially pertinent fare was the specialty of director Kramer, who represented "a new breed of independent producers and directors who had the knack for producing pictures of high artistic merit on low budgets."[4] As an independent producer working in the film industry for thirty years, Kramer had acquired a reputation for producing "message movies" from a "liberal viewpoint"— films consciously made to teach a lesson or correct unworthy attitudes.[5] But the ability of an independent to produce a big-budget film through contracts with a major studio was also due to the economic and institutional changes in the Hollywood film industry that continued to influence its products.

By 1960, what remained of the original studio system had been gradually bought up by corporations, and other studios transformed themselves into huge conglomerates that emphasized distribution and the funding of contracted independents rather than in-house production. Increasingly, films were put together as "deals" by independent producers or agents, who then secured funding for production from the major studios. These major studios then handled national distribution, including television and international releases.

The demise of the traditional studio system gave filmmakers more control over their product than had been the case during the previous era, and this development helped facilitate the production of more socially critical and innovative films. The elimination of the Production Code and the initiation of a new rating system made it possible to experiment with previously forbidden subject matter. Film content was transformed as the major studios lost their power to enforce the strictures of the Production Code Administration. Additionally, until the late 1950s, eight states and ninety cities had licensing boards that reviewed all motion pictures exhibited in their jurisdiction. While in operation, these boards did manage to exert a powerful influence over the film industry and the content of its products. Although the boards primarily focused upon issues of obscenity and sexually explicit material, they sometimes censored political and religious content as well. By the mid-1960s, all but a handful of such boards had been invalidated because of their unconstitutional standards.

Financially, the movie industry's outlook had greatly improved by 1964.[6] The major studios adopted a new strategy in another attempt to differentiate their product from television programming. The blockbuster trend, embodied by the slogan "make them big, show them big, and sell them big," emerged in the late 1950s and continued to accelerate. Meanwhile, the market for cheaply made pictures had dried up by the early 1960s, as television networks increased the number of prime-time hours devoted to the airing of Hollywood film.[7] Changing distribution strategies also took their toll. In the 1950s, a new picture typically opened simultaneously in one or two first-run theaters in each of thirty-five markets. By the early 1960s, distribution had changed to take advantage of the geographical coverage of television advertising, and a picture might play in eight hundred to fifteen hundred theaters on the same day, including drive-ins, which began to play new releases just as they were opening in first-run theaters. This alleviated the need for inexpensive fill-in films, and the production of B movies gradually decreased.[8]

Simultaneously, an emerging baby-boom youth population was quickly becoming central to the evolution of American culture, and audience surveys indicated that a young, liberal audience was responding to newer, more socially conscious and innovative films.[9] The new freedom of expression gave rise to the "art theater," which offered an avenue for independently produced pictures with offbeat themes as well as for foreign products such as French new wave and Italian neorealist films. In 1950, less than a hundred of these specialized theaters existed, whereas by the mid-1960s over six hundred specialized theaters were in operation.[10]

The need to cater to this new audience allowed studios to accept more experimental film content by independent filmmakers. Kramer, labeled a "character" by conservatives in Hollywood, "the foremost of a very few willful independents," had attracted an avid following for his films, which confronted controversial issues such as racial prejudice in *Home of the Brave* (1949) and *The Defiant Ones* (1958). Because of his reputation and his successful track record, Kramer was not entirely motivated by financial or profit considerations. He found that he could produce films for personal reasons that were quite unpopular at the time. Kramer admitted that he was "emotionally drawn to these subjects," and filmed *On the Beach* primarily to "attempt to get people thinking about the arms race."[11]

As a veteran of the Hollywood industry, Kramer was experienced with the compromises required in order to promote his personal vision. He claimed that the managers of large companies were the toughest, most reactionary, and most adamant about what sort of pictures should be made, and independents had to find ways around their censoring pressure. His strategy was to cast big-name stars in controversial scripts, banking upon the star appeal to draw audiences to films with unpopular or particularly sobering themes. This "name casting" made his films competitive with more conventional fare: "If I want to play ball with the big boys, the old entrenched people who still control the industry—the all important machinery of distribution, then I have to play in their park and by their rules. . . . I have to know, for instance, if my budget is going to be a certain figure, I have to satisfy certain rules. If I am going to make a picture about the end of the world, I have to be smart about casting in order to sell it in their park."[12]

Another production strategy involved the formulaic necessity of focusing upon individual lives and romance in order to appeal to a wider audience. Fundamentally, *On the Beach*, as did many of Kramer's other controversial films, told a love story against a backdrop of social of political conflict.[13] Consequently, the film presents various characters played by big-name stars such as Ava Gardner, Gregory Peck, and Fred Astaire involved in romantic entanglements while awaiting their death from a drifting radioactive cloud. Adapted from Nevil Shute's novel about a civilization that created a device for its own destruction, the film begins after the atomic war is already over, and introduces what's left of the world's population as they wait for the drifting radioactive cloud to come and finish the job.

Although Kramer admitted that he ran into more trouble as a "creative producer" from movie industry pressure than from external sources, the production of *On the Beach* stands as one of the earliest confrontations with the Pentagon over film content. Until this time, few people in the film industry had questioned the military's right to ask for changes in scripts or to turn down requests for help if the story was unacceptable. The Pentagon's requirement for script approval on movies that requested its assistance, and the atmosphere of control and influence exerted over film content by the Department of Defense's Directorate for Public Information, eventually was criticized as censorship by many producers. By the time *On the Beach* was in production, few films had dared question the competency and wisdom of the military and its procedures.[14]

The military and Hollywood had historically enjoyed an unwritten partnership that benefited each. On their part, the Pentagon believed that the assistance they provided to filmmakers served their own interests, informing the public of the military's competence and ultimate value. In aiding film production, the Department of Defense was also allowed to change scripts to ensure that it was being presented in the best possible light. Filmmakers sought Pentagon assistance for expertise regarding the technical and procedural aspects of military life, in order to ensure a more accurate martial ambiance. Their aid was also a practical necessity, not only in saving filmmakers large amounts of money for sets and footage but also in providing military equipment unavailable from other sources. To obtain aircraft, aircraft carriers, submarines, and tanks, Hollywood producers had little choice but to submit scripts that portrayed the military establishment in a positive light. This relationship stemmed back to the earliest days of Hollywood production in such movies as *Military Scout* (1911), *Wings* (1927), *Air Force* (1943), and *Above and Beyond* (1954).

But as the Hollywood studio system broke down, traditional contacts and respect for the military simultaneously began to fade.[15] With the House Un-American Activities Committee discredited, the practice of blacklisting revoked and fading into memory, and the Production Code no longer a factor for censoring "unpatriotic themes," independent filmmakers saw the possibility of finding markets for their antimilitary movies, or for films that at least questioned military authority and procedures. Thus, in this evolving atmosphere, Kramer sought to criticize the consequences of the nuclear arms race and in so doing to ultimately criticize the military establishment.

In making the film, Kramer consulted scientists, who were divided on the question of whether the world's civilization would be totally destroyed in the event of a nuclear holocaust. Nevertheless, Kramer remained true to the original novel in its insistence that everyone—without exception—dies in the end. This aroused the ire of civil defense and military authorities; the assistant secretary of state disagreed with Kramer's idea that a nuclear war would wipe out the world's human population, stating that there would only be "eight or nine million casualties." Refusing to alter his script, Kramer was turned down in his request to borrow a nuclear submarine for the picture:[16] "I needed an atomic submarine for the film, but the Pentagon told me, 'No, your story says an atomic war would wipe out the world, and that isn't so. Only about five hundred million people would be killed.' I told them that's the closest I'd like to get to a total wipe out. So, since we would-n't change the script, we didn't get the atomic sub."[17]

Shooting *On the Beach* in Australia with a budget of $2.9 million, Kramer worked under contract with United Artists, who promoted the picture as a "status symbol," as something to be seen despite its grim nature. Banking upon the per-ceived importance of themes such as individual suicide and global extinction, United Artists released the film simultaneously in eighteen cities worldwide, in-cluding Moscow and Tokyo. The film was received with great fanfare and was lauded by some as a deterrent to further nuclear armament.[18] However, the film lost $700,000; according to *Variety,* its unpopularity was not necessarily due to its subject matter but rather to its "preachy quality." The picture was described as be-ing "as heavy as a leaden shroud. . . . The spectator is left with the sick feeling that he's had a preview of Armageddon, in which the contestants lost."[19]

The critical reactions and controversy surrounding the film, including the gov-ernment's attempts to censor it, focused attention upon the film's startling premise. *On the Beach* suggests the complete extinction of humanity, the death of the planet, with no explicit blame upon any specific country's responsibility for the first strike. American society doesn't heroically survive to begin again. Here, there are no survivors. There are also few distractions from the grim message—no invading aliens, no fallout shelters, no struggle back from a dreadful but enervat-ing postwar barbarism. "There are simply a man and a woman reaching the ago-nizing decision to kill their only child in its crib and commit suicide as the rest of the human race expires around them."[20]

The movie also was innovative in that it questioned the complex technology that the military controlled. This point was a conscious criticism. The film states that the fatal nuclear confrontation was started by "a handful of vacuum tubes and transistors, probably faulty." Kramer diverges from Shute's novel, which spec-ified that the war was started by nations deliberately attacking each other. This change in emphasis marks the beginning of the questioning of technology in the early 1960s, the worry that technical systems would grow and become more com-plex until "we couldn't control them."[21] Technical failures and human fallibility could rationally cause a nuclear accident, and the only solution would be to dis-mantle the entire nuclear apparatus.

Some praised the film as "one of the most successful dramatizations of ideas in recent film history, the thorough evolution of a particular nightmare which has been haunting our generation ceaselessly. . . . It is a powerful appeal for sanity in a tremulous world."[22]

Other sectors of American society condemned *On the Beach* as propaganda that distorted scientific fact. Senator Wallace F. Bennett of Utah accused Kramer of being a pacifist and of "playing the Soviet's game" by alarming the public with unjustifiable fears. Questions were raised by officials in President Eisenhower's cabinet, who feared that *On the Beach* would promote "ban the bomb" propaganda and discussed actions they might take to undermine the movie.[23] According to the government view, the movie was extremely misleading because there were not enough weapons in existence to spread the quantity of radioactivity required to sterilize the planet, and "it has been clearly demonstrated that there would be many survivors of an atomic attack."[24]

And, despite its intentions, the film also succumbs to a flowery and unrealistic portrayal of the postnuclear world. As *Time* pointed out:

> Customers are spared any scenes of realistic horror, and are asked to accept the movie notion of what is really horrible about the end of the world: boy (Gregory Peck) does not get girl (Ava Gardner). Though Kramer and company predict that *On the Beach* will "act as a deterrent to further nuclear armaments," the picture actually manages to make the most dangerous conceivable situation in human history seem rather silly and science-fictional.[25]

While waiting for the fatal radioactive cloud, the Earth's last remaining humans are depicted enjoying the conveniences of their doomed civilization. They carelessly cruise the terrain in flashy convertibles and Rolls-Royces, attend cocktail parties, and guzzle vintage wine. Then, calmly resigned to their fate, the last citizens meet their end by conveniently and painlessly consuming government-issued suicide pills. No one suffers radiation sickness; people and animals temporarily flourish while harboring an immense sense of denial about their fate and no sense of regret for their fellow humans' extinction elsewhere on the planet. As the submarine commandeered by Gregory Peck traces a mysterious radio transmission to somewhere near San Diego hoping to find niches of survivors, the cities and streets are portrayed as empty and deserted. The expected corpses, or at least a few scattered skeletal remains, are never shown. Death is hidden from view, a grim reality too discouraging, perhaps, to serve up to movie audiences.

Despite criticism that the film depicts a light-hearted version of suicide, *On the Beach* forced audiences to confront atomic war as a threat to existence, particularly at a time when concerns about the effects of fallout, and the arms race, were at their peak. It stands as the most serious attempt to tackle the issue of human extinction to come out of Hollywood in the 1950s, and was only produced because of Kramer's individual mandate to promote this kind of message, helped along by his fame as an independent producer. Naturally, Hollywood studios weren't anxious to duplicate this theme because of the dismal box-office returns, despite any "prestige" that United Artists might have earned in releasing it. No Hollywood-produced film again attempted to deal so explicitly with this issue until the mid-1970s.

The Postnuclear World

To prevent poor box-office returns while still capitalizing upon the increased public anxiety concerning the nuclear future, Hollywood studios concocted science fiction scenarios that critically speculated upon global nuclear war while offering an avenue of escape for the human species. These films incorporated various science fiction gimmicks such as time travel in presenting the postnuclear Earth far in the future. But, unlike the heroic survivors shown in films of the 1950s, the nuclear survivors of the early 1960s have been transformed into "the other." No longer appearing as familiar human characters simply having to endure a measure of post–nuclear war hardship, these new survivors are changed by their symbolic exposure to the confrontation; they are as different from "us" as if they had mutated through direct radiation exposure. These new concepts consistently assumed the inevitability of a future wide-scale nuclear confrontation and a dismal postnuclear environment for its survivors.

In 1960, media attention was increasingly focused upon the possibility of a Soviet first strike and the ensuing confrontation between the nuclear powers. Only two years earlier, the inevitability of such a confrontation had seemed to fade as both the United States and the Soviet Union had made unilateral commitments to halt to nuclear weapons testing. Prior to this ban, no U.S. administration would accept any restraint on the arms race. However, when the Soviets deployed their intercontinental delivery system, thus posing a real threat to the United States, the first postwar arms limitation agreement became possible and was signed in 1959.

But in May 1960, the Soviet Union shot down an American spy plane flying over Soviet territory, and the test ban was forgotten. As that year's presidential campaign heated up, John Kennedy focused upon the threatening "missile gap" that had supposedly developed between the United States and the Soviet Union, and he pushed for increased weapons development and an institutionalized civil defense program. In a speech he gave the next year after he had been elected president, Kennedy called for increased defense spending, punctuating his address with the slogan "the weapons of war must be abolished before they abolish us."[26] Ironically, Kennedy's prescription for ending war promoted the "peace through strength" doctrine, necessitating further nuclear weapons development to push the United States well ahead of any potentially aggressive nation.

In July 1961, Kennedy again addressed the nation over national radio and television. Implying that the world was on the brink of war because of the Soviet Union's position on West Berlin, Kennedy asked for a multi–billion dollar defense program, including a massive domestic civil defense agenda that stressed the immense gravity of a potential superpower confrontation.[27] As work began on the Berlin Wall in August, the Soviet Union resumed atmospheric testing of nuclear weapons for the first time in three years, and the United States followed suit the next month.

After Kennedy's national address, the Federal Civil Defense Agency was deluged with 6,000 letters a day, more than it used to receive in a month. The public was frantic for information concerning ways to protect life and property from the seemingly inevitable nuclear confrontation. Bomb shelters became a primary domestic concern, a fad verging on hysteria.[28] Predictably, these new opportunities for business development were quickly exploited. Almost overnight, swimming pool contractors became experts on bomb shelters, manufacturers marketed their products as "survival equipment," and banks offered loans for building the shelters. A public controversy arose between those who thought that the shelters would dissuade the enemy from launching a first attack and those who believed that shelters were a foolish waste of time because of the fatal effects of radiation. As a result of this argument, attention was centered upon the perceived effects of fallout, along with issues of social inequities. Many questions emerged in the public debate surrounding the civil defense agenda. Was it possible to survive radioactive dust? Would the environment of the planet be capable of supporting life after being exposed to large amounts of fallout? Since there would never be enough shelters for everybody, who would decide what individuals could utilize the shelters and who would be left outside?

Many believed that the combined effects of the initial nuclear blast, and its accompanying fallout, heat, and radiation, posed insurmountable obstacles to survival. By 1962, a majority of Americans assumed that if a nuclear bomb were dropped upon their city, fallout rather than the explosion would ultimately kill them. A report presented to the Kennedy administration by a panel of leading social scientists stated that many citizens expected "physical destruction to be almost universal and the post-attack world to be a hopeless shambles, in which everything worth living for would be irretrievably lost."[29]

Even so, a number of nuclear war survival manuals were published in the early 1960s that supported the government's position of the survivability of nuclear war. A 1961 "how-to" book entitled *You Can Survive the Bomb* posed this postnuclear scenario that embodied the "heroic survivor" concept so popular in the previous decade: "The aftermath, with its nagging low-level radiation, will create new problems to be solved, new hostile surroundings to be conquered only by courage and wit."[30]

Another manual, entitled *How to Survive an Atomic Bomb*, offered the reader a number of simple rules to follow in case of a nuclear attack. The book included instructions to follow during the initial explosion, such as to "lie down full-length on stomach with face in arms" and to "assume this position next to the nearest building," all the while down playing the effects of radiation.[31] As schoolchildren practiced "duck and cover" exercises in a variety of civil defense drills, government policy began to adopt more complex and convoluted rationales for increasing the nuclear arsenal.

Such public interest in the inevitability and survivability of nuclear war was immediately addressed by Hollywood producers. Film studios churned out scenarios that were contrived to depict the nuclear future as hospitable but dramatically changed from contemporary American society. For example, George Pal, under contract with MGM, produced a film version of H. G. Wells's novel *The Time Machine* (1960). Like *On the Beach*, the film portrayed the complete devastation of human civilization during an atomic war. However, to make the film more palatable to movie audiences, Pal altered the original ending of the novel in order to give humankind some hope for the future. Pal had, by this time, acquired a solid reputation with such other science fiction classics as *Destination Moon* (1950) and *War of the Worlds* (1953), and he sought to promote his own personal vision, a future that was bleak yet survivable.

The Wells novel offered a pessimistic view of the future in which human civilization degenerates into childlike people on the one hand and savages on the other; it presents the fate of humanity as hopeless. At the end of the book, the discouraged hero advances into the distant future only to see Earth orbiting a dying sun, humanity extinct, and large crablike creatures lumbering by the sterile sea awaiting their inevitable death. This was perhaps too gloomy a vision for the fate of human society in the early 1960s, hardly a profit maker. Pal chose to portray the future more optimistically; the hero of his version of *The Time Machine* heads back to the primitive society of the future to rebuild it with the help of the survivors.[32]

And yet the film advances the notion that post–nuclear holocaust survivors would be transformed, turned into something other than human. The time traveler, in venturing far into the future, finds a society divided between a race of blond humans who are raised as livestock to feed the horribly mutated but technologically advanced underground dwellers. Both of these groups have been transformed and are foreign to the humanly compassionate visitor from the past. The naive but beautiful humans have no emotions as we know them; in one scene, they lounge carelessly by a river as one of their companions drowns. They exhibit no interest in their own survival as they are rounded up by the underground dwellers for dinner. On the other hand, the mutated cannibals are also physically and intellectually removed from contemporary humankind as they slaughter their human food supply. It is as if, by 1960, the concept of transmutation and radiation had been inseparably linked, the fear of transformation inescapably linked with issues of nuclear development.

The Time Travelers (1964) also reestablishes the concepts of the inevitable nuclear confrontation, the dismal postnuclear environment, and the transformation of surviving humans into "the other." The story involves a group of present-day civilian scientists who construct and inadvertently enter a space-time continuum that transports them to the Earth of 2071. After fleeing the mutant survivors of a nuclear war who have overrun the surface of the Earth, the time-traveling scientists are given shelter by a group of "normal" humans. Later, it is revealed that this small band represents the only nonmutated survivors left on Earth, "descendants of far thinking scientists" who dwell underground in their technologically advanced society. However, they too must leave the planet in order to avoid eventual radiation sickness. The leader of the survivors offers this elucidation of the Earth's fate; the inevitable nuclear war of the future is presented with familiar stock footage of military atomic bomb tests:

> I wish I could tell you the reason was a natural catastrophe, but it was man's own folly. The destruction was total. Earth, our own hope, is now just a burnt out sterile

slag in space. The last few generations of mutated once humans, the offspring of the radiation saturated survivors, roam the desolate surface possessed by the insanity of crippling deformities of mind and body. When they are gone the Earth will be lifeless and as incapable of sustaining life as the barren moon itself.

However, although these heroic survivors of the future appear "normal," they are obviously lacking in some essential human attributes and are closer in nature and appearance to the alien invaders depicted in previous films. Uncompassionate and calculating, the survivors exterminate the relatively defenseless mutants with ease, referring to them as "deviants," although radiation has only slightly altered their appearance by deforming their hands and causing muteness. The mutants, it is learned, only seek food and assistance from the more advanced survivors, who choose to hoard whatever bounty remains on Earth for themselves. Their advanced technology supplies them with specialized farming, entertainment, and even mechanical androids who act as servants and guards. The film depicts their luxurious lifestyle, while outside the mutants scavenge for food. Additionally, these survivors of the future, while generous with the time travelers, make it clear that they plan to abandon them to a certain death when they complete their rocket. The humans have become transformed as a result of nuclear intervention into "the other," abnormal and not quite human.

With this bleak prospect, the time travelers attempt to reconstruct the time portal in order to return and warn their contemporaries of their possible future. The time travelers are superior human beings, if not in intellect then in their compassion and emotion. They kindly rescue the nuclear survivors after their spaceship explodes before the launch, and they all try to return together to the twentieth century. This also fails, and the travelers are trapped in a time loop, forced to repeat past events over and over and, to the misfortune of humankind, unable to intervene and prevent the future they have witnessed.

Such depictions of the Earth's future established postnuclear civilization as a grim prospect, in which survivors become inhuman alien creatures rather than heroic figures ready to begin civilization anew. This theme was revisited throughout the early 1960s in science fiction films such as *Beyond the Time Barrier* (1960), in which a time-traveling air force pilot finds the mutant survivors of a nuclear war doomed by a deadly "cosmic nuclear plague"; and *Creation of the Humanoids* (1962), in which 92 percent of the human race is wiped out by atomic bombs and the rest are transformed into androids controlled by robotlike automation devices.

Such imaginative visions of humanity's dismal future emphasized the real implications of nuclear warfare, a consideration not usually found in previous films. Hollywood science fiction began to take a critical view of the official policy on nuclear defense and the arms race rather than merely focusing on the perceived effects of domestic testing. Such films as *The Underwater City* (1962) argued against the possibility of finding safe and practical shelter in the event of a nuclear war. *The Flight That Disappeared* (1961) questioned the ethical basis for weapons development, portraying three Pentagon scientists who are put on trial by a heavenly jury of unborn generations regarding the consequences of their nuclear weapons development. In the end, they decide to destroy their research notes and give up the development of atomic weapons. In *Twelve to the Moon* (1960), a crew of scientists representing twelve nations lands on the moon, only to discover a superior civilization whose leaders admonish the Earth people for bearing "the seeds of greed and destruction" and threaten to freeze the Earth unless humankind stops making nuclear weapons.

All these films question the nuclear buildup of the early 1960s and the implications of this buildup for the future of the planet. Survivors no longer merely have to fend off easily eliminated mutated monsters and go on to create a better world. Instead, the future holds mutations more human than monster and worlds that are inhospitable and unsurvivable. The "heroic survivors" in these landscapes are not as attractive as their cinematic predecessors, and they have lost many of their human qualities. The mutated subterranean cannibals in *The Time Machine* may thrive in their technologically advanced civilization with its ingenious system of food supply, but they are far from human.

Hollywood had begun to explore the ethical implications of nuclear technology and to question the consequences of its use, still safely within the science fiction genre. This exploration logically ventured to address the role of the people who had ultimate control over atomic power—the government bureaucracy, the military, and the scientists. Such critical portrayals and direct questioning of government policy began to lead Hollywood away from the science fiction genre and toward more realistic and dramatic productions.

9

Questioning Authority

Government and military officials discuss the worst-case scenario in *Fail-Safe* (1964)

and the erosion of the Cold War ideology during the early 1960s gave Hollywood producers the courage to ignore the potential wrath of the Pentagon and to produce pictures that focused upon the negative side of military leadership. In earlier years, Hollywood products had typically represented the American military as infallible, noble, and all-conquering. But by the time President Kennedy had come to office, the black-and-white delineation of the free world versus the monolithic communist world had become blurred. China and the Soviet Union were no longer allies, Yugoslavia's Tito was a friendly communist, Khrushchev had toured the United States and appeared less cruel and inhumane than his predecessors. Despite the Bay of Pigs invasion and the Cuban Missile Crisis, monolithic ideological Cold War perceptions seemed to be fading away. Gradually, negative depictions of the military evolved from the pervasively positive images promoted since the early 1950s.[1]

Before Dwight Eisenhower left office, he had warned of the dangers of the military industrial complex, and the subsequent Bay of Pigs fiasco was attributed by some to poor military planning and advice.[2] The military confrontation of the Cuban Missile Crisis brought the American people face to face with the reality of potential nuclear confrontation, forcing them, for the first time since the atomic bombing of Japan, to examine the premises on which the military had preserved peace through the ever present threat of massive retaliation to an enemy attack. The threat of nuclear missiles only ninety miles away from the shores of the United States shocked most Americans into an awareness of the continued danger the bomb posed. Yet even with the subsequent signing of the Nuclear Test Ban Treaty in 1963, the military seemed to be conducting business as usual, calling for more bombs, more bombers, more submarines, and more missiles. With this contradiction between national expectations and Pentagon activities, the arms forces found themselves and their methods the subject of question in Congress, in the news media, and on motion picture screens.[3]

Science fiction films about the atomic bomb could provide an avenue for questioning the nature of war and criticizing the military without having to portray combat or raise the issue of so-called "necessary wars." Filmmakers in the 1960s suggested that the bomb's only function was most likely the destruction of modern civilization, and they presented a picture of the disastrous consequences of nuclear power in the hands of a few power-hungry and ultimately fallible individuals. Since the armed forces had committed themselves to nuclear defense, consequently any criticism of the bomb would by its very nature be critical of the military and its reliance upon nuclear weapons. Not only were military officers and scientists scrutinized but also the technology that they controlled, and upon which the smooth operation of the nuclear defense system depended, became suspect as well.

The Military

At first glance, *Voyage to the Bottom of the Sea* (1961) seems to epitomize the lofty summit to which the military, and the military scientist, had aspired in the movies of the previous decade. The film begins by celebrating an imaginary atomic submarine, christened the *Seaview,* designed by the world-renowned scientist-inventor Admiral Nelson. The opening scene presents the admiral commanding his creation; the naval personnel operate with precision, following orders and pushing buttons with unquestioning devotion to their commander and their duty. The admiral beams as he describes the missile room to a group of visitors: "There is more destructive force in this room than all the explosives in World War II." As the submarine surfaces, leaps, and dives in the sea like a slick metallic dolphin, Nelson is hailed by the news media as "the great man, the great inventor, the predominant scientific genius of our time." Nelson himself delivers lines such as these with tongue-twisting precision: "The wild dreams of today are the practical realities of tomorrow. . . . We hope to see sights never before seen by man, and by seeing solve some of the mysteries of the deep!"

But all is not well in this cinematic world, neither below nor above the sea. Upon surfacing in the Antarctic, Nelson discovers that the Van Allen Belt of radiation has suddenly burst into flame and threatens to destroy the Earth. Soon, "the greatest scientific minds in the world are working round the clock for methods of survival." Nelson proposes a plan in which a Polaris missile is shot into the belt, thereby causing it to explode backward and avoid the planet. But the United Nations, dominated by wildly gesticulating foreigners, rejects his theory as being too dangerous. In this "snide and gratuitous caricature of the UN," the scientists are depicted as histrionic, foreign-accented buffoons, who call Nelson's plan "suicidal insanity."[4] Nelson, however, refuses to bend to their questionable authority. Still in sole control of the *Seaview,* "the world's most powerful weapon," he retorts: "I take my orders from the President of the United States." Nelson quickly sets off with his crew to the coordinates from which the missile must be launched, with angry UN police and submarines at his heels.

Soon, his control of the crew and command of the submarine begin to erode. Washington cannot be reached by radio, and presumably all government officials have fled to seek out cooler regions of the planet. Therefore, the Earth's fate is ultimately in Nelson's hands, and he decides unilaterally to go along with his controversial plan. This decision made, his power-hungry and domineering nature reveals itself in his ambition to be the savior of the planet. After rescuing one survivor of a scientific expedition on an iceberg, he brazenly abandons the rest of the party, to the general disgust of his crew. He rationalizes this decision on the basis of implementing his plan: "If we waste any time here, there may be no survivors left anywhere in the world." He knowingly causes the submarine to make an emergency dive before UN police have safely transferred to their own vessel, callously jeopardizing their lives, an act that begins to turn his crew against him.

After fighting off a giant squid and maneuvering through a mine field, the *Seaview* faces an even greater threat from the survivor of the scientific expedition. A foreign-accented religious fanatic, the scientist begins preaching to the disheartened crew that this end is God's will and is inevitable. Soon, a mutiny develops among crew members who are convinced that Nelson's plan will only accelerate the Earth's inevitable demise, and who wish to return to their families to await extinction. Nelson quells the mutiny by allowing those wishing to leave to disembark onto an abandoned ship found floating at sea. Next, saboteurs attempt to kill Nelson, as the remaining crew begins to question his authority and doubt his sanity. Despite all these obstacles, Nelson, in his single-minded obsession with proving his plan correct and saving the world, manages to send the Polaris into space and extinguish the fire. The experiment proves successful and the Earth is prevented from becoming a roasted cinder.

Despite this successful planetary rescue, one is left with the uneasy feeling that it was one individual, scientific genius or not, who single-handedly decided the fate of the world. Because of his position of military power, of control over nuclear technology, Nelson was able to disregard the authority of elected officials and force the implementation of his own risky plan. He is ultimately successful, as most military heroes in Hollywood film are, but questions concerning the fallibility of the individual, particularly one who controls crucial technology, are evident in this movie. Even film critics viewed the basis of the film skeptically: "Essentially, the picture seems to be dedicated to the proposition that an eminent man with a theory ought to be allowed to try it out even though it may be at the risk of the world. . . . [This proposition] made me uneasy about . . . unquestioning obedience to a strong man's will."[5]

Fail-Safe (1964) also focused upon the individuals who hold the atomic arsenal at their command, ultimately questioning this system and its reliance upon human dependability and the technology they supposedly control. Intrinsic weaknesses within the military establishment and the political safeguards meant to avert any possibility of nuclear accidents occurring are critically scrutinized within the narrative of the film. It demonstrates the decisionmaking process in times of potential nuclear crisis, the basic premise being the possibility of a mechanical malfunction or human error leading to the unintentional detonation of a hydrogen bomb.

Here, the paranoia of communist infiltration found in earlier films is replaced with the true horror of the potential of global destruction. A mood of depression pervades the action of the film, as a faulty computer initiates a Strategic Air Command (SAC) strike force. Based on the novel *Fail-Safe* by Eugene Burdick and Harvey Wheeler, the story was serialized in the *Saturday Evening Post* in October 1962, the same month as the Cuban Missile Crisis. Producer Max Youngstein, himself a member of the National Committee for a Sane Nuclear Policy (SANE), produced the film under contract with Paramount.

The story begins a few years in the future, in 1967, and initially provides the audience with voyeuristic glimpses into the lives of certain military employees lives.

Scenes of domestic turmoil and strife, an intimate bedroom conversation between a SAC general and his wife, another SAC officer caring for his aging parents
in a cheap basement apartment, all demonstrate the ordinary humanness of these
individuals who are responsible for the maintenance of the overpowering national defense system. Next, the film introduces guests chatting about the nuclear
future during an elegant dinner party. A pragmatic and cynical professor, who
acts as a civilian advisor to the Pentagon, dominates the conversation, which involves speculation over how many millions of causalities are acceptable in war:

PROFESSOR: Face facts, we're talking about war. I say any war, even thermonuclear war, must have winners and losers. Which would you rather be?
GUEST: In a nuclear war, everyone loses. War isn't what it used to be.
PROFESSOR: It's still the resolution of political and economic conflict.
GUEST: What kind of resolution with 100 million dead? . . . A culture
   with most of its people dead, the food poisoned, the air unbreathable,
   you call that a culture?
PROFESSOR: I'd rather have an American culture survive than a Russian
   one.

A tour of SAC headquarters also erupts into a questioning of the ethics and ra-
tionality of the U.S. defense apparatus. An argument breaks out between a visit-
ing senator and SAC generals concerning the defense system's reliance upon technology and its potential for failure:

SENATOR: Who voted who the power to do it this particular way?
GENERAL: It's the nature of technology, machines are developed to meet
   situations.
SENATOR: Then they take over and begin to make situations.
GENERAL: We have checks on everything, checks and counter checks.
SENATOR: Who checks the checker? Who is ultimately responsible? The
   only thing that everyone can agree upon is that no one is responsible.

Meanwhile, at the SAC's Omaha headquarters, the malfunction of a minor
electronic device creates a coded message that sends an American bomber group
toward the Soviet Union to bomb Moscow. Soon, an ongoing conversation is conducted between the U.S. president; strategizers in a war room, including the professor from the dinner party, the secretary of defense, and other military officials;
the Soviet premier in Moscow; and SAC Omaha Headquarters. Various measures
are adopted in order to stop the planes; American jets and Soviet fighters try to
shoot them down, but special decoy maneuvers foil their attackers. The U.S. president and the SAC bomb squad commander's wife both try, through radio contact, to convince the squadron of the error, but to no avail. SAC personnel have
been indoctrinated to anticipate every kind of countermeasure from the Soviet
enemy, and the very safeguards to foil such gimmickry keeps the bombers on
their course. Since the air force is unable to recall the bombers or to shoot them

down, Moscow is obliterated. The U.S. president, to appease the Soviet leadership and avoid their retaliation, is forced to trade one annihilated city for another, and orders SAC to blow up New York City with two twenty-megaton hydrogen bombs. The pilot who triggers the dropping of these bombs immediately commits suicide. Scenes of New York street life freeze, then the screen goes black. A disclaimer added by the producers to appease the Department of Defense and to avoid any attempts at censorship claims: "A rigidly enforced system of controls and safeguards insure that occurrences such as those depicted in this story cannot happen."

Ironically, such rhetoric is directly echoed by the film's dialogue, and whatever reassurances the Department of Defense hoped to provide with the disclaimer must have been lost—only serving to link the action of the film to the realm of possibility even more.

The issues of human fallibility and an overcomplicated and incomprehensible defense technology were rare topics in the films of this time. The films of the 1950s had avoided serious pondering over the ethical implications of nuclear war and had instead placed all hope and praise in the competency of the military hero. These characters had become almost superhuman in their capacity to handle, fairly and competently, all situations they were faced with. But here, the soundness of the technology and the military system upon the which the nuclear arsenal depended is questioned.

The military characters are portrayed as ultimately human, with human weaknesses, unlike the military heroes of earlier films such as *Above and Beyond*. In *Fail-Safe*, they become victims of the overwhelming technological and security apparatus, of security measures so stringent and dependent on rules that they ultimately create the inability to halt the impending disaster. These military actors are intelligent people trying to use their wits and their techniques to correct an error that has occurred through their overreliance on the efficiency of machines.[6] The U.S. defense system is presented as something inherently flawed, as it is dependent upon elements that have been stressed to the breaking point. Dialogue in *Fail-Safe* continually reiterates this point:

> It doesn't matter, man or machine, something failed. Maybe we'll never know.
> The more complex a machine gets, the more its chance of failure . . . maybe like a person, it just gets tired.
> We're setting up a war machine that acts faster than the ability of men to handle it.

As in films produced during the previous decade, the civilian scientist ultimately fares the worst. The scientist in *Fail-Safe* fanatically insists upon war; his vehement Cold War exclamations seem absurd and even insignificant when juxtaposed to the contemplative and concerned demeanors assumed by the military characters. He shouts: "These are Marxist fanatics, not normal people . . . they are calculating machines," and yet the Soviet premier is portrayed as being ultimately noble and humane, even as he is confronted with his own ultimate destruction. The scientist prods his colleagues in the war room to "take advantage of our chance" and continue a first strike. "Do you believe that communism is not our mortal enemy?" he blasts at a general who insists that the weapons buildup is out of hand, and who has been pushing for an arms reduction agreement. This depiction of the corrupt and fanatical civilian scientist was to emerge even more as a theme in Hollywood productions.

The Scientist

Although members of the military were still depicted as competent and compassionate in most Hollywood productions, the image of civilian scientists continued to degenerate, particularly those in control of nuclear technology. One example of the reemerging theme of control over nuclear power ultimately corrupting an otherwise compassionate and responsible scientist can be found in the 1965 film *Crack in the World*. Here, it is a civilian scientist gone mad with personal ambition who nearly destroys the world. This film also stands as one of the last Hollywood products to incorporate atomic energy into its plot for many years to come, although it is the first to question the effects of the domestic use of nuclear technology.

The film focuses on a nuclear bomb that is exploded in the Earth's crust, creating a giant crack that threatens the continued existence of the planet. The narrative begins at the desert headquarters of "Project Inner Space," where Nobel prize–winning scientist Dr. Sorenson is conducting a tour of his underground laboratory to a UN commission. He is hoping to obtain their approval to use a hydrogen bomb donated by the U.S. military to burn a hole into the Earth's crust. He explains purpose of this endeavor: "Our target is the magma. If we can succeed in bringing this molten mass to the surface, under controlled conditions, we'll have all the energy we can use . . . all the electricity for all kinds of industry."

He goes on echoing the Project Plowshares rhetoric still found in the media of the time: "To obtain limitless energy has been a dream of mankind for thousands of years—now for the first time we can obtain it without poisonous waste materials. . . . If this is successful we can transform all the continents and make a life of plenty for all mankind."

With the blessing of the UN, he begins the countdown to detonation. A gigantic atomic explosion incorporating the ever popular stock footage is presented. After the smoke and fire clears, the experiment is judged a success and the scientist is praised. "A new era has begun," an official joyously exclaims, as fiery red magma flows from the blasted opening, which is soon safely capped. Dr. Sorenson beams at a press conference before the contained magma, speaking of "visions of the future." But all is not well in the Earth's crust. Massive earthquakes, tidal waves, and floods soon begin occurring along a natural earthquake fault. A rival scientist, who had unsuccessfully attempted to block the experiment, finds that his pessimistic predictions are coming true. He explains: "The Earth's crust had already been cracked by the numerous underground explosions set off by the nuclear powers in their years of testing."

The planet, already weakened and vulnerable because of man's nuclear experimentation, has now been dealt its death blow. Soon the Earth will become "merely a cloud of astral dust orbiting the sun." A commission consisting of government officials and scientists meets to debate the immediate future, and uncontrollable squabbling breaks out. A military officer argues with the scientist responsible for the disaster about the problems of civilian nuclear development:

MILITARY OFFICER: You took a calculated risk, which was more risk than calculation.
SCIENTIST: Haven't you, as an officer, ever taken a calculated risk?
MILITARY OFFICER: As a military officer, I can. You, a civilian, cannot. I always said we shouldn't have left this in the hands of civilians.

The scientist, suffering from guilt and dying of a rapidly spreading disease, is admonished for his personal ambition by his fellow scientists: "You're mad. You'll either save the world or destroy it. You've taken an insane risk."

Soon, the scientist drops yet another bomb into a volcano in an attempt to "relieve the pressure in the Earth's crust." This attempt also fails, but the progressing crack changes direction. As the scientist sacrifices his life to "record more information," a huge chunk is blown out of the Earth's crust and becomes an orbiting moon. What remains of the planet, and its population, is saved. The civilian scientist completely disregards his moral responsibilities and takes an unreasonable risk in the interests of personal ambition, while his military counterparts take a saner approach.

Ridicule and Parody: *Dr. Strangelove* (1964)

By 1964, the genre of the Hollywood atomic war film, with its narrative style and ideologically tinged conventions, had become so standard and familiar that it could now be successfully parodied. Such a film was *Dr. Strangelove: Or, How I Learned to Stop Worrying and Love the Bomb* (1964) produced by veteran film director Stanley Kubrick. Kubrick, who had been wondering how to send the world a message about the nuclear buildup, adapted the plot from Peter George's 1958 novel *Red Alert*.[7] Although not a Hollywood product, the film bears mention in this context because it stands as a unique example of parody of Hollywood nuclear films, particularly of the serious endeavor of *Fail-Safe*, and provides a thoughtful criticism of American defense policy and the military establishment. It suggests, as does *Fail-Safe*, that the military does not truly control the bomb and that a nuclear accident is inevitable.

Both *Fail-Safe* and *Dr. Strangelove* were released in 1964, at the time the public seemed more attuned to the humor and pessimism of the latter. When the novel

Fail-Safe was published in 1962, the public was deeply concerned about nuclear issues and the mounting arms race, punctuated by the October Cuban Missile Crisis. But by 1964, the immediate gravity of nuclear topics was waning, partly because of the Nuclear Test Ban Treaty, which had been signed in 1963. *Dr. Strangelove* brazenly raised the question of nuclear annihilation, which had been inhibited and suppressed before this time. The unique tone of *Dr. Strangelove* prefigured the popular rebellion against total and unnecessary war.

To provide assistance in film production, the air force had always insisted on the serious and factual presentation of its procedures and on positive portrayals of those who had their fingers on the switches of the nuclear arsenal. Knowledge that Hollywood was preparing two films about accidental nuclear warfare without Pentagon approval moved air force Chief of Staff Curtis LeMay to encourage producer Sy Bartlett to make *Gathering of Eagles* (1963), in order to show the American people that the air force was doing its job in a responsible manner.[8] The film still relied upon the pseudodocumentary style developed in the 1950s to convey its message. However, poor box-office returns indicated that 1960s audiences were no longer interested in viewing the air force's story in simple and uncritical terms.[9]

By 1961, the Rand Corporation, a think tank of social scientists sponsored by the U.S. Navy, began to study and question the global and economic implications of the arms buildup between the United States and the Soviet Union At the crux of the debate was the concept of deterrence, or "mutually assured destruction," which rested upon the ability to completely destroy the enemy. Herman Kahn, a Rand physicist, published *On Thermonuclear War,* which presented the idea of deterrence through a device that would be set to automatically destroy the world if bombs were detonated over territory of the owner of the device. The aggressor would be committing global suicide by launching a first attack.[10] The concept of a "doomsday machine" was born, only to be ridiculed later in *Dr. Strangelove.*

Dr. Strangelove presents America's national nuclear strategy as irrational, suicidal, and insane. The film's plot, absurdist in style, is parallel to that of *Fail-Safe,* even to its focus upon a war room and a red phone line linking the Soviet premier and the U.S. president. Modern society's accelerating technological inevitability, political impotence, and stupidity are all targets of satire, which reaches its peak with the presentation of the diabolical "doomsday machine" capable of triggering total nuclear annihilation.

Having made an antimilitary statement in *Paths of Glory* (1957), Kubrick began in the late 1950s to read books on nuclear warfare and strategy, and was finally struck by "people's virtually listless acquiescence in the possibility—in fact, increasing probability—of nuclear war."[11] He estimated that he had read seventy books on the subject of the atomic bomb; he also maintained a file of relevant articles and had interviewed Thomas Schelling and Herman Kahn, the author of *On Thermonuclear War* and *Thinking About the Unthinkable.*[12] With Peter George's novel *Red Alert,* Kubrick found a fictional source for his belief in the possibility of an accidental nuclear war, and he intended to develop the novel into a film:

> But after a month or so I began to realize that all things I was throwing out were the things which were most truthful. After all, what could be more absurd than the very idea of two mega powers willing to wipe out all human life because of an accident, spiced up by political differences that will seem as meaningless to people in a hundred years from now as the theological conflicts of the Middle Ages appear to us today?[13]

Kubrick tried to follow the serious tone of the novel in working on the screenplay, but he soon found that each time he created a scene, it turned out to be comic. As a result, the film became a satire. *Dr. Strangelove* criticized not only the bomb but also military and government leaders, and even the system, the premises upon which it operates, and the people who run it.

Kubrick unofficially approached the air force to discuss their cooperation in making the film, and the service told him that his misrepresentation of the Positive Control safeguards against accidental nuclear war precluded any Pentagon assistance. According to military officials, this system was fail-safe, and naturally they refused to give Kubrick any help.[14] Kubrick re-created a B-52 cockpit and cabin from magazine pictures, used a B-52 model in front of a moving matte, and eventually created an ambience that was acceptable as reality.[15]

Dr. Strangelove adopts the familiar routines of the nuclear war film; for example, the opening shot presents a SAC bomber flying over arctic terrain to this explanatory voice-over: "For more than a year, ominous rumors had been privately circulating among high level western leaders that the Soviet Union had been at work on what was darkly hinted to be the ultimate weapon—a doomsday device."

Stock air force footage of bombers refueling midair are combined with elaborate sets of the war room, complete with a round table and an illuminated map of targets in the Soviet Union. Jargon about "code red," "go codes," "plan R," and "operation drop kick" are volleyed with candid tongue-in-cheek delivery by caricatures of a U.S. president, various military officers, and a stereotyped mad scientist known as Dr. Strangelove. The narrative centers on a crazed General Jack Ripper's plan to dispatch his bombers to destroy the Soviet Union and thereby purify the world of evil communist elements. Cold War rhetoric is taken to an extreme of ridicule; the crazed General Ripper talks of "war being too important to be left to politicians," claiming that the air force must take responsibility and try to stop the international communist conspiracy. "The commie has no regard for human life, not even his own. One must be continually on guard," the troops are instructed.

Fun is made of all elements of the military and political bureaucracy involved in the defense system—the "human reliability tests" administered to officers in an attempt to negate the possibility of human fallibility, the complex and paranoid retaliatory safeguards, the squabbling over how many causalities to expect ("we'll come out of this with no more than 10 to 20 million killed, tops"). Finally, the doomsday device, which will automatically trigger itself in the event of atomic attack on the Soviet Union, and is set up to be run by a network of computers; it echoes the "mutually assured destruction" agenda adopted before 1964 by the Department of Defense: "A doomsday shroud, a lethal cloud of radioactivity which will encircle the Earth for 93 years . . . a defense which will destroy all human and animal life of Earth . . . when it is detonated it will produce so much radioactive fallout that it will cause the Earth to become as lifeless as the moon."

Contemporary deterrence arguments are taken to their absurd extremes in the dialogue about "defensive gaps". Missile gaps and defense gaps make way for the competition over a "doomsday gap" (the Soviet Union developed a doomsday device before the United States); and near the end of the film, concern over a "mine shaft gap" emerges when the American citizens who will take refuge from the lethal fallout in mine shafts will compete with the Soviets over space in the shafts. Such extravagant ridicule of the American military, government personnel, and nuclear defense policy was a novel development foreshadowing the social and political discontent that developed as the decade progressed.

Both *Fail-Safe* and *Dr. Strangelove* can be viewed as exploitation films capitalizing upon the intense public interest and debate surrounding the Cuban Missile Crisis. The crisis had reached its peak a year before these films were produced. On October 22, 1962, after weeks of mounting anxiety about whether the Soviets might be installing nuclear-armed missiles on Cuba, President Kennedy delivered a televised address to the nation. He announced that Soviet missiles had been placed in Cuba and warned that in the event missiles were fired from Cuba to any country in the Western Hemisphere, the United States would respond with a direct attack upon the Soviet Union. Demanding that the missiles be immediately removed, Kennedy placed military units on alert and ordered a naval blockade of Cuba. The crisis caused the public's nuclear fear to peak, and food hoarding became prevalent across the country.

It has been noted that the Cuban Missile Crisis marked a turning point in American nuclear policy. The outcome of the crisis amounted to a tacit bilateral arms-control agreement. On a broader scale, the crisis led to a quest for coexistence and a new spirit of accommodation between the leaders of the United States and the Soviet Union.[16] When *Dr. Strangelove* was released in 1964, the Cuban Missile Crisis was still fresh in people's minds, and the film contributed a critical view to public discussion about accidental nuclear warfare. Lewis Mumford, for example, called it a "first break" in the nation's "cold war trance": "What the wacky characters in *Dr. Strangelove* are saying is precisely what needs to be said: this nightmare eventuality that we have concocted for our children is nothing but a crazy fantasy, by nature as horribly crippled and dehumanized as Dr. Strangelove himself.[17]

But these films also marked the end of Hollywood's attempts at exploiting the nuclear issue, for a time. In August 1963, the United States, the Soviet Union, and Great Britain signed the Nuclear Test Ban Treaty, which halted all atmospheric nuclear weapons tests and appeared to alleviate the public's anxiety about wide-scale radiation and nuclear war. The international agreement came after seventeen years of negotiations between the western allies and the Soviet Union. Although at the time of the signing most tests in the United States were already being conducted underground, during the months before the agreement came into effect there was wide public debate over the possible impact of the test ban upon American national security. However, the problems caused by radioactive fallout from atmospheric testing, and concern that testing not pollute the atmosphere or the oceans, pushed the ban through. For instance, Linus Pauling, a leading proponent of the ban, argued for the treaty, supporting his view with evidence from his scientific studies on the damaging effects of radiation exposure.[18]

Predictably, opposition to the ban came from the Atomic Energy Commission (AEC) and the Pentagon. Government scientists argued that radiation control would be a minor factor in a nuclear confrontation and that the dangers of fallout had been exaggerated and falsely linked to atmospheric tests. Pentagon officials claimed that the ban would "weaken our military capabilities" in the race to retain military superiority over the Soviet Union.[19] Finally, the treaty was signed not with the primary motivation to "rid the world from fears and dangers of radioactive fallout" but for political advantages. In a speech before the UN by President Kennedy in 1963, Kennedy presented the ban as a way of "reducing world tension, preventing the spread of nuclear weapons to nations not possessing them, and limiting the arms race." It was promoted as simply a "symbolic first step" toward reducing world tension and resolving international conflict.[20]

The treaty prohibited any nuclear explosions that would create "radioactive debris" detectable outside the originating country. This move did reduce environmental fallout, in spite of the facts that France and China refused to sign the treaty and continued to test in the atmosphere and that venting from underground tests also released radioactive particles into the air. As an arms control measure, the treaty was disappointing. Tests continued in underground shafts at a faster pace than before; the United States tested more weapons in the five years after the "test ban" than in the previous five years. And the treaty was not a deterrent to the arms race, since both the Soviet Union and the United States began developing ballistic and antiballistic missile systems that did not rely upon atmospheric testing.

The treaty did, however, create a false sense of security and helped shift the nuclear arms race out of the public limelight. When testing moved underground in 1963, the familiar mushroom cloud disappeared from the horizon and most of its critics went with it, resulting in a sharp decline in culturally expressed engagement with the atomic bomb issue. The nuclear theme largely disappeared from film and television, emerging rarely in fiction and popular music.[21] Whereas in 1959 64 percent of Americans believed that nuclear war was the nation's most urgent problem, by 1964 the figure had dropped to 16 percent. Soon, the topic completely vanished from the surveys.[22]

The fear of the effects of fallout gradually subsided as the public's attention turned to the more immediate problems of the Vietnam War and domestic issues such as the civil rights movement. The war in Vietnam began to monopolize the attention of the media, the government, and the antiwar groups, particularly when the major escalation took place in 1965. The growing loss of life created a sense of urgency and immediacy, and the consequences of nuclear weapons development and testing became more abstract and remote. By the mid-1960s, even SANE's directives had focused entirely upon Vietnam.

The editor of *Bulletin of Atomic Scientists,* Eugene Rabinowitch, set the hands of the "clock of doom" back a few minutes when he wrote:

> We are not succumbing to a facile optimism engendered by a change in climate of our diplomatic relations with the Soviet Union, or to the exhilaration engendered by the personal contacts of the leaders of the great powers and their visits to different countries of the world. We want to express in this move our belief that a new cohesive force has entered the interplay of forces shaping the fate of mankind, and is making the future . . . a little less foreboding.[23]

With radioactive fallout presumably contained in shafts below the Earth's surface, the fears of the dangers of atomic testing were put to rest. Even so, at this time researchers began to investigate the health of those directly affected by the testing program in the American Southwest. In 1963, AEC scientists found that the original estimates of the hazards caused by radiation exposure were too low, citing increased incidents of death from leukemia in Utah from 1950 to 1964 and an increase in deaths overall from 1959 to 1960. Fearing that publicity concerning this issue would be detrimental to the continuing underground testing program, the AEC advised against formal investigation, and the problem was temporarily forgotten.[24]

The American public paid relatively little heed to the continuing development of bigger and more deadly nuclear weaponry, while the bomb shelter craze died out shortly after the Cuban Missile Crisis. Over the next decade, two politically contradictory reactions to national defense directives emerged. One mandate sought to develop more powerful and effective defense systems in order to gain, and maintain, superiority over the Soviet Union. The other strove to attain security from such weaponry development by attempting to contain it with treaties.[25] The various arms limitations negotiations and treaties during these years did not stop the arms race, but they did give the impression that progress was being made to avoid the hazards of nuclear war and that the experts had the problem well in hand.

After the early 1960s, films in the science fiction genre had all but disappeared, giving way to Westerns, spy movies, and social dramas. After the post-Sputnik burst of film that climaxed in *Dr. Strangelove* and other works released in 1964, the ensuing years were marked by surprisingly little explicit cultural concern with nuclear issues. The topic of nuclear war and its implications had been exploited to the point of satire, and had inevitably lost its viability as a successful Hollywood product.

10

From Mutually Assured Destruction to Mutant Ninja Turtles

Last surviving humans ponder the future in *On the Beach* (1959)

THE FINDINGS IN THIS STUDY REAFFIRM THE THEORY that any area of popular culture is made up of a very complex mix of residual, dominant, and emergent elements, with many internal conflicts and contradictions among these.[1] Film content consists of a large number of "texts," often standard and repetitive, which are composed on the basis of certain stylized conventions, often drawing on familiar images present in the culture of the makers and receivers of texts, a reworking or incorporation of themes and images from the historic past of a culture. Film content can sometimes capitalize upon popular anxieties through the use of metaphor and the selection of specific genres. In the case of atomic technology, Hollywood selectively incorporated an existing body of residual themes available within the culture in order to address the fears and anxieties of audiences and to allow a venue for questioning the wisdom of the official government agenda. At the same time, these potentially oppositional sentiments were defused, and governmental criticism and pressure was avoided by holding the images within the margins of Cold War ideology.

This Cold War ideology operated as a pervasive and deliberate cultural influence that served to interpret the development of atomic issues in a covert but consistent manner. The potentially oppositional metaphors that could not necessarily be contained by the prevailing ideological notions, such as the residual themes of transmutation and death rays, were in one sense appropriated by the dominant culture and rendered unthreatening in their film resolutions. On the other hand, these retribution metaphors were allowed to flourish, because they were harmless enough and apparently posed no threat. Whatever their degree of internal controversy and variation, they did not in the end exceed the limits of the central definitions of the culture.[2] The selective tradition in which Hollywood operates, the way in which an entire range of meaning and practices from the past and/or present are adopted, reinterpreted, and diluted, are involved in the making and remaking of the dominant culture. It is continuously active and adjusting, and alternative senses of the world, differing opinions and attitudes, can be tolerated and accommodated to a certain extent within this culture.

Depictions of nuclear technology and the consequences of its use continue to appear in Hollywood film. However, the development of the imagery associated with the bomb and the selection of its pertinent issues, its technology, the individuals and institutions that controlled it, and radiation's effects upon the environment, occurred between the years 1945 to 1963. The success and influence of films incorporating atomic themes coincided with larger social issues such as the rapid technological advances in nuclear fusion, ICBMs and satellite technology; political events and policies like the Korean War and the Atomic Energy Commission's domestic testing program; and a growing public awareness of and concern with political and strategic postures like "mutually assured destruction," the Cuban Missile Crisis, and the growing dangers of fallout.[3] Changes in the economic structure of the

Hollywood industry contributed to variable freedom in the selection of product content throughout these years. Direct governmental pressure from agencies such as the House Un-American Activities Committee determined that questioning the ethical implications of the bomb would be confined within the texts of Cold War rhetoric, which emphasized concerns for national security and the glorification of the military establishment. The requirement of Hollywood filmmakers to present issues surrounding the new technology in an understandable, interesting, and attractive form to audiences, exploiting their fears and anxieties in the interest of profits, motivated filmmakers to develop and capitalize upon the science fiction genre, which incorporated residual themes already in the culture. These residual elements were appropriated to define and give meaning to the atomic age and some of the issues it entailed, simultaneously opening a venue for views contradictory or even potentially oppositional to the official government stance.

Hence, while early attempts at exploiting atomic issues in entertainment film involved a mixture that reiterated official government policy and also questioned the ethical implications of bomb development, Cold War dictates overtly pressured Hollywood to discover subtle ways to exploit audience interest in imagining the consequences of the atomic program. Soon, filmmakers found that the depiction of the transmutational properties of radiation linked to fears of nature's retribution for its violation in the science fiction genre was popular among specific audiences. By the end of the 1950s, the science fiction genre had run its course with nuclear themes, and as the public debate shifted to other issues, filmmakers looked to the development of other genres.

After 1964 and the barrage of nuclear themes and images generated by the Hollywood industry comes a fifteen-year period of relative public apathy toward the issue. Again, many factors contributed to this phenomenon. Organized popular opposition to the nuclear arms race all but disappeared from the public agenda after 1965, perhaps because the Cuban Missile Crisis, the closest the United States and the Soviet Union had come to actually using their nuclear arsenals, had been resolved without a missile being fired. Many argued that the policy of "mutually assured destruction" had worked, as evidenced by the peaceful resolution of the crisis.[4] The 1963 ban on atmospheric testing removed the most immediate biological threat of the Pentagon's weapons development program, and fears of fallout and environmental contamination faded in the public debate. In 1964, the covert command in Vietnam was transformed into an open war that became a national crisis later in the decade, while in the same year the first of a number of urban upheavals commenced. Political activism from then on focused upon Vietnam and America's inner cities instead of on nuclear weapons, which seemed to have become an accepted and integral part of normal existence. The atomic issue receded into the background, as a potentially frightening but generally accepted feature of everyday life.[5]

As always, the Hollywood industry sought to capitalize upon the contemporary social agenda and shifting audience demand. In catering to the increasingly sophisticated young adult audience, filmmakers addressed more issues from a liberal viewpoint than it had in the 1950s. The science fiction genre faded in favor of more realistic portrayals of contemporary social problems. The final end to studio blacklisting, the demise of the Production Code, and the restructuring of Hollywood production, particularly with regard to exhibition venues, allowed more options for film content and production. Described as conveying themes acceptable to movie audiences and Hollywood producers, the "creeping leftism" of the 1960s suggested themes for films such as *Spartacus* (1960), depicting a slave revolt; *Inherit the Wind* (1960) and *Sweet Bird of Youth* (1962), criticizing fundamentalist religion; and *Raisin in the Sun* (1961), *The Outsider* (1961), *West Side Story* (1961), *To Kill a Mockingbird* (1963), and *Nothing But a Man* (1964), attacking racial intolerance.[6]

Slowly, the images of nuclear technology began to reemerge in Hollywood products of the 1970s, as the domestic usage of nuclear power became a contemporary issue. In spite of the variety of new special effects and innovative film technology now available to studio production, and the demand for higher-quality television fare, representations of nuclear issues were merely appropriated from previous Hollywood productions. The fear of transmutation, the inevitable but largely survivable nuclear war of the future, the "heroic survivors" who go on the create a new world, are surprisingly familiar formulas after reviewing the films of the 1950s. Rather than exploring new themes and issues surrounding nuclear development, the representations remained linked to their original portrayals.

For example, radiation and its transmutational effects had been so closely linked in films of the 1950s that with the expanding development of domestic usage of nuclear power, and the increasing number of nuclear accidents, fears of radioactive contamination were rekindled and familiar cinematic mutations reappeared. In 1971, radioactive wastewater contaminated the drinking water supply in St. Paul, Minnesota, while a thousand people were exposed to radioactive waste in an 1979 accident in Tennessee. Soon, Hollywood productions again offered up mutated insects and humans in films such as *The Swarm* (1978), *Slithis* (1975), and *Night of the Lepus* (1972). These apparitions were presented to 1970 audiences basically unchanged from their radiated predecessors of 1950 Hollywood, again the unforeseen and unhappy consequence of the development of nuclear technology and of humanity's tampering with nature's forbidden secrets. Although these films had the deadly radiation emerging from nuclear waste dumps instead of from the underground and all-but-forgotten nuclear testing program, they followed the same basic search-and-destroy scenario as developed in the radiation-produced monster genre. Hollywood, as always, found inventive new ways in which old themes and formulas were reshaped to meet the times.[7]

In similar fashion, the continuing notion of the inevitable nuclear confrontation of the future was resurrected in the 1970s. The depiction of a dismal post–nuclear holocaust environment, where through their oblique exposure to nuclear war survivors are transformed, either manifestly or symbolically, into "the

Other," remained basically unchanged. For example, *The Omega Man* (1971) presented the one remaining nonmutated human battling an army of doomed malformed religious fanatics in a postholocaust city. *Logan's Run* (1976) drew upon the survivors depicted in *The Time Machine* (1960) in portraying a civilization of survivors who had been transformed into pleasure-loving but emotionless individuals ruled by a robot government. The pessimistic *Planet of the Apes* series (begun in 1969) adapted the concept of human post–nuclear war transformation to its extreme. Here, set in the distant future, humans have ultimately devolved either into apes or into a primitive cave-dwelling society of speechless humans. In one of many sequels to *Planet of the Apes,* another mutant human civilization, which worships an undetonated nuclear warhead, is introduced, and members of this civilization intentionally cause the complete obliteration of the planet.

In the post-Vietnam and Watergate era, the Hollywood industry found an audience for films portraying the cultural disenchantment with military, political, and corporate corruption, and again questions of the human fallibility of those in control of the nation's atomic arsenal emerged. Worries of civilian accidents linked with nuclear power plants, and increasing suspicion of military and civilian competence, can be found in *Stronger Than the Sun* (1977), *Red Alert* (1977), and *The Uranium Conspiracy* (1978). Concern about media and government cover-ups of nuclear accidents surfaced in the highly successful *The China Syndrome* (1979), released the same year equipment failures and human mistakes led to the nation's worst nuclear accident at Three Mile Island in Middletown, Pennsylvania.

The 1980s witnessed a renewed Cold War agenda in official government rhetoric and a new emphasis upon arms development, missile gaps, and the Soviet Union as the "evil empire." Again, Hollywood produced depictions of atomic warfare and its effects that remained within the confines of the representations evolved in the 1950s. An important example of this can be found in television special *The Day After* (1983). Intentionally made to offer a critical view of continued arms development, the production set a record for the number of viewers watching a single television show; it has been described as "the most controversial television show of its time."[8] Proposing to depict the catastrophic aftereffects of a nuclear bomb on a small midwestern town, *The Day After* was overwhelmed by a media blitz before it ever aired. Pentagon criticism of its "misleading" depiction of radiation's effects, and more crucially the withdrawal of all important commercial sponsors, caused some stations to cancel the program. Ultimately, the entrenched ideological positions embodied within the movie counteracted its "unrelenting grimness" and any controversial message the producers may have intended. The television drama still maintained that the United States would survive with a working governmental system in spite of widespread destruction, as demonstrated by scenes of military personnel dispensing food and medical supplies to an irradiated but orderly population. American life continued after a Soviet first strike, reaffirming the official stance that limited nuclear war was possible and survivable.

The Cold War rhetoric rediscovered in the 1980s American political agenda was soon recognized and exploited by Hollywood. *Invasion of the Body Snatchers* (1978), *Invasion U.S.A.* (1983), and *Not of This Earth* (1985), all classics from the 1950s, were remade but still remained true to their original Cold War position in emphasizing the fear of foreign invasion and transformation. New Cold War offerings like *Wargames* (1983) again glorified the military establishment in their ability to control wayward scientists and the entire nuclear defense system. Hollywood in the 1980s also began to specifically draw upon the heroic survivor formula in the familiar post–nuclear holocaust scenario. Films such as *Aftermath* (1980), *DefCon 4* (1983), *The Survivor* (1988), *The Terminator* (1984), *Future Hunters* (1985), and *Mad Max* (1979) all typically allude to a global atomic confrontation of the historical past, then show the future as a pioneering frontier. Despite the increasing evidence at this time of the devastating environmental effects of nuclear use, these films continued to incorporate earlier atomic assumptions and suggest a continued determination to avoid coming to terms with the present.[9] Again and again, a surviving hero is confronted with a frontier to conquer, a civilization to rebuild, and a post–nuclear war environment unsullied by the effects of radiation or nuclear winter.

The conscious selection of these themes by Hollywood filmmakers to encapsulate and convey a specific view of nuclear issues continues to replicate the original ideas developed in the early fifteen-year evolution of nuclear films. This is due in part to three interrelated factors: the continued acceptability of these images by the audience, the intertextual nature of Hollywood film production, and the functioning of ideology. Primarily, portraying nuclear issues within this relatively narrow array of themes and images continues to draw acceptably large audiences and still produces the sought-after profit. Then as now, the Hollywood industry's challenge lay in developing themes that would work for the audience as a whole and that would provide correlatives for the common wishes and fears of the largest possible audience. Hollywood's initial and continuing commercial success proves that it meets this challenge.

Because of the intertextual nature of Hollywood production, new film texts continue to draw upon previous ones, endlessly replicating the successfully received formulas and discarding unsuccessful narratives. Hence, the early experimentation gave way to the repetition of proven successful formulas; films about nuclear spies and radiation-produced monsters proliferated while the docudrama and comic portrayals of nuclear issues, earlier made possible by the monopolistic market conditions of the 1940s, fell by the wayside as competition for shrinking audiences increased. Movies with nuclear themes simply reused those successful visions that had come before, with little change in formula or presentation. Although there were slight innovations in style and format, there was little motivation to go beyond the boundaries of standardized successful plots.

Hence, the atomic images generated by Hollywood have remained within the confines of one view, with one set of contradictory and potentially oppositional images associated with it. Nuclear war is portrayed as survivable and usually as inevitable, with an exciting new world of social possibility following it. Nuclear use is linked to transmutation, whether directly through radiation exposure or vicariously through nuclear survival. The military and social system can contain any threat but can never fully contain the horrors they ultimately are responsible for creating. Hollywood filmmakers don't seem to be able to go beyond these notions and present alternatives to this established repertoire of themes. These apparent limits on the imagination, the unspoken assumption that these narrow issues are all that nuclear development entails, are the essence of the workings of ideology. Conceiving of a future nuclear confrontation as inevitable and portraying the lucky survivors' daily existence as exciting and attractive promotes the idea that the American nuclear policy is "natural," "right," and acceptable, an inevitable product of nature rather than of history. The continual dissemination of these notions in popular culture chronically distorts our perception of such events and potentially cripples our response to them.

Hence, public rhetoric continually evokes the limited range of nuclear images created and replicated, in part, by Hollywood. Public concern over the nuclear capabilities of other countries with unstable governments evokes the vision of the power-hungry madman's finger on the nuclear button, waiting to bring on the inevitable Armageddon. Themes of atomic espionage are still viable, with the defense of the nation's nuclear secrets from ever present subversives ready to invade the United States. Whether the threat originates from Asia or the Middle East, nuclear terrorism promises to continue as an exploitable Hollywood theme. So too do the imagined effects of radiation emerging from nuclear dump sites, as the nation's nuclear arsenal is slowly disarmed. And still, every so often one comes across a contemporary magazine article that links local earthquakes to the continued underground testing in Nevada, or that elaborates upon the dangers of radiation's effects on food preservation. As an accepted part of popular culture, kindergartners play with plastic "action figures" who have the ability to transmutate from human being into super-powered rodent. "He mutated with a rat" is the simple and self-evident explanation offered by the condescending five-year-old. The images continue to shape our lives.

Appendix

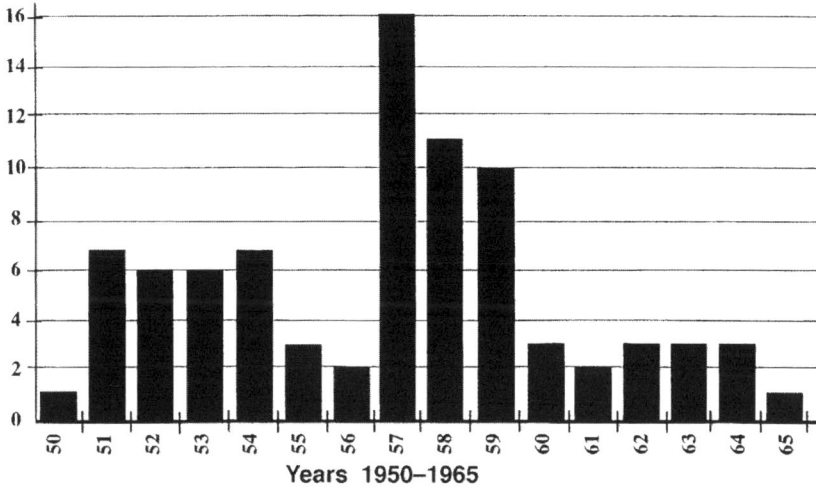

Figure A.1   Number of Nuclear Genre Films per Year

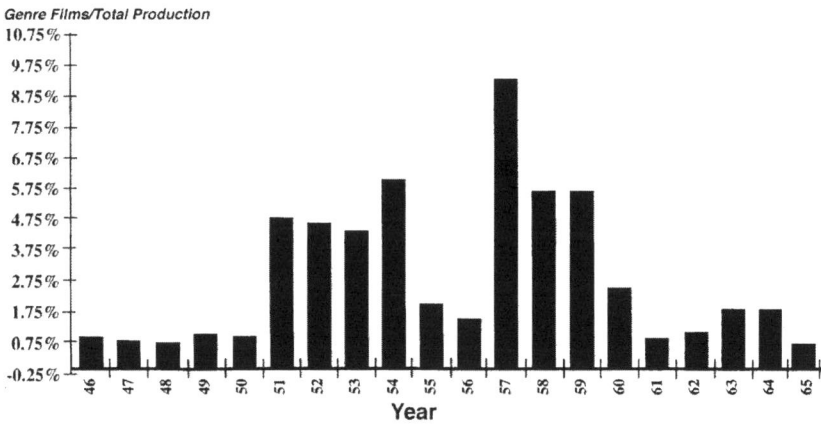

Figure A.2   Nuclear Genre Films as Percentage of Total Hollywood Production

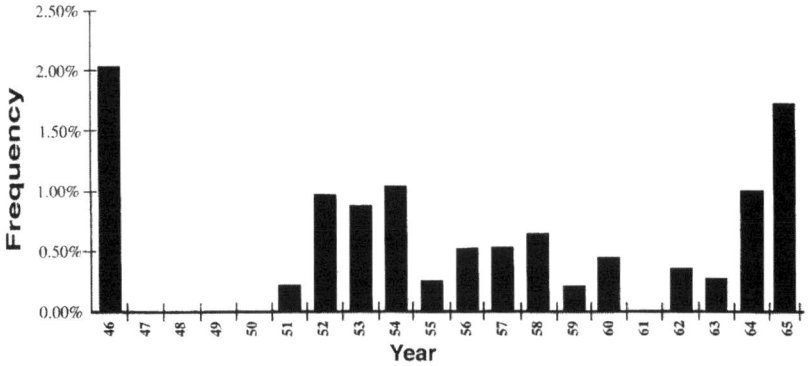

Figure A.3   Frequency of Images of Atomic Explosions in Nuclear Genre Movies

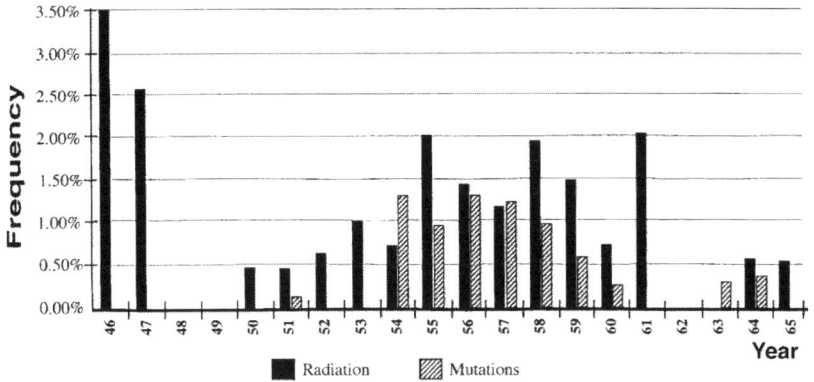

Figure A.4   Frequency of Images of Radiation and Radiation-Produced Mutations in Nuclear Genre Movies

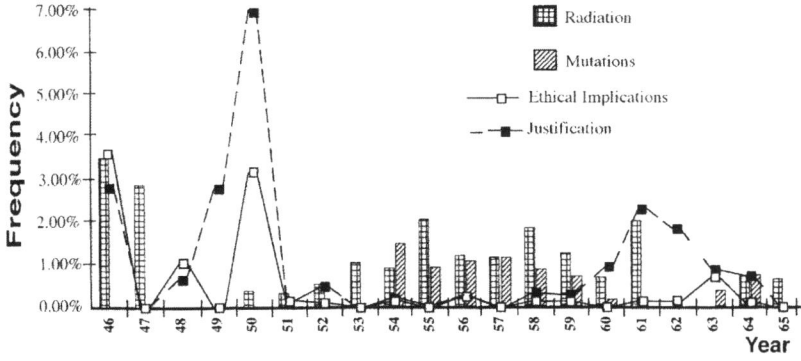

Figure A.5   Frequency of Images of Radiation, Mutations, and Dialogue Devoted to Ethical Implications and Justification of Atomic Development

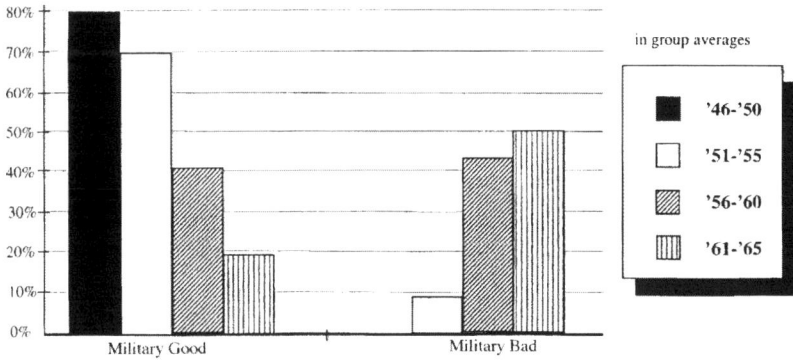

Figure A.6   Negative Images of Military

Notes

INTRODUCTION

1. I use the words "nuclear" and "atomic" interchangeably, no distinction between them being intended. The term "atomic" was more commonly used in the 1940s and 1950s, with "nuclear" used thereafter.

2. Robert Ray, *A Certain Tendency of the Hollywood Cinema, 1930–1980* (Princeton: Princeton University Press, 1985), pp. 6–7.

3. Louis Althusser, *For Marx* (London: New Left Books, 1979), p. 231.

4. D. Swanson, "Popular Art As Political Communication," in *Politics in Familiar Contexts,* ed. Robert L. Savage and Dan Nimmo (New York: Ablex Publishing Co., 1990), pp. 13–62.

5. The Federation of Atomic Scientists was formed in October 1945.

6. See H. Bruce Franklin, *War Stars: The Superweapon and the American Imagination* (New York: Oxford University Press, 1988), pp. 137–141; and Paul Boyer, *By the Bomb's Early Light* (New York: Pantheon Books, 1985), pp. 9–17.

7. George Gallup, *The Gallup Poll, 1935–1971* (New York: Random House, 1972), p. 895.

8. Mick Broderick, *Nuclear Movies* (Jefferson, N.C.: McFarland and Co., 1991), p.5.

9. *Atom Bomb,* Paramount newsreel, August 1945.

10. Such films include *The Red Menace* (1949), *The Whip Hand* (1951), *I Was a Communist for the FBI* (1951), *The Thief* (1952), and *Atomic Attack* (1954). See John Cogley, *Report on Blacklisting* (New York: Fund for the Republic, 1956), p. 115.

11. Raymond Williams, *Problems in Materialism and Culture: Selected Essays* (London: Verso Publishers, 1980), pp. 38–45.

12. Emanuel Levy, *Small Town America in Film* (New York: Frederick Ungar, 1991), p. 19.

13. Peter Golding and Graham Murdock, "Culture, Communication, and Political Economy," in *Mass Media and Society,* ed. James Curran and Michael Gurevitch (London: Edward Arnold, 1991), p. 18.

14. Graham Murdock, "Cultural Studies: Missing Links," *Critical Studies in Mass Communication* (December 1989):437.

15. Stuart Hall, "The Problem of Ideology: Marxism Without Guarantees," in *Marx: A Hundred Years On,* ed. Brian Matthews (London: Lawrence and Wishart, 1983), pp. 57–85.

16. James Linton, "But It's Only a Movie," *Jump Cut* 17 (April 1978):16–19.

17. For a view of the powerful role of the audience, see A. R. Bauer, "The Obstinate Audience: The Influence Process from the Point of View of Social Communication," in *The*

Process and Effects of Mass Communication, ed. Wilbur Lang Schramm (Urbana: University of Illinois Press, 1971); for an opposing view, see Herbert Schiller, *Mass Communication and American Empire* (Boston: Beacon Press, 1989).

18. John Strick, "The Economics of the Motion Picture Industry: A Survey," *Philosophy of the Social Sciences* 8 (December 1978):406–417.

19. Garth Jowett and James Linton, eds., *Movies As Mass Communication* (Beverly Hills, Calif.: Sage, 1980), p. 27.

20. Joseph Turow, "A Mass Communication Perspective on Entertainment Industries," in *Movies As Mass Communication,* ed. Garth Jowett and James Linton (Beverly Hills, Calif.: Sage, 1980), pp. 166–167.

21. Janet Staiger, "The Hollywood Mode of Production," in *The Classical Hollywood Cinema,* ed. David Bordwell, Janet Staiger, and Kristin Thompson (New York: Columbia University Press, 1985), p. 96.

22. Tony Bennett, "Media, Reality, Signification," in *Culture, Society and the Media,* ed. Michael Gurevitch, Tony Bennett, James Curran, and Janet Woollacott (London: Methuen, 1980), pp. 287–303.

23. Hugh Edmunds and John Strick, "Economic Determinants of Violence in Television and Motion Pictures and the Implications of Newer Technologies," in *The Report of the Royal Commission on Violence in the Communications Industry* (Toronto: Queen's Printer for Ontario, 1977), pp. 71–184.

24. See Herbert Gans, "The Creator-Audience Relationship in the Mass Media: An Analysis of Movie Making," in *Mass Culture: The Popular Arts in America,* ed. B. Rosenberg and D. M. White (New York: The Free Press, 1957), pp. 315–324.

25. Gans, "The Creator-Audience Relationship," p. 322.

26. Dennis McQuail, "The Uncertainty About the Audience and the Organization of Mass Communications," *The Sociological Review, Monograph 14: The Sociology of Mass Media Communicators,* ed. Paul Halmos (January 1969):75–84.

27. Ian Jarvie, *Movies and Society* (New York: Basic Books, 1970), p. 42.

28. See Howard Newcomb and Robert S. Alley, eds., *The Producer's Medium: Conversations with the Creators of American TV* (New York: Oxford University Press, 1983); and Neal Gabler, *An Empire of Their Own: How the Jews Invented Hollywood* (New York: Crown, 1988).

29. By focusing upon American depictions of nuclear usage, I do not mean to suggest that American culture was solely responsible for originating and disseminating such depictions. However, the atomic bomb was first developed and used by the United States, and thus its population was the first to face the unprecedented power and the ethical implications of such technology. The Hollywood film industry was also a leader in exploiting the newly developed technology in its products.

30. Spencer Weart, *Nuclear Fear: A History of Images* (Cambridge: Harvard University Press, 1988); Constantina Titus, *Bombs in the Backyard: Atomic Testing and American Politics* (Reno: University of Nevada Press, 1986); and Ira Chernus, *Dr. Strangegod: On the Symbolic Meaning of Nuclear Weapons* (Columbia: University of South Carolina Press, 1986).

31. Michael Rogin, "*Kiss Me Deadly*: Communism, Motherhood and Cold War Movies," *Representations* 6 (1984):3.

32. David Dowling, *Fictions of Nuclear Disaster* (Iowa City: University of Iowa Press, 1987); Paul Brians, *Nuclear Holocausts: Atomic War in Fiction 1895–1984* (Kent, Ohio: Kent State University Press, 1987); Peter Biskind, *Seeing Is Believing: How Hollywood Taught Us*

to Stop Worrying and Love the Bomb (New York: Pantheon Books, 1983); and Peter Biskind, "Pods, Blobs, and Ideology in American Films of the Fifties," in *Shadows of the Magic Lamp*, ed. George Slusser and Eric S. Rabkin (Carbondale: Southern Illinois University Press, 1985).

33. Robert J. Lifton and Greg Mitchell, *Hiroshima in America* (New York: Putnam's Sons, 1995).

34. For film analysis from a psychoanalytic view, see Patrick Lucanio, *Them or Us: Archetypal Interpretations of Fifties Alien Invasion Films* (Bloomington: University of Indiana Press, 1987); and M. Tarratt, "Monsters from the Id," in *Film Genre Reader*, ed. Barry Keith Grant (Austin: University of Texas Press, 1986), pp. 258–277. For film as reflection of society, see Jack Shaheen, *Nuclear War Films* (Carbondale: Southern Illinois University Press, 1978).

35. Robert Sklar, *Movie-Made America: A Social History of American Movies* (New York: Random House, 1975); and Andrew Tudor, *Monsters and Mad Scientists: A Cultural History of the Horror Movie* (Cambridge, England: Basil Blackwell, 1989).

CHAPTER ONE

1. *Life*, March 17, 1947, p. 74.

2. Paul Boyer, *By the Bomb's Early Light* (New York: Pantheon Books, 1985), p. 30.

3. Rob Paarlberg, "Forgetting About the Unthinkable," *Foreign Policy* 10 (1973):132.

4. In terms of actual percentage of time shown, atomic explosions appeared more prominently in the years 1946, 1964, and 1965 than in the period from 1951 to 1960. In the nuclear films of the mid-1950s, the predominant themes of the effects of radiation from atmospheric testing displaced most serious depictions of the bomb itself and its effects in war. Later, in the 1960s, as the arms race escalated into a potential confrontation between the United States and the Soviet Union, Hollywood again began to examine the consequences of atomic war. Depictions of atomic explosions emerged again at this time. (See Chart A.3 in the Appendix.)

5. Tino Balio, *The American Film Industry* (Madison: University of Wisconsin Press, 1985), p. 254.

6. Ibid., p. 288.

7. Boyer, *By the Bomb's Early Light*, p. 194.

8. John Eames, *The MGM Story* (New York: Crown, 1979), p. 209.

9. *Life*, March 17, 1947, p. 75.

10. Nathan Reingold, "MGM Meets the Atomic Bomb," *Wilson Quarterly* (Autumn 1984):157.

11. Ibid., p. 158.

12. Lawrence Suid, *Guts and Glory: Great American War Movies* (Reading, Mass.: Addison-Wesley Publishing Co., 1978), p. 188.

13. C. Barry, *Collier's Yearbook, 1947* (New York: Collier and Son, 1947), p. 49.

14. Parsons to Norman Ramsey, October 30, 1946, quoted in Boyer,(1985), p.317.

15. See Jack Shaheen and Richard Taylor, "The Beginning or the End?" in *Nuclear War Films*, ed. Jack Shaheen (Carbondale: Southern Illinois University Press, 1978), p. 7.

16. Reingold, "MGM Meets the Atomic Bomb," 162.

17. Bernard Feld, "Einstein and the Politics of Nuclear Weapons," *The Bulletin of the Atomic Scientists* 35 (1979):5–16.

18. Constantina Titus, *Bombs in the Backyard: Atomic Testing and American Politics* (Reno: University of Nevada Press, 1986), p. 6.

19. *Life,* March 17, 1947, p. 78.

20. H. W. Baldwin, *Mistakes of the War* (New York: Harper and Brothers, 1950).

21. Ibid., p. 97.

22. Baldwin, *Mistakes of the War;* and Herbert Feis, *The Atomic Bomb and the End of World War II* (Princeton: Princeton University Press, 1950).

23. *Variety,* February 13, 1947.

24. Reingold, "MGM Meets the Atomic Bomb," p. 161.

25. Ibid., p. 160

26. Robert J. Lifton and Greg Mitchell, *Hiroshima in America* (New York: Putnam's Sons, 1995), p. 361

27. Alice Kimball Smith, *A Peril and a Hope: The Scientists' Movement in America, 1945–1947* (Chicago: University of Chicago Press, 1965), p. 356.

28. Ibid., p. 358.

29. Norman Moss, *Men Who Play God* (New York: Harper and Row, 1968), p. 127.

30. Albert Einstein, quoted in Heinz Nathan and Otto Norden, eds., *Einstein on Peace* (New York: Simon and Schuster, 1960), p. 376.

31. Daniel Land, *Early Tales of the Atomic Age* (Garden City, N.Y.: Doubleday, 1948), p. 75.

32. Boyer, *By the Bomb's Early Light,* p. 106, and chap. 9.

33. Spencer Weart, *Nuclear Fear: A History of Images* (Cambridge: Harvard University Press, 1988), p. 117.

34. Boyer, *By the Bomb's Early Light,* p. 269.

35. Noam Chomsky, *Language and Responsibility* (Hassocks, England: Harvester Press, 1979), p. 20.

36. Raymond Williams, *Problems in Materialism and Culture: Selected Essays* (London: Verso Publishers, 1980), pp. 40–43.

37. Paul Chilton, "Nukespeak: Nuclear language, Culture and Propaganda," *Nukespeak: The Media and the Bomb.* (London: Comedia Publishing, 1982), p.96–98.

38. Joseph Rotblatt, quoted in John Cox, *Overkill* (New York: Pelican, 1981), p. 10.

39. William Laurence, *Men and Atoms: The Discovery, the Uses, and the Future of Atomic Energy* (New York: Simon and Schuster, 1980), pp. 117–120.

40. Henry De Wolf, *Atomic Energy for Military Purposes: The Official Report on the Development of the Atomic Bomb Under the Auspices of the United States Government, 1* (Princeton: Princeton University Press, 1976).

41. *New York Times,* August 7, 1945.

42. *Atom Bomb,* Paramount newsreel, August 1945.

43. Weart, *Nuclear Fear,* p. 10.

44. See M. R. Langer, "Fast New World," *Colliers,* January 1940, 19–54.

45. Weart, *Nuclear Fear,* p. 73.

46. Frederick Soddy, *The Interpretation of Radium and the Structure of the Atom,* 3rd ed. (London: John Murray, 1920), p. 251. First published in 1909.

47. Frederick Soddy, "Some Recent Advances in Radioactivity," *Contemporary Review* 83 (1903):708–720.

48. Edwin E. Slosson, "Death-Dealing and Labor Saving Rays," *Scientific Monthly* 20 (1925):108–111.

49. *Variety,* February 13, 1947.

50. Shaheen and Taylor, *"The Beginning or the End?"* p. 9.

51. Reingold, "MGM Meets the Atomic Bomb," p. 163.

52. *Life*, March 17, 1947, p. 76.

53. *Variety*, February 13, 1947.

54. *Time*, February 24, 1947, p. 106.

55. Leonard Maltin, *Movie and Video Guide* (New York: Signet, 1995), p. 93.

CHAPTER TWO

1. H. Bruce Franklin, *War Stars: The Superweapon and the American Imagination.* (New York: Oxford University Press, 1988), p. 182.

2. Herbert York, *The Advisors: Oppenheimer, Teller, and the Superbomb* (San Francisco: W. H. Freeman, 1976), p. 34.

3. See Constantina Titus, "Selling the Bomb: Hollywood and the Government Join Forces at Ground Zero," *Halcyon* 7 (1985):16–29.

4. Paul Boyer, *By the Bomb's Early Light* (New York: Pantheon Books, 1985), p. 102.

5. William Sweet, *The Nuclear Age: Atomic Energy, Proliferation, and the Arms Race* (Washington, D.C.: The Congressional Quarterly, 1988), p. 8.

6. Eugene Rabinowitch, "Five Years After," *The Bulletin of the Atomic Scientists* (January 1951):3–12; and Boyer, *By the Bomb's Early Light*, p. 274.

7. Boyer, *By the Bomb's Early Light*, p. 96.

8. Paul A. Carter, *Another Part of the Fifties* (New York: Columbia University Press, 1983), p. 273.

9. Leslie R. Groves, *Now It Can Be Told* (New York: Harper and Row, 1962), p. 70.

10. Ibid., pp. 438–439.

11. Spencer Weart, *Nuclear Fear: A History of Images* (Cambridge: Harvard University Press, 1988), p. 121.

12. Roland Barthes, *Mythologies* (New York: Hill and Wang, 1972), p. 117.

13. Charles Olson, *The Cold War . . . And After* (Englewood Cliffs, N.J.: Prentice Hall, 1975), p. 7.

14. Stuart M. Speiser, *How to End the Nuclear Nightmare* (New York: North River Press, 1984), p. 62.

15. Edward T. Thompson, *Beyond the Cold War* (New York: Pantheon Books, 1982), p. 67.

16. Ibid., p. 37.

17. Gregg Herken, *The Winning Weapon: The Atomic Bomb in the Cold War, 1945–1950* (New York: Knopf, 1980), p. 153.

18. Robert Divine, *Eisenhower and the Cold War* (New York: Oxford University Press, 1981), p. 13.

19. Constantina Titus, *Bombs in the Backyard: Atomic Testing and American Politics* (Reno: University of Nevada Press, 1986), p. 70.

20. Robert Griffith, *The Politics of Fear: Joseph R. McCarthy and the Senate* (Amherst: University of Massachusetts Press, 1987).

21. McCarran International Security Act, Public Law 414, 82nd Congress, 2nd sess. (June 27, 1952), chap. 477, 66 Stat., 163; 8 U.S.C., 1101–1503.

22. Communist Control Act, Public Law 637, 83rd Congress, 2nd sess. (August 24, 1954), chap. 886, 68 Stat., 775; 50 U.S.C., 841.

23. William Manchester, *The Glory and the Dream: A Narrative History of America, 1932–1972* (New York: Bantam Books, 1974), pp. 671–672.

24. Michael Uhl and Tod Ensign, *G.I. Guinea Pigs: How the Pentagon Exposed Our Troops to Dangers More Deadly Than War* (New York: Wideview Books, 1980), p. 58.

25. L. L. Strauss, *Men and Decisions* (New York: Doubleday, 1962).

26. Ralph B. Levering, *The Public and American Foreign Policy, 1918–1978* (New York: William Morrow, 1978), p. 97.

27. George Gallup, "Attitudes Toward U.S.-Russian Relations," in *The Gallup Poll, 1935–1971* (New York: Random House, 1972), pp. 567, 581–582.

28. Ibid., pp. 827, 1366.

29. Leo Bogart, *Premises for Propaganda* (New York: The Free Press, 1976), pp. vi, xv.

30. Ibid., p. 96.

31. A. H. Dawson, "Motion Picture Economics," *Hollywood Quarterly* 3, 3 (1947): 217–240.

32. Russell Earl Shain, *An Analysis of Motion Pictures about War Released by the American Film Industry, 1930–1970* (New York: Arno Press, 1976), p. 77.

33. George Kahn, *Hollywood on Trial* (New York: Boni and Gaer, 1948), pp. 184–185.

34. "Mayer Says Films Feared Censoring," *New York Times*, December 10, 1948, p. A5.

35. Nora Sayre, *Running Time: Films of the Cold War* (New York: Dial Press, 1982), p. 22.

36. Tino Balio, *The American Film Industry* (Madison: University of Wisconsin Press, 1985) p. 412.

37. Sayre, *Running Time*, p. 22.

38. John Cogley, *Report on Blacklisting* (New York: Fund for the Republic, 1956), p. 113.

39. Attendance figures are taken from *Film Daily Yearbook of Motion Pictures*.

40. Michael Conant, *Antitrust in the Motion Picture Industry* (Berkeley: University of California Press, 1960), p. 13.

41. Bureau of the Census, *Historical Statistics of the United States* (Washington, D.C.: Bureau of the Census, 1958), p. 10.

42. Ibid., p. 224.

43. *Variety*, July 7, 1948, p. 3.

44. Cogley, *Report on Blacklisting*, p. 115.

45. Balio, *American Film Industry*, p. 412.

CHAPTER THREE

1. Spencer Weart, *Nuclear Fear: A History of Images.* (Cambridge: Harvard University Press, 1988), p. 130.

2. Andrew Furtwanger, "Growing Up Nuclear," *The Bulletin of the Atomic Scientists* 37, 1 (1981):44–48.

3. *Las Vegas Review-Journal,* May 6, 1955.

4. Bill Warren, *Keep Watching the Skies: American Science Fiction Movies of the Fifties.* (Jefferson, N.C.: McFarland and Co., 1982), p. 11.

5. James Savage and B. Storms, *Reach to the Unknown* (Los Alamos, N.Mex.: University of California and U.S. Atomic Energy Commission, 1965), p. 29.

6. Louis Lamont, *Day of Trinity* (New York: Antheum, 1965), pp. 251–253.

7. Ibid., p. 255.

8. William A. Shurcliff, *Bombs at Bikini: The Official Report of Operation Crossroads* (New York: William H. Wise, 1947), p. 36.

9. David Bradley, *No Place to Hide* (Boston: Little, Brown and Co., 1948), p. 104.

10. D. B. Parker, "Mist of Death over New York," *Reader's Digest*, 1947, pp. 7–10.

11. Patrick Lucanio, *Them or Us: Archetypal Interpretations of Fifties Alien Invasion Films* (Bloomington: Indiana University Press, 1987), p. 27.

12. Review of *The Day the Earth Stood Still, New York Times*, August 28, 1951.

13. Bruce Kawin, "Children of the Light," in *Shadows of the Magic Lamp*, ed. George Slusser and Eric S. Rabkin (Carbondale: Southern Illinois University Press, 1985), pp. 14–29.

14. Peter Biskind, *Seeing is Believing: How Hollywood Taught Us to Stop Worrying and Love the Bomb* (New York: Pantheon Books, 1983), p. 153.

15. Paul Brians, *Nuclear Holocausts: Atomic War in Fiction 1895–1984* (Kent, Ohio: Kent State University Press, 1987).

16. Martha Bartter, *The Way to Ground Zero: The Atomic Bomb in American Science Fiction* (Westport, Conn.: Greenwood Press, 1988), p. 129.

17. See Martha Bartter, "Nuclear Holocaust As Urban Renewal," *Science Fiction Studies* 13 (1986):148–158.

51. Corman, *How I Made a Hundred Movies*, p. 31.

CHAPTER FOUR

1. H. L. Gold, the editor of *Galaxy Science Fiction*, quoted by Kingsley Amis, *New Maps of Hell* (London: Gollancz, 1961), p. 64.

2. Paul Michaels, *The American Movies Reference Book: The Sound Era* (Englewood Cliffs, N.J.: Prentice Hall, 1969), p. 29.

3. Mick Broderick, *Nuclear Movies* (Jefferson, N.C.: McFarland and Co., 1991), p. 17.

4. Concern with and general discussion about radiation can be found in the early period of 1947–1953, but depictions of actual radiation-induced mutations appear in 1954 and continue to 1960. (See Chart A.7 in the Appendix.)

5. See Chart A.8 in the Appendix.

6. Steven Neale, *Genre* (London: British Film Institute, 1981).

7. Spencer Weart, *Nuclear Fear: A History of Images* (Cambridge: Harvard University Press, 1988), p. 266.

8. W. A. Scott, "The Avoidance of Threatening Material in Imaginative Behavior," in *Motives in Fantasy, Action, and Society*, ed. John W. Atkinson (Princeton: Van Nostrand Press, 1958), pp. 572–585.

9. See Joel Kovel, *Against the State of Nuclear Terror* (Boston: South End Press, 1983).

10. Susan Sontag, *Against Interpretation and Other Essays* (New York: Delta, 1966), pp. 208–225.

11. Ibid., p. 212.

12. H. G. Wells, *The World Set Free* (London: Macmillan, 1914).

13. Thomas Schatz, "The Structural Influence: New Directions in Film Genre Study," in *Film Genre Reader*, ed. Barry Keith Grant (Austin: University of Texas Press, 1986), pp. 91–101.

14. Bill Warren, *Keep Watching the Skies: American Science Fiction Movies of the Fifties* (Jefferson, N.C.: McFarland and Co., 1982), p. xiii.

15. H. L. Gold, the editor of *Galaxy Science Fiction*, quoted by Kingsley Amis, *New Maps of Hell* (London: Gollancz, 1961), p. 64.

16. Francis Arnold, "Out of this World," *Films and Filming* 9 (1963):14–18.

17. Nora Sayre, *Running Time: Films of the Cold War* (New York: Dial Press, 1982), p. 191.

18. Robert Cassady, "Impact of the Paramount Decision on Motion Picture Distribution and Price Making," *Southern California Law Review* 31 (1958):155.

19. Calvin Pryluck, "Front Office, Box Office, and Artistic Freedom: An Aspect of the Film Industry, 1945–1969," in *Movies as Artifacts,* ed. Michael Marsden and John Nachbar (Chicago: Nelson-Hall, 1982), p. 45.

20. Michael Conant, *Antitrust in the Motion Picture Industry* (Berkeley: University of California Press, 1960).

21. Tino Balio, *The American Film Industry* (Madison: University of Wisconsin Press, 1985), p. 401.

22. "How Hollywood Hopes to Hit the Comeback Road," *Newsweek,* January 12, 1953, pp. 66–67.

23. Balio, *American Film Industry,* p. 404.

24. Hy Hollinger, "Teenage Biz vs. Repair Bills," *Variety,* December 19, 1956, pp. 1,20.

25. Warren, *Keep Watching the Skies,* p. xi.

26. Evidence of this trend can be found in the changing release dates for science fiction films and in the increase in drive-in theaters. Until 1953, science fiction movies tended to be released in the fall, early winter, and spring, the periods when the studios were trying to capture adult audiences. By the mid-1950s, the bulk of these films were being released in the March to September period, when teenagers and children were more likely to attend movies on their own. Drive-in outdoor theaters were also built to lure the younger audience. In 1946, 300 drive-in theaters were in existence in the United States; by 1956, the number had risen to 4,500. See Fredric Stuart, "The Effects of Television on the Motion Picture Industry," in *The American Movie Industry,* ed. Gorham Kindem (Carbondale: Southern Illinois University Press, 1982), pp. 257–307, esp. 263.

27. Abel Green, "Tri Dimension's Hectic Race," *Variety,* January 28, 1953, p. 18.

28. "3-D Crowded Out of Conversation," *Variety,* February 10, 1954, p. 11.

29. Bob Bernstein, "Horror Era Looms on Video Front; Opinion Divided," *Billboard,* December 9, 1957, pp. 1, 4.

30. Fred MacDonald, "The Cold War as Entertainment in Fifties Television," *Journal of Popular Film and Television* 7 (1978):18.

31. Thomas Doherty, *Teenagers and Teenpics: The Juvenilization of American Movies in the 1950s* (Boston: Unwin Hyman, 1988), p. 3.

32. Whitney Williams, "Exploitation Pictures Paid Off Big for Majors, Also Indie Producers," *Variety,* January 9, 1946, p. 36.

33. Ibid., p. 8.

34. "U.S. Showbiz Angles on Soviet Satellite: Gags, New Space Cadet Spree," *Variety,* October 9, 1957, p. 1.

35. George Yousling, "Bank Financing of the Independent Motion Picture Producer," quoted in Balio, *American Film Industry,* p. 417.

36. Roger Corman's films concerning nuclear issues also include *Monster from the Ocean Floor* (1954), *Not of This Earth* (1956), *It Conquered the World* (1956), *War of the Satellites* (1958), and *Last Woman on Earth* (1960).

37. Ed Naha, *The Films of Roger Corman* (New York: Arco Publishers, 1982), p. 13.

38. Roger Corman, *How I Made a Hundred Movies in Hollywood* (New York: Random House, 1990), p. 37.

39. "Despite Shortage, Double Bills Flourish," *Variety,* February 4, 1959, p. 14.

40. Roger Corman, quoted in Naha, *Films of Roger Corman,* p. 112.

41. Corman, *How I Made a Hundred Movies,* p. 32.

42. "AIP Offers Package: Dual Bill, One Story," *Motion Picture Herald,* December 6, 1958, p. 10.

43. Richard Gehman, "The Hollywood Horrors," *Cosmopolitan,* November 1958, p. 40.

44. "Youth Wants to Know About the Movies!" *Motion Picture Herald,* October 11, 1958, p. 21.

45. Balio, *American Film Industry,* p. 378.

46. Irving Rubine, "Boys Meet Ghouls, Make Money," *New York Times,* March 16, 1958, sec. 2, p. 7, col. 3.

47. Roger Corman, quoted in Naha, *Films of Roger Corman,* p. 14.

48. Corman, *How I Made a Hundred Movies,* p. 19.

49. Ibid., p. 17.

50. Gary Morris, *Roger Corman* (Boston: Twayne Publishers, 1985), p. 6.

51. Corman, *How I Made a Hundred Movies,* p. 31.

CHAPTER FIVE

1. Mick Broderick, *Nuclear Movies* (Jefferson, N.C.: McFarland and Co., 1991), p. 17.

2. Harry S. Truman, "Moscow Divides the World," in *The American Image of Russia,* ed. Benson L. Grayson (New York: Frederick Ungar, 1978), p. 219.

3. Howard Ball, *Justice Downwind: America's Testing Program in the 1950s* (New York: Oxford University Press, 1986).

4. Brian Murphy, "Monster Movies: They Came from Beneath the Fifties," in *Movies as Artifacts,* ed. Michael Marsden and John Nachbar (Chicago: Nelson-Hall, 1982), p. 42.

5. *New York Times,* April 1, 1954, p. 20; and U.S. House, Subcommittee on Oversight and Investigations of the Committee on Interstate and Foreign Commerce, and Senate, Health and Scientific Research Subcommittee of the Labor and Human Resources Committee, and Senate, Committee on the Judiciary, *Health Effects of Low-Level Radiation,* 96th Congress, 1st sess. (April 19, 1954), serial no. 96–41, vol. 1, "Diary of Gordon Dean, Entry Date May 27, 1953," 151.

6. See *Invasion U.S.A.* (1952).

7. Thomas Doherty, *Teenagers and Teenpics: The Juvenilization of American Movies in the 1950s* (Boston: Unwin Hyman, 1988), p.145.

8. Peter Biskind, *Seeing Is Believing: How Hollywood Taught Us to Stop Worrying and Love the Bomb* (New York: Pantheon Books, 1983), p. 132.

9. For a discussion of this view, see Ira Chernus, *Dr. Strangegod: On the Symbolic Meaning of Nuclear Weapons* (Columbia: University of South Carolina Press, 1986), pp. 32–37.

10. Norman Moss, *Men Who Play God* (New York: Harper and Row, 1968), p. 31.

11. For an elaboration of this concept, see Paul Fussell, *The Great War and Modern Memory* (New York: Oxford University Press, 1975), pp. 76–78.

12. G. Gray, *The Warriors* (New York: Harper and Row, 1970), p. 132.

13. James Aho, *Religious Mythology and the Art of War* (Westport, Conn.: Greenwood Press, 1981), p. 10.

14. Edward T. Thompson, *Beyond the Cold War* (New York: Pantheon Books, 1982), p. 23.

15. Kurt London, *The Permanent Crisis* (Waltham, Mass.: Blaisdell Publishers, 1968), p. 2.

16. H. Bruce Franklin, *War Stars: The Superweapon and the American Imagination* (New York: Oxford University Press, 1988), p. 162.

17. Truman, "Moscow Divides the World," p. 220.

18. Arthur Knight, quoted in Bill Warren, *Keep Watching the Skies: American Science Fiction Movies of the Fifties* (Jefferson, N.C.: McFarland and Co., 1982), p. 195.

19. See Spencer Weart, *Nuclear Fear: A History of Images* (Cambridge: Harvard University Press, 1988), pp. 38–43.

20. Ball, *Justice Downwind*.

21. George Gallup, *The Gallup Poll, 1935–1971* (New York: Random House, 1972), p. 1229.

22. Report issued by the Atomic Energy Commission on the effects of hydrogen bomb explosions. *New York Times*, February 16, 1955, p. 18.

23. Constantina Titus, *Bombs in the Backyard: Atomic Testing and American Politics* (Reno: University of Nevada Press, 1986), p. 84.

24. U.S. Atomic Energy Commission, *Atomic Tests in Nevada* (Washington, D.C.: U.S. Atomic Energy Commission, 1957), pp. 33–34.

25. Gladwin Hill, "Desert 'Capital' of the A-Bomb," *New York Times Magazine*, February 13, 1955, p. 22.

26. Lewis L. Strass, (1955) NA/RG 326, 5–6.

27. Titus, *Bombs in the Backyard*, pp. 75–78.

28. *Las Vegas Review-Journal*, March 17, 1953.

29. David Wallechinsky and Irving Wallace, *The People's Almanac* (New York: Doubleday, 1975), p. 242.

30. Gallup, *Gallup Poll*, pp. 1486, 1452.

31. Ibid., pp. 1488, 1553.

32. World Health Organization, *Mental Health*, annex 1, "Statement of the Sub-committee on the Peaceful Uses of Atomic Energy of the World Federation for Mental Health, Approved by the 25th Meeting of the Executive Board of the WFMH, London, 8–12 Feb. 1957," pp. 47–48.

33. Weart, *Nuclear Fear*, p. 73.

34. *New York Times*, February 25, 1939, p. 17.

35. Dr. Morton's theory of the therapeutic value of radium solutions was discussed in *Scientific American* 90, 5 (January 30, 1904):90.

36. Hermann Muller, *Science* 66 (1927):84–87.

37. Frederick Soddy, "The Frustration of Science," in *Frederick Soddy*, ed. George B. Kauffman (Dordrecht, Netherlands: Reidel, 1986), p. 24.

38. William Whetham, "Matter and Electricity," *Quarterly Review* 397 (1904):126.

39. *New York Times*, 1929.

40. T. Martyn, "In Science Lies the Challenge to War," *The New York Times Magazine*, June 30, 1929, pp. 4–5, 20.

41. Taylor Stoehr, *Hawthorne's Mad Scientists: Pseudoscience and Social Science in 19th Century Life and Letters* (Hamden, Conn.: Archon Publishers, 1978).

42. E. M. Butler, *Myth of the Magus* (Cambridge: Cambridge University Press, 1948), pp. 3–6.

43. H. G. Wells, *The Island of Dr. Moreau* (London: William Heinemann, 1896).

44. J. B. Priestley, *The Doomsday Men* (New York: Harper and Brothers, 1938).

45. Anatole France, *Penguin Island* (New York: J. Lane Publishers, 1908).

46. Douglas Alver Menville and Robert Reginald, *Things to Come: An Illustrated History of the Science Fiction Film* (New York: New York Times Books, 1977), pp. 68–72.

47. H. G. Wells, *Things to Come* (1935), in *Focus on the Science Fiction Film*, ed. William Johnson (Englewood Cliffs, N.J.: Prentice Hall, 1972), p. 35.

48. François Truffaut, *Dr. Cyclops* (1940), in *Focus on the Science Fiction Film*, ed. William Johnson (Englewood Cliffs, N.J.: Prentice Hall, 1972), p. 48.

49. *The Invisible Ray*, Universal Studios, directed by Lambert Hillyer (1936).

50. Paul A. Carter, *Another Part of the Fifties* (New York: Columbia University Press, 1983) p. 274.

51. John Bronsan, *Future Tense* (London: MacDonald and Jane's, 1978), p. 95.

52. *First Man into Space*, directed by Robert Day (1959).

53. Japan's Toho studios created one of the most famous mutated monsters, Godzilla, which was said to have been influenced by *The Beast from 20,000 Fathoms*. Some scholars believe that the Japanese monsters are metaphors for the atomic bomb and nuclear destruction while also symbolizing the United States as an occupying force that was literally the country. Just as Hollywood avoided realistic depictions of the consequences of atomic bombing, so too did Japanese studios, opting instead for less direct means of venting and exploiting sublimated nuclear anxiety. See Broderick, *Nuclear Movies*, pp. 19–21.

CHAPTER SIX

1. Andrew Tudor, *Monsters and Mad Scientists: A Cultural History of the Horror Movie* (Cambridge, England: Basil Blackwell, 1989), p. 39.

2. Ibid., p. 42.

3. See Peter Biskind, *Seeing Is Believing: How Hollywood Taught Us to Stop Worrying and Love the Bomb*. (New York: Pantheon Books, 1983), which explores this idea in relation to a wide range of Hollywood films.

4. Nora Sayre, *Running Time: Films of the Cold War* (New York: Dial Press, 1982), p. 191.

5. J. H. Wright, "Genre Films and the Status Quo," in *Film Genre Reader*, ed. Barry Keith Grant (Austin: University of Texas Press, 1986), p. 46.

6. George Kennan, *The Nuclear Delusion: Soviet-American Relations in the Atomic Age*. (New York: Pantheon Books, 1976), p. 18.

7. Sayre, *Running Time*, p. 201.

8. Tudor, *Monsters and Mad Scientists*, p. 220.

9. Spencer Weart, *Nuclear Fear: A History of Images* (Cambridge: Harvard University Press, 1988), p. 170.

10. Peter Pringle and John Spigelman, *The Nuclear Barons* (New York: Holt, Rinehart and Winston, 1981), pp. 125–126.

11. A. M. Rosenthal, "Eisenhower Tries New Atomic Tack," *New York Times*, December 9, 1953, p. 2.

12. H. Haber, *The Walt Disney Story of Our Friend the Atom* (New York: Simon and Schuster, 1957), p. 13.

13. U.S. Atomic Energy Commission, *Annual Report to Congress of the Atomic Energy Commission for 1960* (January 1961), p. 245.

14. Constantina Titus, *Bombs in the Backyard: Atomic Testing and American Politics* (Reno: University of Nevada Press, 1986) p. 79.

15. Edward Teller, *The Legacy of Hiroshima* (Garden City, N.Y.: Doubleday, 1962).

16. Glenn Seaborg and William Corliss, *Man and Atom* (New York: Dutton, 1971), p. 184.

17. Despite the public heralding of a utopian "white city" powered by atomic technology in the early 1950s, little time in Hollywood film is devoted to the use of atomic power. (See Chart A.5 in the Appendix.) When atomic power is shown, Hollywood products tend to concentrate upon the negative consequences of its use. Nuclear power is shown as having negative consequences more than twice as much as having positive consequences in the film sample. (See Chart A.6 in the Appendix.)

18. Dwight D. Eisenhower, "The Soviet Threat," in *The American Image of Russia*, ed. Benson L. Grayson (New York: Frederick Ungar, 1978), p. 214.

19. M. Eastman, "Worse Than Fascism," in *The American Image of Russia*, ed. Benson L. Grayson (New York: Frederick Ungar, 1978), p. 146.

20. Harry S. Truman, "Moscow Divides the World," in *The American Image of Russia*, ed. Benson L. Grayson (New York: Frederick Ungar, 1978), p. 215.

21. Eastman, "Worse than Fascism," p. 148.

22. Joel Kovel, *Against the State of Nuclear Terror* (Boston: South End Press, 1983).

23. Michael Rogin, *Ronald Reagan the Movie and Other Episodes in Political Demonology* (Berkeley: University of California Press, 1987), p. 219.

24. George Gallup, *The Gallup Poll, 1935–1971* (New York: Random House, 1972), p. 1716.

25. Kurt London, *The Permanent Crisis* (Waltham, Mass.: Blaisdell Publishers, 1968), p. 2.

26. Ibid., p. 46.

27. Benson L. Grayson, ed., *The American Image of Russia* (New York: Frederick Ungar, 1978), p. 39.

28. Eastman, "Worse than Fascism," p. 143.

29. London, *Permanent Crisis*, p. 2.

30. Ibid., p. 41.

31. Phillip Elliott, "Some Aspects of Communism As a Cultural Category," *Media, Culture, and Society* 1, (1980):201.

32. Truman, "Moscow Divides the World," p. 220.

33. Mick Broderick, *Nuclear Movies* (Jefferson, N.C.: McFarland and Co., 1991), pp. 10–12.

34. Michael Ryan and Douglas Kellner, *Camera Politica: The Politics and Ideology of Contemporary Hollywood Film* (Bloomington: Indiana University Press, 1988), p. 83.

35. Broderick, *Nuclear Movies*, p. 12.

36. Biskind, *Seeing is Believing*, p. 56.

CHAPTER SEVEN

1. Thomas Doherty, *Teenagers and Teenpics: The Juvenilization of American Movies in the 1950s* (Boston: Unwin Hyman, 1988), pp. 170–172.

2. George T. Mazuzan and J. Samuel Walker, *Controlling the Atom: The Beginnings of Nuclear Regulation, 1946–1962* (Berkeley: University of California Press, 1984), p. 57.

3. H.B. Franklin, *War Stars: The Superweapon and the American Imagination* (New York: Oxford U. Press, 1988), p.181.

4. William Sweet, *The Nuclear Age* (Washington, D.C.: The Congressional Quarterly, 1988), p. 206.

5. Paul A. Carter, *Another Part of the Fifties* (New York: Columbia University Press, 1983), p. 194.

6. Edward Teller, quoted in Carter, *Another Part of the Fifties*, p. 276.

7. See Ira Chernus, *Nuclear Madness* (New York: State of New York Press, 1991), pp. 150–155.

8. *Life*, November 19, 1945, pp. 27–35.

9. Ira Chernus, *Dr. Strangegod: On the Symbolic Meaning of Nuclear Weapons* (Columbia: University of South Carolina Press, 1986), p. 88.

10. Philip Strick, *Science Fiction Movies* (London: Gallery Press, 1977), p. 82.

11. *Time*, June 1, 1959; and *Monthly Film Bulletin*, September 1959, p. 121.

12. Bosley Crowther, review of *The World, the Flesh and the Devil*, *New York Times*, May 21, 1959, p. 35.

13. H. Bruce Franklin, *War Stars: The Superweapon and the American Imagination* (New York: Oxford University Press, 1988), p. 194

CHAPTER EIGHT

1. Robert Hatch, "The Garden of Atom," *New Republic* 14 (May, 1951):23.

2. Bob Salmaggi, review of *Flight That Disappeared*, "Filmfacts," *New York Herald Tribune*, October 1961, p. 216.

3. *The Nation*, January 2, 1960, p. 20; *Commentary*, June 1960, pp. 522–523; and Joseph Keyerleber, "On the Beach," in *Nuclear War Films*, ed. Jack Shaheen (Carbondale: Southern Illinois University Press, 1978), p. 31.

4. Tino Balio, *United Artists* (Madison: University of Wisconsin Press, 1987), p. 139.

5. Donald Spoto, *Stanley Kramer* (New York: Putnam's Sons, 1978), p. 11.

6. Balio, *United Artists*, p. 126.

7. Robert Ray, *A Certain Tendency of the Hollywood Cinema, 1930–1980* (Princeton: Princeton University Press, 1985), p. 264.

8. Balio, *United Artists*, p. 124.

9. Michael Ryan and Douglas Kellner, *Camera Politica: The Politics and Ideology of Contemporary Hollywood Film* (Bloomington: Indiana University Press, 1988), p. 6.

10. Tino Balio, *The American Film Industry* (Madison: University of Wisconsin Press, 1985), p. 405.

11. Bosley Crowther, "'A' Movies on 'B' Budgets," *New York Times Magazine*, November 12, 1950, pp. 20–25.

12. Stanley Kramer, quoted in Bosley Crowther, "Hollywood's Producer of Controversy" *New York Times Magazine*, 1959, p. 80.

13. Crowther, "'A' Movies on 'B' Budgets," p. 18.

14. Lawrence Suid, "The Pentagon and Hollywood: *Dr. Strangelove*," in *American History/American Film*, ed. John E. O'Connor and Martin A. Jackson (New York: Continuum, 1988), p. 222.

15. Ibid., p. 223.

16. Keyerleber, "On the Beach," p. 34.

17. Stanley Kramer, quoted in Spoto, *Stanley Kramer*, p. 211.

18. Keyerleber, "On the Beach," p. 31.

19. *Variety Film Reviews*, December 2, 1959.

20. Paul Brians, *Nuclear Holocausts: Atomic War in Fiction 1895–1984* (Kent, Ohio: Kent State University Press, 1987), p. 20.

21. *On the Beach*, United Artists, directed by Stanley Kramer.

22. Paul V. Beckley, *New York Herald Tribune,* December 20 1959.

23. Spencer Weart, *Nuclear Fear: A History of Images* (Cambridge: Harvard University Press: 1988), p. 218.

24. Crowther, "Hollywood's Producer of Controversy," p. 76.

25. *Time,* December 29, 1959, p. 44.

26. It is interesting to note that this line was borrowed from H. G. Wells's 1936 science fiction movie *Of Things To Come*—"If we don't end war, war will end us."

27. Robert Divine, *Since 1945: Politics and Diplomacy in Recent American History* (New York: Wiley, 1979), p. 117.

28. A. I. Waskow and Stanley L. Newman, *America in Hiding* (New York: Ballantine, 1962).

29. National Academy of Sciences and National Research Council, *Emergency Planning and Behavioral Research* (Washington, D.C.: National Academy of Sciences), p. 5.

30. Mel Mawrence and John C. Kimball, *You Can Survive the Bomb* (Chicago: Quadrangle Books, 1961), pp. 1–17.

31. Robert Gerstell, *How to Survive an Atomic Bomb* (New York: Bantam Books, 1960), p. 52.

32. Gail Morgan Hickman, *The Films of George Pal* (New York: A. S. Barnes and Co., 1977), p. 123.

CHAPTER NINE

1. See Chart A.9 in the Appendix.

2. Robert F. Kennedy, *Thirteen Days: A Memoir of the Cuban Missile Crisis* (New York: W. W. Norton, 1969), p. 112; and Arthur M. Schlesinger, *A Thousand Days* (Boston: Houghton Mifflin, 1965), pp. 250–297.

3. Schlesinger, *Thousand Days,* pp. 260–290.

4. Arthur Knight, *"Voyage to the Bottom of the Sea," Filmfacts,* August 1961, p. 190

5. *New York Herald Tribune,* July 20, 1961.

6. Bosley Crowther, "Film Festival: Fonda in Sidney Lumet's *Fail-Safe,"* *New York Times,* September 16, 1964, p. 36.

7. Interestingly, Peter George had sued the authors of the novel *Fail-Safe,* Eugene Burdick and Harvey Wheeler, for plagiarism.

8. Lawrence Suid, "The Pentagon and Hollywood: *Dr. Strangelove,"* in *American History/American Film,* ed. John E. O'Connor and Martin A. Jackson (New York: Continuum, 1988), p. 224.

9. *Newsweek,* July 22, 1963, p. 86; *Daily Variety,* June 4, 1963.

10. Herbert Kahn, *On Thermonuclear War* (Princeton: Princeton University Press, 1961).

11. Alexander Walker, *Stanley Kubrick Directs* (New York: Harcourt Brace Jovanovich, 1972), p. 158.

12. Leon Minoff, "Nerve Center for a Nuclear Nightmare," *New York Times,* April 21, 1963, sec. 2, p. 7.

13. Joseph Glemis, *The Film Director As Superstar* (Garden City, N.Y.: Doubleday, 1970), p. 309.

14. Suid, "The Pentagon and Hollywood," p. 226.

15. *Newsweek,* February 3, 1964, pp. 70–80; Minoff, "Nerve Center," p. 7.

16. H. Bruce Franklin, *War Stars: The Superweapon and the American Imagination* (New York: Oxford University Press, 1988), p. 192.

17. Lewis Mumford, quoted in William O'Neill, *Coming Apart* (Chicago: Quadrangle Books, 1971), pp. 214–215.

18. Constantina Titus, *Bombs in the Backyard: Atomic Testing and American Politics* (Reno: University of Nevada Press, 1986), p. 102.

19. James H. McBride, *The Test Ban Treaty: Military, Political, and Technological Implications* (Chicago: Henry Regnery Co., 1967), pp. 76–119.

20. *Congressional Quarterly Weekly Report* (September 27, 1963):1962.

21. Paul Boyer, *By the Bomb's Early Light* (New York: Pantheon Books, 1985), p. 356.

22. George Gallup, *The Gallup Poll, 1935–1971* (New York: Random House, 1972), p. 1944.

23. Eugene Rabinowitch, Editorial, *The Bulletin of the Atomic Scientists*, January 1960.

24. Titus, *Bombs in the Backyard,* pp. 104–105.

25. Franklin, *War Stars,* p. 191.

CHAPTER TEN

1. Raymond Williams, *The Sociology of Culture* (New York: Schocken Books, 1981), p. 228.

2. Raymond Williams, *Problems in Materialism and Culture: Selected Essays* (London: Verso Publishers, 1980), p. 40.

3. See for example, Ira Chernus, *Dr. Strangegod: On the Symbolic Meaning of Nuclear Weapons* (Columbia: University of South Carolina Press, 1986), p. 134.

4. Robert Divine, *Since 1945: Politics and Diplomacy in Recent American History* (New York: Wiley Publishers, 1979), p. 117.

5. Ira Chernus, *Dr. Strangegod,* p. 156.

6. Peter Biskind, *Seeing Is Believing: How Hollywood Taught Us to Stop Worrying and Love the Bomb* (New York: Pantheon Books, 1983).

7. Robert Sklar, *Movie-Made America: A Social History of American Movies* (New York: Random House, 1975), p. 280.

8. Leonard Maltin, *TV Movie and Video Guide* (New York: New American Library, 1988), p. 223.

9. Mick Broderick, *Nuclear Movies* (Jefferson, N.C.: McFarland and Co., 1991), p. 45.

References

Aho, James. 1981. *The Warriors*. New York: Harper and Row.

Althusser, Louis. 1979. *For Marx*. London: New Left Books.

Amis, Kingsley. 1961. *New Maps of Hell*. London: Gollancz.

Aptheker, Herbert. 1962. *The Era of McCarthyism*. New York: Marzani.

Arnold, Francis. 1963. "Out of This World." *Films and Filming* 9:14–18.

Badash, Lawrence. 1979. *Radioactivity in America: Growth and Decay of a Science*. Baltimore: Johns Hopkins University Press.

Baldwin, H. W. 1950. *Mistakes of the War*. New York: Harper and Brothers.

Balio, Tino. 1985. *The American Film Industry*. Madison: University of Wisconsin Press.

_____. 1987. *United Artists*. Madison: University of Wisconsin Press.

Ball, Howard. 1986. *Justice Downwind: America's Testing Program in the 1950s*. New York: Oxford University Press.

Barry, C. 1947. *Collier's Yearbook, 1947*. New York: Collier and Son.

Barthes, Roland. 1972. *Mythologies*. New York: Hill and Wang.

Bartter, Martha. 1986. "Nuclear Holocaust As Urban Renewal." *Science Fiction Studies* 13:148–158.

_____. 1988. *The Way to Ground Zero: The Atomic Bomb in American Science Fiction*. Westport, Conn.: Greenwood Press.

Bennett, Tony. 1982. "Theories of the Media, Theories of Society." In *Culture, Society and the Media,* ed. Michael Gurevitch, Tony Bennett, James Curran, and Janet Woollacott. London: Methuen.

Berger, A. 1979. "Nuclear Energy: Science Fiction's Metaphor of Power." *Science Fiction Studies* 6:121–129.

Biskind, Peter. 1983. *Seeing Is Believing: How Hollywood Taught Us to Stop Worrying and Love the Bomb*. New York: Pantheon Books.

_____. 1985. "Pods, Blobs, and Ideology in American Films of the Fifties." In *Shadows of the Magic Lamp,* ed. George Slusser and Eric S. Rabkin. Carbondale: Southern Illinois University Press.

Bogart, Leo. 1976. *Premises for Propaganda*. New York: The Free Press.

Bordwell, David, Janet Staiger, and Kristin Thompson. 1985. *The Classical Hollywood Cinema*. New York: Columbia University Press.

Bourget, J. L. 1986. "Social Implications in the Hollywood Genres." In *Film Genre Reader,* ed. Barry Keith Grant. Austin: University of Texas Press.

Boyer, Paul. 1985. *By the Bomb's Early Light*. New York: Pantheon Books.

Bradley, David. 1948. *No Place to Hide*. Boston: Little, Brown and Co.

Brians, Paul. 1987. *Nuclear Holocausts: Atomic War in Fiction 1895–1984*. Kent, Ohio: Kent State University Press.

Broderick, Mick. 1991. *Nuclear Movies*. Jefferson, N.C.: McFarland and Co.

Brody, P. J. 1987. "Adults' Memories of Growing Up in the Atomic Age." Boston University Dissertation Abstracts, vol. 48/07-B, p. 2089.

Bronsan, John. 1978. *Future Tense*. London: MacDonald and Jane's.

Buscombe, Edward. 1986. "The Idea of Genre in the American Cinema." In *Film Genre Reader*, ed. Barry Keith Grant. Austin: University of Texas Press.

Butler, E. M. 1948. *Myth of the Magus*. Cambridge: Cambridge University Press.

Carter, Paul A. 1983. *Another Part of the Fifties*. New York: Columbia University Press.

Caute, David. 1979. *The Great Fear*. New York: Simon and Schuster.

Ceplair, Larry, and Steven Englund. 1980. *The Inquisition in Hollywood: Politics in the Film Community, 1930–1960*. Garden City, N.Y.: Doubleday.

Chernus, Ira. 1986. *Dr. Strangegod: On the Symbolic Meaning of Nuclear Weapons*. Columbia: University of South Carolina Press.

_____. 1991. *Nuclear Madness*. New York: State of New York Press.

Chomsky, Noam. 1979. *Language and Responsibility*. Hassocks, England: Harvester Press.

Cogley, John 1956. *Report on Blacklisting*. New York: Fund for the Republic.

Combs, James E. 1984. *Polpop: Politics and Popular Culture in America*. Bowling Green, Ohio: Bowling Green State University Popular Press.

Conant, Michael. 1960. *Antitrust in the Motion Picture Industry*. Berkeley: University of California Press.

Corman, Roger. 1990. *How I Made a Hundred Movies in Hollywood*. New York: Random House.

Dawson, A. H. 1947. "Motion Picture Economics." *Hollywood Quarterly* 3, 3:217–240.

De Wolf, Henry. 1976. *Atomic Energy for Military Purposes: The Official Report on the Development of the Atomic Bomb Under the Auspices of the United States Government, 1.* Princeton: Princeton University Press.

Divine, Robert. 1979. *Since 1945: Politics and Diplomacy in Recent American History*. New York: Wiley Publishers.

_____. 1981. *Eisenhower and the Cold War*. New York: Oxford University Press.

Doherty, Thomas. 1988. *Teenagers and Teenpics: The Juvenilization of American Movies in the 1950s*. Boston: Unwin Hyman.

Donahue, Susan Mary. 1987. *American Film Distribution*. Ann Arbor: University of Michigan Research Press.

Dorman, W. 1985. "The Media: Playing the Government's Game," *The Bulletin of the Atomic Scientists* 41:118–124.

Dowling, David. 1987. *Fictions of Nuclear Disaster*. Iowa City: University of Iowa Press.

Eames, John. 1979. *The MGM Story*. New York: Crown.

Edelson, Edward. 1975. *Visions of Tomorrow: Great Science Fiction from the Movies*. New York: Doubleday.

Edmunds, Hugh, and John Strick. 1977. "Economic Determinants of Violence in Television and Motion Pictures and the Implications of Newer Technologies." In *The Report of the Royal Commission on Violence in the Communications Industry*. Toronto: Queen's Printer for Ontario, pp. 71–184.

Elliot, Phillip. 1980. "Some Aspects of Communism As a Cultural Category." *Media, Culture, and Society* 1:195–210.

Farrell, James. 1987. "The Crossroads of Bikini." *Journal of American Culture* 10, 2:55–66.

Feenberg, Andrew. 1978. "The Politics of Survival: Science Fiction in the Nuclear Age." *Alternative Futures* 1, 2:3–23.

Feld, Bernard. 1979. "Einstein and the Politics of Nuclear Weapons." *The Bulletin of the Atomic Scientists* 35:5–16.

France, Anatole. 1908. *Penguin Island*. New York: J. Lane Publishers.

Franklin, H. Bruce. 1988. *War Stars: The Superweapon and the American Imagination*. New York: Oxford University Press.

Fulton, R. 1987. "Death and Society in 20th-Century America." *Omega* 18, 4:379–395.

Furtwanger, Andrew. 1981. "Growing Up Nuclear." *The Bulletin of the Atomic Scientists* 37, 1:44–48.

Gallup, George. 1972. *The Gallup Poll, 1935–1971*. New York: Random House.

Gans, Herbert. 1957. "The Creator-Audience Relationship in the Mass Media: An Analysis of Movie Making." In *Mass Culture: The Popular Arts in America*, ed. B. Rosenberg and D. M. White. New York: The Free Press.

Gerstell, Richard. 1960. *How to Survive an Atomic Bomb*. New York: Bantam Books.

Glasser, O. 1934. *William Conrad and the Early History of the Roentgen Rays*. Springfield: Charles C. Thomas.

Glemis, Joseph. 1970. *The Film Director As Superstar*. Garden City, N.Y.: Doubleday.

Golding, Peter, and Graham Murdock. 1991. "Culture, Communication, and Political Economy." In *Mass Media and Society*, ed. James Curran and Michael Gurevitch. London: Edward Arnold.

Grant, Barry Keith, ed. 1986. *Film Genre Reader*. Austin: University of Texas Press.

Gray, G. 1970. *The Warriors*. New York: Harper and Row.

Grayson, Benson L., ed. 1978. *The American Image of Russia*. New York: Frederick Ungar.

Griffith, Robert. 1987. *The Politics of Fear: Joseph R. McCarthy and the Senate*. Amherst: University of Massachusetts Press.

Groves, Leslie R. 1962. *Now It Can Be Told*. New York: Harper and Row.

Haber, H. 1957. *The Walt Disney Story of Our Friend the Atom*. New York: Simon and Schuster.

Hall, Stuart. 1983. "The Problem of Ideology: Marxism Without Guarantees." In *Marx: A Hundred Years On*, ed. Brian Matthews. London: Lawrence and Wishart.

Herkin, Gregg. 1980. *The Winning Weapon: The Atomic Bomb in the Cold War, 1945–1950*. New York: Knopf.

Hickman, Gail Morgan. 1977. *The Films of George Pal*. New York: A. S. Barnes and Co.

Hilgartner, Stephen 1982. *Nukespeak: Nuclear Language, Visions, and Mindset*. San Francisco: Sierra Club.

Jacobsen, C. G. 1984. *The Nuclear Era: Its History, Its Implications*. New York: Spokesman Books.

Jarvie, Ian. 1970. *Movies and Society*. New York: Basic Books.

Johnson, William. 1972. *Focus on the Science Fiction Film*. Englewood Cliffs, N.J.: Prentice-Hall.

Jowett, Garth, and James Linton, eds. 1980. *Movies As Mass Communication*. Beverly Hills, Calif.: Sage.

Kahn, George. 1948. *Hollywood on Trial*. New York: Boni and Gaer.

Kahn, Herbert. 1961. *On Thermonuclear War*. Princeton: Princeton University Press.

Kaplan, Morton A. 1976. *The Life and Death of the Cold War*. Chicago: Nelson Hall.

Kennan, George. 1976. *The Nuclear Delusion: Soviet-American Relations in the Atomic Age*. New York: Pantheon Books.

Kennedy, Robert F. 1969. *Thirteen Days: A Memoir of the Cuban Missile Crisis*. New York: W. W. Norton.

Kovel, Joel. 1983. *Against the State of Nuclear Terror.* Boston: South End Press.

Krepon, M. 1986. "Neoconservative War of the Worlds." *The Bulletin of the Atomic Scientists* 42, 3:6–7.

Kuhn, Annette. 1990. *Alien Zone: Cultural Theory and Contemporary Science Fiction Cinema.* London and New York: Verso Publishers.

Lamont, Louis. 1965. *Day of Trinity.* New York: Antheum.

Land, Daniel 1948. *Early Tales of the Atomic Age.* Garden City, N.Y.: Doubleday.

Laurence, William 1980. *Men and Atoms: The Discovery, the Uses, and the Future of Atomic Energy.* New York: Simon and Schuster.

Lens, S. 1964. *The Futile Crusade: Anti-Communism As American Credo.* Chicago: Quadrangle Books.

Levering, Ralph B. 1978. *The Public and American Foreign Policy, 1918–1978.* New York: William Morrow.

Levy, Emanuel. 1991. *Small Town America in Film.* New York: Frederick Ungar.

Lifton, Robert J., and Greg Mitchell. 1995. *Hiroshima in America.* New York: Putnam's Sons.

Linton, James. 1978. "But It's Only a Movie." *Jump Cut* 17 (April):16–19.

London, Kurt. 1968. *The Permanent Crisis.* Waltham, Mass.: Blaisdell Publishers.

_____. 1984. "Of Arms and Culture." *Current Research on Peace and Violence* 7:1–64.

Lucanio, Patrick. 1987. *Them or Us: Archetypal Interpretations of Fifties Alien Invasion Films.* Bloomington: University of Indiana Press.

MacDonald, Fred. 1978. "The Cold War as Entertainment in Fifties Television." *Journal of Popular Film and Television* 7:3–29.

Maier, Charles S. 1978. *The Origins of the Cold War and Contemporary Europe.* New York: Viewpoints.

Maland, C. 1964. "*Dr. Strangelove* (1964): Nightmare Comedy and the Ideology of Liberal Consensus." *American Quarterly* 5:697–717.

Maltin, Leonard. 1995. *Movie and Video Guide.* New York: Signet.

Manchester, William. 1974. *The Glory and the Dream: A Narrative History of America, 1932–1972.* New York: Bantam Books.

Marchino, M. L. 1978. "No Place to Hide." *The Progressive* 42, 4.

Marsh, C., and C. Fraser. 1989. "Nuclear Issues and the Nature of Public Opinion." In *Public Opinion and Nuclear Weapons,* ed. C. Marsh and C. Fraser. London: Macmillan.

Maurer, M. 1985. "Screening Nuclear War and Vietnam." *Culture and* Society 23:68–73.

Mawrence, Mel, and John C. Kimball. 1961. *You Can Survive the Bomb.* Chicago: Quadrangle Books.

Mazuzan, George T., and J. Samuel Walker. 1984. *Controlling the Atom: The Beginnings of Nuclear Regulation, 1946–1962.* Berkeley: University of California Press.

McBride, James H. 1967. *The Test Ban Treaty: Military, Political, and Technological Implications.* Chicago: Henry Regnery Co.

McQuail, Dennis. 1969. "The Uncertainty About the Audience and the Organization of Mass Communications." *The Sociological Review, Monograph 14: The Sociology of Mass Media Communicators,* ed. Paul Halmos (January):75–84.

Menville, Douglas Alver, and Robert Reginald. 1977. *Things to Come: An Illustrated History of the Science Fiction Film.* New York: New York Times Books.

Miller, Douglas T., and Marion Nowak. 1977. *The Fifties: The Way We Really Were.* Garden City, N.Y.: Doubleday.

Morris, Gary. 1985. *Roger Corman*. Boston: Twayne Publishers.

Moss, Norman. 1968. *Men Who Play God*. New York: Harper and Row.

Mueller, John E. 1979. "Public Expectations of War During the Cold War." *American Journal of Political Science* 23:301–329.

Murdock, Graham. 1989. "Cultural Studies: Missing Links." *Critical Studies in Mass Communication* (December):436–440.

Murphy, Brian. 1982. "Monster Movies: They Came from Beneath the Fifties." In *Movies as Artifacts*, ed. Michael Marsden and John Nachbar. Chicago: Nelson Hall.

Murray, L. 1975. "The Film Industry Responds to the Cold War, 1945–1955: Monsters, Spies, and Subversives." *Jump Cut* 9:14–16.

Naha, Ed. 1982. *The Films of Roger Corman*. New York: Arco Publishers.

Neale, Steven. 1981. *Genre*. London: British Film Institute.

Nimmo, Dan D. 1974. *Popular Images of Politics*. Englewood Cliffs, N.J.: Prentice Hall.

Noel, D. C. 1987. "The Nuclear Horror and the Hounding of Nature: Listening to Images." *Soundings: An Interdisciplinary Journal* 70:289–308.

O'Connor, Jack E., and Martin A. Jackson, eds. 1988. *American History/American Film*. New York: Continuum.

Olson, Charles. 1975. *The Cold War . . . And After*. Englewood Cliffs, N.J.: Prentice Hall.

O'Neill, William. 1971. *Coming Apart*. Chicago: Quadrangle Books.

Paarlberg, Rob. 1973. "Forgetting About the Unthinkable." *Foreign Policy* 10:132.

Papademas, D. 1984. "Nuclear Propaganda: A Review Essay." *Humanity and Society* 8:104–109.

Parnas, D. 1986. "Pentagon Links Change in Script, Eastwood Aid." *Arkansas Gazette*, May 26.

Price, J. 1982. *The Anti-Nuclear Movement*. New York: Twayne Publishers.

Priestley, J. B. 1938. *The Doomsday Men*. New York: Harper and Brothers.

Pringle, Peter, and John Spigelman. 1981. *The Nuclear Barons*. New York: Holt, Rinehart and Winston.

Pruessen, R. W. 1974. "The Objectives of American Foreign Policy and the Nature of the Cold War." In *Reflections on the Cold War*, ed. L. Miller. Philadelphia: Temple University Press.

Pryluck, Calvin. 1982. "Front Office, Box Office, and Artistic Freedom: An Aspect of the Film Industry, 1945–1969." In *Movies as Artifacts*, ed. Michael Marsden and John Nachbar. Chicago: Nelson-Hall.

Rabinowitch, Eugene. 1951. "Five Years After." *The Bulletin of the Atomic Scientists* (January):3–12.

Ray, Robert. 1985. *A Certain Tendency of the Hollywood Cinema, 1930–1980*. Princeton: Princeton University Press.

Reingold, Nathan. 1984. "MGM Meets the Atomic Bomb." *Wilson Quarterly* (Autumn):155–163.

Rogin, Michael. 1984. "*Kiss Me Deadly*: Communism, Motherhood, and Cold War Movies." *Representations* 6:1–36.

———. 1987. *Ronald Reagan the Movie and Other Episodes in Political Demonology*. Berkeley: University of California Press.

Rollins, P. C. 1973. "*Victory at Sea*: Cold War Epic." *Journal of Popular Culture* 2:463–482.

Ross, A. 1987. "Containing Culture in the Cold War." *Cultural Studies* 1:329–348.

Ryan, Michael, and Douglas Kellner. 1988. *Camera Politica: The Politics and Ideology of Contemporary Hollywood Film*. Bloomington: Indiana University Press.

Sanders, J. 1980. "Shaping the Cold War Consensus: The Soviet Threat, Interelite Conflict, and Mass Politics in the Korean War Era." *Journal of Sociology* 24-25:67–136.

Savage, James, and B. Storms. 1965. *Reach to the Unknown*. Los Alamos, N.Mex.: University of California and U.S. Atomic Energy Commission.

Sayre, Nora. 1982. *Running Time: Films of the Cold War*. New York: Dial Press.

Schlesinger, Arthur M. 1965. *A Thousand Days*. Boston: Houghton Mifflin.

Scott, W. A. 1958. "The Avoidance of Threatening Material in Imaginative Behavior." In *Motives in Fantasy, Action, and Society*, ed. John W. Atkinson. Princeton: Van Nostrand Press.

Seaborg, Glenn, and William Corliss. 1971. *Man and Atom*. New York: Dutton.

Seldes, George. 1949. *The People Don't Know: The American Press and the Cold War*. New York: Gaer.

Shaheen, Jack. 1978. *Nuclear War Films*. Carbondale: Southern Illinois University Press.

Shain, Russell Earl. 1974. "Hollywood's Cold War Films, 1948–1952: An Annotated Filmography." *Journal of Popular Film and Television* 3:165–172.

_____. 1974. "Hollywood's Cold War." *Journal of Popular Film and Television* 3:334–350.

_____. 1976. *An Analysis of Motion Pictures About War Released by the American Film Industry, 1939–1970*. New York: Arno Press.

Shurcliff, William A. 1947. *Bombs at Bikini: The Official Report of Operation Crossroads*. New York: William H. Wise.

Sklar, Robert. 1975. *Movie-Made America: A Social History of American Movies*. New York: Random House.

Slosson, Edwin E. 1925. "Death-Dealing and Labor Saving Rays." *Scientific Monthly* 20:108–111.

Slusser, George, and Eric S. Rabkin, eds. 1985. *Shadows of the Magic Lamp*. Carbondale: Southern Illinois University Press.

Smith, T. W. 1983. "The Polls: American Attitudes Toward the Soviet Union and Communism." *Public Opinion Quarterly* 47:277–292.

Soddy, Frederick. 1903. "Some Recent Advances in Radioactivity." *Contemporary Review* 83:708–720.

_____. 1920. *The Interpretation of Radium and the Structure of the Atom*. 3rd ed. London: John Murray. First published in 1909.

_____. 1986. "The Frustration of Science." In *Frederick Soddy*, ed. George B. Kauffman. Dordrecht, Netherlands: Reidel.

Solomon, James Fisher. 1988. *Discourse and Reference in the Nuclear Age*. Norman: University of Oklahoma Press.

Sontag, Susan. 1966. *Against Interpretation and Other Essays*. New York: Delta.

Speiser, Stuart M. 1984. *How to End the Nuclear Nightmare*. New York: North River Press.

Spoto, Donald. 1978. *Stanley Kramer*. New York: Putnam's Sons.

Stoehr, Taylor. 1978. *Hawthorne's Mad Scientists: Pseudoscience and Social Science in 19th Century Life and Letters*. Hamden, Conn.: Archon Publishers.

Strauss, L. L. 1962. *Men and Decisions*. New York: Doubleday.

Strick, John. 1978. "The Economics of the Motion Picture Industry: A Survey." *Philosophy of the Social Sciences* 8 (December):406–417.

Strick, Philip. 1977. *Science Fiction Movies*. London: Gallery Press.

Suid, Lawrence. 1978. *Guts and Glory: Great American War Movies*. Reading, Mass.: Addison-Wesley Publishing Co.

_____. 1988. "The Pentagon and Hollywood: *Dr. Strangelove*." In *American History/ American Film*, ed. John E. O'Connor and Martin A. Jackson. New York: Continuum.

Swanson, D. 1990. "Popular Art As Political Communication." In *Politics in Familiar Contexts*, ed. Robert L. Savage and Dan Nimmo. New York: Ablex Publishing Co.

Sweet, William. 1988. *The Nuclear Age: Atomic Energy, Proliferation, and the Arms Race*. Washington, D.C.: The Congressional Quarterly.

Teller, Edward. 1962. *The Legacy of Hiroshima*. Garden City, N.Y.: Doubleday.

Thompson, Edward T. 1982. *Beyond the Cold War*. New York: Pantheon Books.

Titus, Constantina. 1983. "Back to Ground Zero: Old Footage Through New Lenses." *Journal of Popular Film and Television* 2:3–11.

_____. 1985. "Selling the Bomb: Hollywood and the Government Join Forces at Ground Zero." *Halcyon* 7:16–29.

_____. 1986. *Bombs in the Backyard: Atomic Testing and American Politics*. Reno: University of Nevada Press.

Truman, Harry S. 1978. "Moscow Divides the World." In *The American Image of Russia*, ed. B. Grayson. New York: Frederick Ungar.

Tudor, Andrew. 1989. *Monsters and Mad Scientists: A Cultural History of the Horror Movie*. Cambridge, England: Basil Blackwell.

Uhl, Michael, and Tod Ensign. 1980. *G.I. Guinea Pigs: How the Pentagon Exposed Our Troops to Dangers More Deadly Than War*. New York: Wideview Books.

Walker, Alexander. 1972. *Stanley Kubrick Directs*. New York: Harcourt Brace Jovanovich.

Wallechinsky, David, and Irving Wallace. 1975. *The People's Almanac*. New York: Doubleday.

Warren, Bill. 1982. *Keep Watching the Skies: American Science Fiction Movies of the Fifties*. Jefferson, N.C.: McFarland and Co.

Wasko, Janet. 1982. *Movies and Money: Financing the American Film Industry*. Norwood: Ablex Publishing Corp.

Waskow, A. I., and Stanley Newman. 1962. *America in Hiding*. New York: Ballantine.

Weart, Spencer. 1988. *Nuclear Fear: A History of Images*. Cambridge: Harvard University Press.

Wells, H. G. 1896. *The Island of Dr. Moreau*. London: William Heinemann.

_____. 1914. *The World Set Free*. London: Macmillan.

Weyer, J. 1976. "The Image of Alchemy in 19th and 20th Century Histories of Chemistry." *Ambix* 23:65–79.

Williams, Raymond. 1980. *Problems in Materialism and Culture: Selected Essays*. London: Verso Publishers.

_____. 1981. *The Sociology of Culture*. New York: Schocken Books.

Winks, Robin W. 1964. *The Cold War*. New York: Macmillan.

Wolfe, G. K. 1976. "*Dr. Strangelove, Red Alert*, and Patterns of Paranoia in the 1950s." *Journal of Popular Film and Television* 5:57–67.

York, Herbert. 1976. *The Advisors: Oppenheimer, Teller, and the Superbomb*. San Francisco: W. H. Freeman.

Index

1968786R00121

Printed in Great Britain
by Amazon.co.uk, Ltd.,
Marston Gate.